★ PYONGYANG

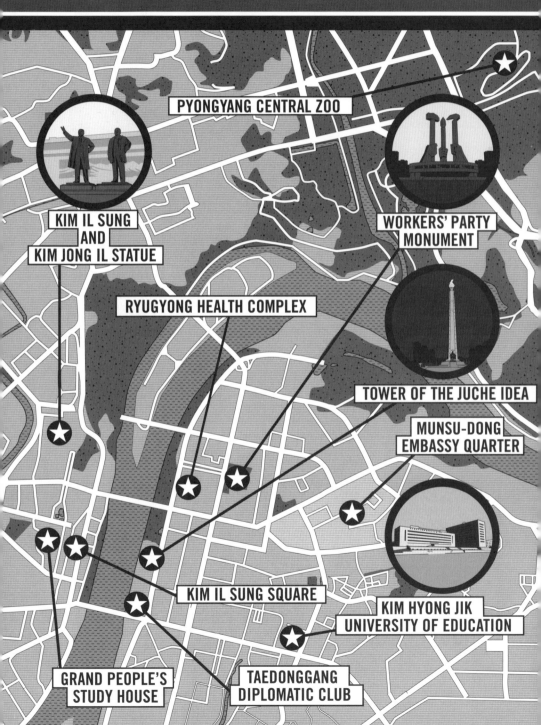

PYONGYANG CENTRAL ZOO

KIM IL SUNG
AND
KIM JONG IL STATUE

WORKERS' PARTY
MONUMENT

RYUGYONG HEALTH COMPLEX

TOWER OF THE JUCHE IDEA

MUNSU-DONG
EMBASSY QUARTER

KIM IL SUNG SQUARE

KIM HYONG JIK
UNIVERSITY OF EDUCATION

GRAND PEOPLE'S
STUDY HOUSE

TAEDONGGANG
DIPLOMATIC CLUB

SEE YOU AGAIN IN PYONGYANG

ALSO BY TRAVIS JEPPESEN

All Fall: Two Novellas

16 Sculptures

The Suiciders: A Novel

Dicklung & Others

Disorientations: Art on the Margins of the "Contemporary"

Wolf at the Door: A Novel

Poems I Wrote While Watching TV

Victims: A Novel

SEE YOU AGAIN IN PYONGYANG

A JOURNEY INTO KIM JONG UN'S NORTH KOREA

TRAVIS JEPPESEN

hachette
BOOKS

NEW YORK   BOSTON

Hachette Books
Hachette Book Group
1290 Avenue of the Americas
New York, NY 10104
hachettebooks.com
twitter.com/hachettebooks

First Edition: May 2018

Hachette Books is a division of Hachette Book Group, Inc.
The Hachette Books name and logo are trademarks of Hachette Book Group, Inc.

The publisher is not responsible for websites (or their content) that are not owned by the publisher.

The Hachette Speakers Bureau provides a wide range of authors for speaking events. To find out more, go to www.hachettespeakersbureau.com or call (866) 376-6591.

Photo opening Part 5 courtesy of the author.
All other photos courtesy of John Monteith.
Map of Pyongyang/North Korea courtesy of Miles Clement.

Library of Congress Control Number: 2018934067

ISBNs: 978-0-316-50915-2 (hardcover), 978-0-316-50913-8 (ebook)

Printed in the United States of America

LSC-C

10 9 8 7 6 5 4 3 2 1

CONTENTS

Acknowledgments . . . . *vii*

Author's Note . . . . *ix*

Prologue 1

Part One: Dreams of a Forgotten City 9

Part Two: "World's Worst Country" 49

Part Three: Norkorealism 81

Part Four: Us and Them 111

Part Five: The Atrocity Exhibition 137

Part Six: Victory Day 163

Part Seven: Houses of Friendship 193

Part Eight: Folding Screen 215

Part Nine: Reconciliation 267

Epilogue 297

Bibliography *303*

ACKNOWLEDGMENTS

THE FIRST WORDS I published on my travels to the DPRK focused on the country's visual art and culture. Much of that early material was expanded upon in this book. I want to thank David Velasco at *Artforum* and Lindsay Pollock, Richard Vine, and Cathy Lebowitz at *Art in America* for commissioning and editing those initial pieces.

After my study trip to Pyongyang in 2016, Spring Workshop in Hong Kong provided me with a luxurious landing pad, a place to spend a month sorting through hundreds of pages of diaries and notes I'd accumulated. It was a nurturing place to start work on a book. I am indebted to Defne Ayas, who recommended me for the residency, and the entire staff of Spring Workshop, especially Mimi Brown and Christina Li.

I flew from that urban megalopolis halfway across the globe to the forested environs on the outskirts of Vilnius, Lithuania, where I was hosted by the art center Rupert. There, I had the dual task of beginning the earliest draft of the book while simultaneously preparing for an exhibition that opened the same month. It was an invigorating and productive few weeks of work of the most gratifying sort, and I'm grateful to Juste Jonutyte and the entire staff of Rupert for allowing it to happen.

In 2017, I was an international research fellow at the National Museum of Modern and Contemporary Art (MMCA) Seoul, where a good chunk of the book's first draft was written. The experiences I had living and working in this fabulous city enriched and expanded my understanding of the depths of the Korean experience—historically, culturally, linguistically. I met many former residents of North Korea, most of whom I sadly cannot name; each forced me to make profound revisions to my understanding of life above the thirty-eighth parallel and collectively made me realize just how multifaceted, misunderstood, and unsummarizable those diverse life experiences really are. Their contribution to my project is inestimable. From my time in Seoul, I particularly wish to thank Sun Mu, Jang Jin Sung, Kim Kyung-mook, Kim Bom-hee, Dirk Fleischmann, Bartomeu Mari, Misa Shin, Barbara Cueto, Emily Bates, Son Kwang-ju, Park Hee-jung, Choi Sun, Yeo Gyeong-hwan, Eugene Kwon, and Emma Corrall.

Finally, the Hordaland Kunstsenter welcomed me as writer-in-residence in Bergen, Norway, while I was completing the final draft. Many thanks to Scott Elliott and Anthea Buys for the kind invitation and support.

Thanks to Alek Sigley and Tongil Tours for making the study trip happen. Also to Simon Cockerell and Koryo Tours for organizing my first visits to the DPRK. Pernille Skar Nordby was on one of those trips, and I gained much from reading her subsequent MA thesis on North Korean architecture. To John Monteith, who was with me on my first visit to North Korea, and whose photographs adorn these pages. And special thanks to Tom Masters for inspiring my interest in the country to begin with.

Miek Coccia has been more than just an agent—a sounding board, a therapist, and, most of all, a friend. Certainly this book never would have seen fruition were he not nearby every step of the way.

Many thanks to Paul Whitlatch for his immediate and enthusiastic interest in the project and for his editorial insights that were vital in the manuscript's final revisions. And to the entire team at Hachette, especially Lauren Hummel, Carolyn Kurek, Joanna Pinsker, and Odette Fleming.

To my great friend and mentor Bruce Benderson, who knows more than me about the potential *richesses* that can be mined from getting lost. To Bertie Marshall for hosting me in London. To my late friend Brian Tennessee Claflin, who was both my muse and my biggest cheerleader and who knew I eventually would write this book. To all the friends in Berlin and elsewhere who have put up with my hours-long rants and conversations about North Korea over the years, thank you so much. To my parents, Debi and Jon Jeppesen, and my grandmother, Elizabeth Blackburn, for enduring it all. To Wang Ping-Hsiang— home is wherever you are.

To all the friends in Pyongyang I cannot name—see you again someday.

AUTHOR'S NOTE

WRITING IS A predatory activity; you're always stalking some amorphous ideals, often ones that cannot be named or readily summarized, in the attainment of truth and accuracy—hence the need *to write*. When human lives are involved, the process can become hazardous—an awareness that any writer who ventures into North Korean terrain should attain. North Korea throws into question the very nature of reality and reminded me, again and again, the ways in which "truth" is constantly being remolded by its surrounding context.

North Korea poses any number of daunting challenges to outside researchers. As I've been working on this book, one issue that has remained at the forefront of my thoughts is safety—less for myself and more for those I have met along the way. A compromise had to be reached in order to protect these sources. While everything in this book is truthful, in that it happened to either me or those I know well, many figures in the book are, in fact, composites of at least two or more people; and most names have been changed. Comrade Kim Nam Ryong, for instance, is a composite of men I have encountered, befriended, or otherwise learned about, some current and others former residents of Pyongyang, and the Korean State Travel Company he works for is a fictional hybrid based on knowledge I have gleaned about the operations at several of the country's state-owned tourism bureaus.

Among the North Korean defectors I have interviewed in the South and elsewhere, I have tried to seek out those who purposefully avoid speaking with the media. Certain defectors expect to be paid in exchange for an interview; I pointedly avoided those individuals. By being careful not to compromise people's safety but offering no cash incentive, I tried to create an interview scenario in which my sources had no motivation to mislead me about their experiences and perspectives.

In addition to the camouflaging devices outlined previously, I have employed other mechanisms from the writer's tool kit for clarity and brevity. Namely, I've shifted the order of some events and merged some conversations to improve the flow of the narrative. My intention is to present not a play-by-play accounting of my days in North Korea but rather a representation of the range of experiences I had over multiple trips. Although the narrative primarily centers on my 2016 study program, I have, in some cases, inserted a particularly vivid experience from an earlier trip or a subsequent visit in 2017 into the sequence of events.

I also had to grapple with the issue of sourcing and fact-checking. As anyone who has studied North Korea can confirm, the standard journalistic and academic requirements of conducting research are often impossible to fulfill in this context. Fact has to be distinguished from rumor and hearsay. (Ironically, this mirrors the lived experience of the average North Korean citizen, for whom most precious information is received via word of mouth.) As this conflict arose again and again throughout my work on the book, I felt that the honest thing to do would be to articulate these philosophical quandaries as I recall them occurring. Some of those moments have been rendered as dialogues between myself and my travel companions.

Other problems are linguistic in nature. Somewhat confusingly, there exist two systems for romanizing Korean words. A variant of the older McCune-Reischauer system is still used in North Korea, while in South Korea, a Revised Romanization system has been in official use since 2000. To add more confusion to the matter, most proper nouns retain the old McCune-Reischauer system in both Koreas (for example, the romanization of the common last name remains "Kim" rather than the Revised Romanized "Gim," and "Pyongyang" has still not shifted to the revised "Pyeongyang"). Given the predominance of this convention across most English-language literature and since it was in North Korea where I first began to learn the language, I have mostly retained the North's version of the McCune-Reischauer romanization system throughout the book, going so far as to retain the practice of de-hyphenating first names, which are always written after the last name (in the South, it would be "Jong-un"; in the North, it's "Jong Un.")

Despite all these challenges, I have tried to put forth only things that I know and firmly believe to be true. Any mistakes are mine and mine alone.

SEE YOU AGAIN IN PYONGYANG

PROLOGUE

OBSESSIONS LEAD PEOPLE on strange detours, and sometimes those detours come to define the entire geography of a person's existence. Watching the fall of the Berlin Wall as a ten-year-old in the living room of a suburban house in the American south, I could not have fathomed the immense significance of what I was seeing. Sure, I had been taught that communism was something bad, the polar opposite of the pristine democracy I had been raised in and programmed to cherish, and I could understand that this evil was now coming to an end. Everything was black and white, good and bad, rough and smooth. A ten-year-old growing up in those sheltered circumstances has no real cognizance of the actual texture of things, of ways of life that differ tremendously from one's own. A little more than a decade later, I'd be walking the streets of those same gray Central European cities my childhood eyes had witnessed coming undone on the evening news.

I've lived in two of those cities, Prague and Berlin, for most of my twenties and thirties. Whenever I'm asked what brought me to live in these capitals of some of the past century's darkest and most significant moments, I fail to offer a pithy reply. Something along that stretch of adolescence and early adulthood derailed me from the standard life trajectory that my southern suburban upbringing implied. A growing fascination with other ways of life led me first to New York City to study art, literature, and philosophy at a left-leaning university where nearly all subjects were viewed through the lens of a Marxist interpretation of history. I became fascinated with cultic systems of belief and their twistings of ideology, with the notion of escape, with revising my limited means of perception. The best way to do this, I discovered, was through constant movement—never staying in the same place for long. Shirking any scene that might come too close to resembling the dreaded "comfort zone." As my friends in Berlin, where

I have been lately based, will tell you, I spend a lot of my time escaping that city for others, the notion of a static, stable place called *home* being increasingly nebulous.

In short, I became a writer. My model the Baudelairean *flâneur*, Robert Walser's destinationless *Spaziergänger*, the wanderer whose ultimate allegiance is to no nation, no collective, and no ideology but to the City in the broadest sense—the chaotic and confused metropolis, the crazed church of constant motion where poetic creation is born. Unlike Baudelaire, who had to stick with Paris—the possibilities of travel being what they were in the nineteenth century—I am fortunate to live in an era when travel is easier and cheaper than ever before. The cities of the world, in all their rich plurality, have become my extended stomping ground.

Since my addiction to motion is what feeds my writing, the main purpose of travel for me is to get lost. Losing myself in the strangeness of new environs, marveling at the process each time as what is strange transforms into something familiar. I will go to great lengths, travel far distances, for the sole purpose of getting lost—of losing myself.

So it is strange that someone like me would be drawn to the one city on the planet where it is forbidden to get lost, a city with strange customs that is officially governed by an even stranger ideological system. The capital of a strange country with a strange leader, a country universally demonized, laughed at, feared, and generally misunderstood. The type of place that even a traveler like me, with my perennial search for freedom from all the trappings of a conventional existence via writing and constant movement, would be likely to shrug off. No *flâneurs* allowed in Pyongyang. You can't even wander around on your own without the supervision of a local, government-licensed guide, whose duty it is to lead you on a strict itinerary. What could such a place possibly offer someone like me?

Quite a lot, it turns out. Because the fuel for my wanderlust has perennially been a sense of intrigue, a need to gauge and decode the seemingly incomprehensible. To find the sense in the seemingly outlandish. My first novel, written when I was twenty-three, was in part about a UFO religious cult. North Korea, from a distance, appeared like a cultish exaggeration in the present of the history I was forced to confront every day, living in two of the capitals of Europe's ill-fated experiments with communism. Over there, in North Korea, was a veritable *other* way of life. Like many, I didn't even know it was possible to *go* there. Then it happened to come up in conversation with my friend Tom Masters, a travel writer, that not only had he visited the country several times in the past, he would soon be returning to revise the North Korea chapter of a guidebook he was working on. Would I be interested in coming along?

We landed in Pyongyang in the spring of 2012, just a few months after the death of Kim Jong Il. The country was suddenly in the hands of his son, about whom the people of North Korea and the world knew next to nothing. An aura of uncertainty hovered over the streets of Pyongyang, where whispered gossip and rumor form the unofficial currency. There were other currents flowing through the air, of course—the omnipresent whiffs of paranoia and suspicion. But there was also a palpable sense of hopefulness, an optimism of the potential changes that the new young leader might bring.

I hadn't expected to find such a colorful place. I certainly didn't expect to be received with as much warmth as I was. Although I have spent the entirety of my adult life as an expatriate, I still hold a US passport, so in the eyes of the North Korean authorities and citizens alike, I am an American through and through. (In a country led by an ultra-nationalist ideology where international travel is forbidden for all but a chosen few, the notion of expatriation was and is perplexing for most North Koreans to fathom.) A citizen of the enemy state. Yet none of the hostilities typically directed toward the United States by the state media of the Democratic People's Republic of Korea (the country's official name, DPRK for short) were ever articulated toward me by any of the North Koreans I met on that trip. I was the only American in the delegation but was treated with as much graciousness as the others. As in other countries in East Asia, foreign visitors are considered honored guests and are treated with gratitude; hospitality is intrinsic to the culture. A highly musical country, North Korea even has a song, "Pan-gap-sum-ni-da" ("Nice to Meet You"), which North Koreans delight in singing to all foreign visitors. Above all, North Koreans want you not only to feel welcome but to be impressed by their country, of which they are immensely proud.

I knew better than to be seduced by it all, but I couldn't help being charmed. I knew about the nukes, I knew about the concentration camps, I knew about the systematic injustices perpetrated by the regime against the populace. But is that really all there is to it? I knew going in that there would be limits to what I could find out. Somewhat perversely, not only was I able to accept the highly proscribed nature of North Korean tourism borrowed from the former Soviet Union, but I was quickly able to comprehend the reasons why. In a country where everyone, more or less, is being watched, why should I, a tourist and a citizen of an enemy state, be exempt from this?

After that initial visit in 2012, I returned to North Korea several times. The first was just a month later, to see the Arirang Mass Games, which I wrote about for *Artforum*. I returned again in 2014 for an architecture-themed tour that enabled me to see the extent to which the city had changed in just two years. That visit gave me further insight into the priorities of the country's new leadership beyond the headlines, the ways that the capital was being transformed and reshaped according to those goals.

Over the years, I devoured every book on North Korea I could get my hands on, from best-selling defectors' narratives to academic treatises focused on art, film, sociology, and the economy. Anything to gain some insight into the realities of daily life beyond the multiple layers of propaganda and mythmaking. Then, in early 2016, I came upon an article on an online news site devoted to North Korea. It was about a new company, Tongil Tours. Unlike the other tourism companies offering three-to-eight-day package tours to North Korea with fairly uniform and standardized itineraries, Tongil intended to specialize in educational exchanges with the North. The brainchild of Alek Sigley, a young East Asian studies undergrad from Australia, Tongil would be offering that summer, for the first time in North Korea's history, a month-long intensive Korean language course for foreigners at one of Pyongyang's foremost educational institutions, Kim Hyong Jik University of Education. I immediately clicked on the link to the Tongil Tours website and applied.

There wasn't a moment of hesitation on my part. I had just finished my PhD, shutting the book on a five-year chapter of my life, and needed to lose myself in a new adventure. And there it was, spelled out in front of me. To dive into, to partake in—albeit in a very minor observer's role—this "history of the present." At the same time, I've had a love of languages ever since a comparative literature professor in college instilled in me the idea that you can't properly come to understand a place until you have learned to speak the language. This, I immediately understood, was the opportunity I had long yearned for but never thought would be possible—to come to understand the DPRK inside out, through its lingo—through an immersion, albeit limited, in daily life over an extended period of time. A chance to spend an entire month there, rather than the paltry few days of the typical tourist, absorbing all of the nuances that evade most foreigners.

Some family and friends feared I might lose myself in a more literal way. Just months before, University of Virginia student Otto Warmbier had been arrested in Pyongyang for attempting to steal a propaganda banner. Some voices in the

American media speculated that his detention was political and symbolic, that no American was truly safe to visit North Korea. But I had been in Pyongyang before when other American prisoners were being held. The media fury didn't faze me. By then, I was well aware of the rules one must submit to when journeying to the DPRK and had already debated the risks and rewards, both in my mind and in conversation with others.

I had also carefully considered the ethics of traveling to North Korea. Many are against it on principle—the old "torture porn" argument, which views travels to such dictatorships to be a cheap exercise in the lurid exploitation of "dark tourism," where all citizens one encounters should be viewed as nothing more or less than prisoners of the regime, human propaganda posters. And: the possibility of providing financial aid to the development of nuclear weapons.

No one has ever been able to prove that tourism funds the DPRK's military operations. Given the country's refusal to publicly disclose statistics about budgets and spending, the truth will likely never be known. Yet that doesn't stop a number of Western media outlets from asserting tourism's financial contribution to the nuclear program as though it were a fact. The North Korean government, for all the terrible things it undeniably and inexcusably does, also builds housing, schools, and hospitals for its citizens. If you had concrete proof that your tourism money was being spent on the construction of an orphanage, would this be the deciding factor that would persuade you to travel there? Are there not aspects of every country one might object to—including your own? Once we begin to impose travel boycotts on ethical grounds, we quickly run out of places we can go.

The "torture porn" argument is harder to engage because it really comes down to the attitude and intentions of the individual traveler, which is the one thing no one can control. North Korea is an impoverished country whose people live under the ever-shifting whims of an oppressive police state. Since nearly anyone, save for South Korean passport holders, can legally visit, then it follows that anyone can go to gawk, if that is one's main intention. But the implication that this is the primary motive of *everyone* who goes to North Korea is ridiculous and groundless. On my earlier visits to the country, I had met people from all walks of life on my tours, from doctors to architectural historians to flight attendants, who were visiting the country for any number of reasons. Given the difficulty and expense of traveling to such a place, there is little logic that can be unearthed in the assertion that the few souls who venture there have cynical motives for doing so.

Actually, the travel companies comprising the tiny market of North Korean tourism tend to emphasize the eye-opening, mind-changing vitality of one-on-one engagement between foreigners and North Koreans on these admittedly proscribed tours. And while I think it is right to be skeptical of any sales pitch, I have seen that this sort of engagement *is* effective. I have watched North Koreans, in conversing for the first time with an alien from the outside world, forced to alter and revise certain truisms they had been taught to believe. What's more surprising is that this process also happens in reverse. I've learned things from North Korea about the world I come from that I never would have figured out otherwise. I learned that a lot of what I had been taught to believe about North Korea is false, exaggerated, or distorted.

While I always dimly perceived that all media, no matter the degree of its asserted objectivity, is ideologically biased, I've come to understand that much of the reporting on North Korea in the West, reporting that shapes our understanding of North Korea, is especially ideological. The North Korean regime and its leaders have often been described as irrational. My experiences have made me question that contention and wonder if this "irrationality" is more often than not a label applied by those who do not wish to understand an opponent's worldview.

I believe there is a fundamental and flawed humanity that unites the people I have met there with those I have encountered elsewhere, a humanity that is often overlooked in the opportunistic pursuits of warspeak and political advantage. I have seen how agency continues to creep in and operate—even thrive—under conditions of top-down repression. My interactions with North Koreans have largely taken place in approved and monitored settings. But even in such situations, there are certain things that simply cannot be controlled—and the generation of new ideas is one of them. In that sense, travel to North Korea is actually a deeply subversive activity—one that has rich benefits for both parties. It is a fruitful substitute for the more consequential forms of diplomacy that should be taking place on a higher level but, as of this writing, are not.

The month I spent in Pyongyang made me realize that despite the frequency and reach of my peregrinations across the planet's surface, my foreignness, that ingrained sense of American privilege that is so unique and difficult to shake off, had always enabled me to put a certain distance between myself and the worlds I was exploring. That I myself, as a writer, was somehow outside of everything I was observing, outside of history even; that writing somehow made me a ghosted presence, an invisible vehicle that might serve as a mediation filter. It is a distance, I now realize, that precludes true understanding. Getting there was the easy part; in order to really *be* there, to reach that point where I could begin to understand the seemingly incomprehensible, I had to dissolve that artificial distance within myself—that invisible wall that separates "us" from "them." I took a long walk, and in the end, despite all appearances to the contrary, it was unguided.

After five years, I ended up somewhere that looked a lot different from the place where I started off. That's the best kind of getting lost—where in the end, you find so much more than just your way.

PART ONE

DREAMS OF A FORGOTTEN CITY

ONE

THERE'S A MIST that covers the entire city every morning. Waking up, it's like you haven't awoken at all. More like you are stepping from one dream into another. An enchanted otherworld. The mist doesn't blot out entirely all those vertical facades forming the cityscape. Rather, it enshrouds them, so the colorful buildings stand as actors behind a transparent stage curtain.

Staring through that curtain, your eyes can just make out the cherry-red flame crowning the Tower of the Juche Idea, perhaps even the apex of the Ryugyong Hotel. The mist curls like smoke over the Taedong River, snaking its way unhurriedly through the city center, a dredging boat or two punctuating its flow. Everything as still as these waters. You feel, at that moment, as though you are in a forgotten place, a world away from the dense mosaic of people and traffic and noise and neon signage of the twenty-first-century capital city.

In the midst of this reverie, a single tone pierces the silence. A tone so ethereal that for a moment, you might believe that it is borne by the wind. Its source could be an antiquated synthesizer, a theremin. You open your window to investigate. Seems to be coming from the main train station down the road. Could it be an air raid siren? No...for then it is followed by a second note. An eerie cinematic melody coalesces from the sonic ether.

It is a song. A plaintive cry. A gentle command. It is also, you realize, an alarm clock for the people of central Pyongyang, the signal that ignites the morning ritual. All around you, in the apartments of those pastel buildings, people are rising from their beds, water is splashed on faces, uniforms pressed, red pins installed on the left breast over each citizen's heart. The question posed by the song's title—"Where Are You, Dear General?"—is answered in its resounding, omnipresent sonority, reminding all who have been roused from their dream-land, and who inevitably know its absent words by heart, exactly where they are.

The capital's more ambitious denizens tend to rise even before the morning anthem's blare. Over in east Pyongyang—in a formerly rundown area that has in recent years become a bastion of the *nouveau riche,* replete with the alluring glitz of new shops, restaurants, recreation centers, and apartment complexes—Comrade Kim Nam Ryong is up at 4 a.m. to the theme from *Titanic,* set as the alarm on his Arirang smartphone. While his wife and eight-year-old daughter sleep, Comrade Kim does his morning exercises in the living room before sitting down with a cup of tea in the kitchen to read the morning newspapers. There's the *Rodong Sinmun,* the Worker's Newspaper—the country's main news organ—but also a slew of broadsheets reserved for the eyes of business elites. There are documents that have arrived from the Workers' Party related to his position as managing director of one of the state's international tourism companies outlining crucial policy and administrative directives that he will be obliged to carry out or at least pay lip service to. Turning back to the *Rodong Sinmun,* he carefully reads the daily editorial to gauge the day's tone from the government. Like most sophisticated Pyongyangites, he's become adept at reading between the lines; it is often what is glaringly absent in these rant-like missives that is most revealing.

At half past five, it is time to wake his wife and daughter. Together, they sit for a shared breakfast of maize porridge and hardboiled eggs, washed down with a sour yogurt drink imported from China, which his daughter will opt to substitute with powdered milk.

Shortly after Comrade Kim departs for the office at 7, a loud knock resounds. "Get up!" shouts a familiar voice. "Time to clean!"

Comrade Lee at the door. Head of the *inminban,* the People's residential unit. Every North Korean belongs to one. The units consist of anywhere between twenty and forty dwellings. In the Kims' building, all apartments sharing the central staircase constitute one *inminban.* The *inminbanjang* is usually a middle-aged or elderly woman. Her job is to "heighten revolutionary vigilance," as one propaganda poster has it. Keeping a watchful eye over the comings and goings in her assigned unit, down to the smallest detail. As Comrade Lee remembers well from her training, a good *inminbanjang* knows exactly how many spoons and chopsticks are in each family's kitchen, and can spill that information on cue if the need should arise.

The *inminbanjang* is, in a sense, the nosy neighbor elevated to the status of official position. They are residential spies required to keep track of the most intimate details of their charges' private lives. Up until 1995, *inminbanjang* were even required to report on the spending habits of citizens—especially large and luxurious items that suspiciously exceeded one's household income.

Like all jobs in the Democratic People's Republic of Korea, *inminbanjang* are selected. Women like Comrade Lee and their families can live quite well by local standards. In theory, they're supposed to inspect each apartment at least once a week. But in many *inminban* units—including the Kims'—this task has been neglected over time, reflecting the ever-widening gap between theory and practice since the new young leader took over. Still, an *inminbanjang* has the capacity to make one's life a living hell. Every enterprising wife, upon moving in to a new building, will go out of her way to make friends with the *inminbanjang*, flattering her with compliments and, more importantly, gifts. In return, minor blunders may be agreeably overlooked.

Some duties, however, cannot be avoided. As professional busybody, the *inminbanjang* is responsible for greeting and registering each and every visitor to the property. That way, no vendors, burglars, foreigners, or counterrevolutionaries are able to make their way onto the premises. When a visitor arrives from out of town—even if it's a relative who simply wishes to stay for one night—the *inminbanjang* dutifully inspects their travel permit so as to determine exactly how many nights the traveler may stay in Pyongyang. Travel permits to the capital are notoriously difficult to obtain—though bribes can make that process go much faster.

Then there are the unannounced midnight checks *inminbanjang* conduct together with the police a few times each month. Families woken up, apartments searched for illegal media and literature. The main concern is to make sure no one is sleeping on the premises without permission. Anyone caught— even if it happens to be a Pyongyang citizen who has failed to fill out the proper paperwork with the *inminbanjang*—faces interrogation, a fine, and a report filed with their own *inminban* and work unit. Such infractions can result in hours-long arguments with the police. Often those caught are lovers engaged in illicit affairs and so eager to avoid having their activities widely circulated. Luckily for Comrade Kim's family and their neighbors, Comrade Lee is a rather motherly *inminbanjang.* She discreetly warns her charges when those midnight inspections are imminent, especially the elderly widow next door to the Kims, who is known to rent out her second room as an hourly love hotel for extra income.

Comrade Lee is tough, however, on the morning discipline. In addition to serving as a *de facto* extension of the state security apparatus, the *inminbanjang* oversees the daily cleaning of the building's public spaces. It is the responsibility of one adult family member from each apartment—generally the wife, as married women, unlike men, are not required to hold day jobs in the DPRK—to spend an hour each morning on this activity. Mopping floors, trimming bushes, sweeping the sidewalk in front of the building, plucking any weeds that might have sprouted amid the landscaping. The result, as any visitor to Pyongyang immediately notices, is that the city is perpetually pristine.

Pyongyang has awoken. On Comrade Kim's commute, the streets bustle with activity. Impeccably dressed white-collar workers walking steadfastly toward dimly lit offices, red-scarved Young Pioneers, members of the obligatory Korean Children's Union, making their way in flocks to school. There are the drab gray-and-green uniforms denoting civil servants, government officials, police, military—a motley collection of functionary traffic forging pathways through the broad avenues, the alleyways between the bright-pastel buildings. At one time nearly everyone—every man, at least—was in uniform. Now restrictions have relaxed, and fashion has diversified, though it's still formally conservative: everything impeccably tailored, pressed, tidy. Still, there is some variety now. It's the middle of summer, so for men, that means short-sleeve shirts of all colors and designs, the only conforming feature a collar. For members of the burgeoning middle to upper classes, a wristwatch is *de rigueur,* with the more expensive European brands like Rolex being the most sought after—though upon closer inspection, most reveal themselves as knockoffs from neighboring China. Women's wear is more colorful and diverse. It was only in recent years, toward the end of Kim Jong Il's life, that women were permitted to wear trousers in public. Skirts still predominate and are required for many positions—always long enough to conceal the knees—but among the younger and more rebellious upper echelons, trousers or even pantsuits can be seen. Where the men have watches as their bling, women like to show off with fancy footwear. High heels combined with socks is a new look.

The morning rush hour brings long lines at bus stops and crowding on the subway cars, donated by the city of Berlin, and red trams, a familiar sight to anyone who's been to Prague; they were ordered in the early 1990s from what was then Czechoslovakia. Congestion in the center each morning is managed by the robotic choreography of turquoise-uniformed traffic girls. All vehicles are government- or military-owned, officially, though the policy has become lax enough in recent years that they are often used by well-connected private citizens on business that would hardly be regarded as official elsewhere in the world. Hundreds of taxicabs, run by some half-dozen companies, compete.

Comrade Kim arrives to find his office at the Korean State Travel Company glistening, as it is the duty of his underlings to arrive each morning an hour early to clean. The workday commences with a meeting. Comrade Kim's colleague reads aloud from the editorial of the *Rodong Sinmun,* its content breezily discussed, directives on daily tasks given. Although his organization's name is Korean State Travel Company, tourism is but one of the many businesses Comrade Kim, a managing director, engages in at work each day.

Since 2012, around the time that Kim Jong Un assumed power after his father's demise, the line dividing *private and unofficial* from *state-run and official* business has grown increasingly murkier, though this obfuscation has its roots in the unofficial forms of capitalism that arose in the black markets during the famine of the 1990s. In Pyongyang, senior-level officials with good political connections and the ability to travel abroad can, in essence, do whatever they want. Comrade Kim is ambitious and enterprising; he oversees a number of import-export ventures—food, medicine, consumer electronics, high-end cosmetics. His foreign contacts were made during the years he spent as an employee at two DPRK embassies abroad, a position that enabled him to travel to some two dozen countries. He is an emblem of what locals call the *donju,* the money-masters, the new rich. Different from the elites, whose privilege is handed to them at birth as a consequence of familial allegiance to the Kim family and who still form the topmost layer of prestige, the *donju* are more like second-tier elites, those who have acquired their power and wealth as a result of the accidental incursion of capitalism. The yuppies. Like other *donju,* Comrade Kim carries his activities out under the auspices of a more powerful sponsor working in the Ministry of Foreign Affairs, one of his old classmates from the Foreign Languages High School he attended. Such connections are not unlike the structure at big corporations in South Korea, where classmates go on to employ or do business with one another for life, forming guarded networks that are almost impossible for an outsider to break into. Each time a big deal goes through, Comrade Kim pays kickbacks to his sponsor—who, in turn, will pay a little to his own protector, all the way up to the very top of the command, the ruling family and their associates. Whether these chains make for an alternate taxation system in a country where there is officially no income tax or a mafia-style protection racket is neither discussed nor talked about. It's simply how it works these days and accounts for the increasing displays of wealth on the city's streets. It's trickle-down economics, East Asian–style. The elites enrich themselves and, in doing so, create new jobs and opportunities for the classes below them.

★

Across town, Kim Kum Hui begins her day singing and marching in single file behind her classmates into Pyongyang Primary School No. 4. Songs like "Defend the Headquarters of the Revolution," which describes the Korean people as "bullets and bombs," teach her that her duty as a Korean is to defend Marshal Kim Jong Un no matter what. Even acting as a human shield, if need be. When she learns about her country's biggest enemy, she is taught that the correct way to refer to one of its citizens is "American bastard."

Inside the main entrance, the students are greeted with a large painting of Kim Il Sung and Kim Jong Il standing in front of Mount Paekdu, toothy smiles plastered across the leaders' faces. Following her classmates, she bows before their likenesses on her way into the classroom.

Kum Hui spends twelve to sixteen hours away from her parents each school day. In George Orwell's *Animal Farm,* all the puppies are taken away from their mothers at birth, only to reemerge later as the warrior guard dogs that have been put into place to protect the system. Something similar happens here. In Confucian philosophy, the family is the most sacred and self-protecting unit—a highly suspect position to the North Korean state. It has to be reoriented: the state as the family. The paternal and maternal figures are wrapped up in two men, the saviors of the nation, and now the third descendant: the unblemished Paekdu bloodline. The patriarchs of the state-family formation.

A large part of the school curriculum is devoted to the study of their lives.

What they sacrificed. What they won. So that little children like Kum Hui could be the happiest in the world. She will learn that the correct way is to love them, to worship them. She will learn to accept everything she is taught without question. The questions will come later. But by then, she will know better than to voice them aloud. She will instead learn to form her own conclusions.

✪

Another tone slices through the day, signaling lunch hour. There is a burgeoning restaurant scene catering to elites, though most prefer to dine out for dinner, not lunch. Some will return home to eat with their spouses. Certain offices, like Comrade Kim's, offer an on-site cantina.

Over rice, kimchi, and bean paste soup, Comrade Kim chats with his colleagues. He'll be leaving work early, he tells them, along with Comrade Min. They're going to the airport. No, he's not going anywhere this time. He has to pick up a delegation—three foreigners. All young men. They'll be studying for a month at Kim Hyong Jik University of Education—an endeavor he himself set up. Such an undertaking would have been unthinkable just a couple years ago. But thanks to his standing, his connections, and the way things have been shifting around of late, the program was given the go-ahead.

His colleagues chew over this thoughtfully as a couple of the men light up post-meal cigarettes.

"And you're not going to believe this," he smiles as they lean in for the whispered punch line. "One of them is an American bastard."

TWO

IT'S THE MIDDLE of July 2016, and Beijing is as humid and muggy as always this time of year, with temperatures rising to the upper nineties in Fahrenheit. Sunbaked streets swarm with slow-moving traffic. My taxi finally makes it down the car-clogged six-lane highway to the flashy shopping district of Sanlitun, its showcase shops of Western brands ringed by a concentration of trashy bars catering to tourists and expats. I'm having lunch with my friend Simon Cockerell, who runs Koryo Tours, a travel agency that organizes group excursions to North Korea. I traveled with Koryo on my first four treks there. Tomorrow, however, I'm headed back on a different kind of trip. I've enrolled in a month-long Korean language intensive at Kim Hyong Jik University of Education. The university has a department offering bachelor's and master's degrees in Korean for foreigners, though currently only Chinese students are able to study there full-time. In an effort to expand its reach, not to mention its income, the university is making this first-time experiment in opening its doors to Western foreigners. It's not likely it will be viewed as a major triumph; I'm one of three students who have signed up. And another of the three is the owner of the company, Tongil Tours, a new competitor of Koryo, that arranged the trip with the North Koreans. So technically, I'm one of two.

Simon isn't surprised to hear of the low turnout. "Our numbers have been flat across the board this year," he tells me. "We're not losing any business. But we're certainly not gaining any."

I ask him if the situation has to do with recent tensions. "Not really," he says. "There are always *tensions*."

He stares into his plate of pasta, as though reconsidering that statement. "If it's anything, then it's Warmbier."

Over New Year's 2016, twenty-one-year-old University of Virginia student Otto Warmbier traveled to North Korea for a five-day trip with a company called Young Pioneers, named after the red-scarved socialist youth organization that all North Korean children must join. The company is known for its hard-partying tours targeting college-age students. Its motto: "providing budget travel to destinations your mother would rather you stayed away from." According to the accounts of group members, on their last night in Pyongyang, Warmbier got wasted with other tourists in the lobby bar of the Yanggakdo Hotel. Then, in the middle of the night, as the result of either a dare or drunken hubris, he snuck off into a staff-only room of the hotel and attempted to steal a propaganda banner. When he realized it was attached to a wooden partition, making it impossible to fold up and stuff in a suitcase, he simply left the banner, partition and all, on the ground and then went back to his room.

"The next morning," says Simon, "the staff shows up for work. 'What's this banner doing on the ground?' It's written in Korean, which of course Warmbier can't read. So he doesn't realize that it actually has Kim Jong Il's name written on it. Of course no Korean would leave it on the floor like that! They had to go back and watch the previous night's video surveillance footage to see what had happened. By that time, it was too late—there were too many people involved. They had to report it."

As his group was about to depart Pyongyang that morning, Warmbier was stopped at passport control. The police took him into custody.

In the aftermath, DPRK state media presented Otto Warmbier as an under-cover CIA agent on a mission. The American media asserted that Warmbier was an innocent pawn that the evil North Korean regime was attempting to use as a bargaining chip to extract more "aid" that it would actually use to develop its nuclear weapons program. Calls for banning US tourism to North Korea reso-nated throughout Congress and the media. Any American, the reasoning went, could be arrested on the flimsiest of grounds.

The bad press is taking its toll. "We've had some cancellations," Simon admits.

I wonder out loud whether Young Pioneers even bothers to brief its tour par-ticipants on the dos and don'ts of travel to North Korea like Koryo does. If it had, then Warmbier should have been well aware that, no matter your national-ity, stealing a propaganda banner would not go down well with the authorities. Meddling with a banner, after all, would result in serious, perhaps even deadly, punishment for a North Korean; why would a foreigner be considered exempt from similarly punitive measures? If anything, when traveling on an American passport to such a place, one intuits the need to be extra-vigilant in respecting local laws and customs.

I had heard that Warmbier originally intended to travel to Pyongyang with Koryo Tours. In his televised confession after his arrest in Pyongyang, Otto asserted that he contacted both Koryo and Young Pioneer Tours and that his father and brother considered coming along on the trip. Ultimately, Otto claimed in the confession, he decided to go with Young Pioneer Tours because their tours are less costly. I ask Simon if this is true. Instead of answering me, he looks down at his pasta and sighs.

"I don't know why his father didn't go with him in the end," says Simon. "I can't help but wonder if his father were with him on the trip—would he really have been wandering around in the staff-only section of the hotel at 2 a.m. on New Year's Eve? It's true that Young Pioneers is less expensive. And it's not that Koryo is *better*. We're just... Well, it's a different sort of culture."

He stops there, with characteristic modesty—in all the years we've known each other, I've never once heard Simon say anything remotely critical or unfriendly about any of Koryo's competitors in the industry. And I have to say that Koryo does offer a more *cultured* version of tourism to North Korea, which is precisely why its trips are slightly more expensive. It has also been in the business much longer than its competition in this tiny niche market, has good relations with its colleagues at the state-owned travel companies in Pyongyang, and, as the most successful company in terms of pure numbers, has been able to open doors to cities and entire regions of the DPRK that were previously off-limits to foreign tourists. While the itineraries are often similar, there is a distinction between the marketing and implicit philosophy between the two companies. Young Pioneers runs a DPRK-themed bar in the backpackers' paradise of Yangshuo in western China where you get a free shot if you book a tour. A 2017 Associated Press article about the company's "gung-ho culture" reported that the founder of Young Pioneer Tours was once hospitalized in Pyongyang after breaking his ankle stepping off a moving train in a state of inebriation. Koryo, on the other hand, stresses the mutual benefits of intercultural exchange, has coproduced films, art exhibitions, and sporting events with its North Korean partners, and raised funds for orphanages in the country.

"He probably wouldn't have gotten shitfaced drunk and done such a stupid thing is what you're saying."

Simon shrugs his shoulders. "I saw the video surveillance footage. The timer clearly shows it was 2 a.m. on the first of January. I don't know, mate. Do you think a sober person—in the middle of the night on New Year's Eve, no less—would have done such a thing?"

In the lobby of my hotel off the Northern 4th Ring Road, I shake hands with Alek Sigley. We had spoken on Skype shortly after I applied to the program, but this is our first time meeting in person. The son of an Australian sinologist and a Shanghainese mother, Alek is an East Asian studies undergrad who speaks fluent Chinese, Japanese, and Korean and has spent most of the past five years hopping between universities throughout the region. On his fifth visit to North Korea in 2013, his tour guide appeared one morning with her boss from the Korean State Travel Company, one Comrade Kim, who said he was eager to have an Australian business partner. He had the idea of importing the famous Australian beef. Alek told Comrade Kim politely that, while he appreciated the suggestion, he didn't want to jeopardize his entire future by violating international sanctions. Comrade Kim nodded his understanding and then suggested they team up to start a new travel company.

Comrade Kim's gentlemanly demeanor left a strong impression on Alek. Along with the guide, who went by her last name, Min, he had never met such sophisticated, worldly North Koreans on any of his previous visits. Both had spent a lot of time outside the country and had a good understanding of the world Alek came from; they were able to speak a common language. What's more, Pyongyang Project, the educational endeavor that Alek was traveling with, was falling apart. He and Comrade Kim both knew it. Kim suggested that Alek pick up where Pyongyang Project left off: a student-run initiative offering educational tours to the DPRK. Tongil Tours, named after the famous Tongil (Reunification) Street in Pyongyang, was born.

It's attributable to Kim's worldliness and internal contacts in the Ministry of Foreign Affairs and Ministry of Education that this study trip was able to happen. Many other organizations had attempted similar initiatives with the DPRK in the past, but none had come to fruition. Until now. Alek, who already speaks Korean to a relatively advanced degree, has to come along to see and experience it for himself. Since only a French graduate student and I have signed up, Tongil Tours is losing money on the trip, but in this case, Alek doesn't mind. Quiet and serious, he has the determination of someone who is led by his passions. He might be operating at a financial loss, but he is also breaking new ground. He takes the idea of engagement one step further than Koryo.

"We're at three different levels of Korean," Alek tells me as we wait in the lobby for our third party to show. "You're a total beginner, and I think Alexandre, the French guy, has studied for a year or so. I told them that we will need three different teachers, so we'll see. I think there shouldn't be any problems, though. I have a good relationship with our partners in Pyongyang. We're friends."

Our classes are to be held Monday through Friday, two hours each morning, at Kim Hyong Jik University of Education in east Pyongyang. Named after Kim Il Sung's father, who was himself a teacher, the university is the country's most prestigious training ground for future pedagogues and is also home to a Korean linguistics department. Afternoons and weekends will be devoted to homework and excursions.

"Here comes Alexandre." Alek nods toward the door. Outside, a tall, strapping figure hurriedly removes his luggage from the trunk of a taxi and ambles his way through the rain into the hotel lobby. Like me, Alek has only previously met Alexandre through Skype. They instantly recognize each other.

"Guys," says Alexandre, using the unlikely American vernacular as he takes turns shaking our hands, "great to meet you both." He has the gregarious confidence of someone twice his twenty-one years. Someone who has clearly seen much of the world. Whereas Alek, with a slight hunch he attributes to an adolescence spent playing computer games, holds himself with a certain amount of reserve and shyness—though he can also cut loose and be quite funny when opening up about his secret non-intellectual passions like death metal, geeking out about his love of the North Korean girl group the Moranbong Band, and revealing himself to be a secret stoner—Alexandre radiates a jovial openness so unlike the common stereotype of impossible complexity foreigners often hold of the French. His exuberance is underlined by his stocky, solid build and handsome face. He's also a travel addict, has a deep-sea diving license, and studied abroad in Dubai before gaining his recent place at the Sciences Po in Paris. I realize I'm at least twelve years older than the others, but it's fine. We go for beers and barbecue across the street.

"Guys, just to let you know," Alexandre says, suddenly turning serious, "I won't be drinking on this trip. As a rule, I do not drink when I go there. I'm very sorry. It's just..."

"You're afraid something might slip out?" I venture.

"I know myself." Alexandre smiles self-consciously.

And he knows the DPRK. He's been four times before, the same number as me. Alek has us dwarfed, at ten prior visits. Though probably none of us will ever manage to top Simon, who's visited on a record hundred and fifty occasions. This is how DPRK obsessives get to know each other. Where you've been. What you've done. What you still haven't seen but would like to.

It's this latter piece we get stuck on. Alek has sent us a proposed itinerary composed largely of excursions all three of us have already seen and done. Any wiggle room?

Alek assures us it can all be adjusted tomorrow on the ground, with Kim and Min. We head back to our rooms across the street, agreeing to meet in the lobby at nine the next morning and share a taxi to the airport.

THREE

"PYONGYANG," AS ONE of the city's first foreign explorers described it in 1894, "has a truly beautiful situation on the right or north bank of the clear, bright Taedong, 400 yards wide at the ferry. It occupies an undulating plateau, and its wall, parallel for two miles and a half, rises at the stately Water Gate from the river level, and following its windings, mounts escarped hills to a height of over 400 feet, turning westwards at the crest of the cliff at a sharp angle marked by a pavilion, one of several, and follows the western ridge of the plateau, where it falls steeply down to a fertile rolling plain."

Throughout history, Pyongyang has gone by as many different names as it has identities. The city has been cursed with a cyclical history of war, defeat, and rebirth. It was once known as the "capital of willows," but owing to the ravages of constant battle and rapid industrialization, there are far fewer willow trees around today.

The name "Pyongyang" means "flatland," an apt description for the landscape surrounding the city, which is irrigated by the strength of the wide Taedong River, making it ideal for both farming and habitation. The mountainous northern half of the country is largely inhospitable to both agriculture and human habitation. By contrast, Pyongyang and its surroundings seem like a natural idyll in otherwise hostile environs.

As DPRK official history would have it—a version of history contested virtually everywhere else on the planet—the origins of the Korean people can be traced to Pyongyang, or at least the outskirts of the modern city, the northwestern suburb of Kangdong, not far, as it happens, from the summer residence of Kim Jong Un. Here, the North Koreans believe, was the ancient city of Asadal, where a king named Tangun established his capital some five thousand years ago.

Historians outside the DPRK have positioned the kingdom in what is now Liaoning Province in northeastern China. Most regard Tangun's existence as myth. His mother was said to have been a bear. Kim Il Sung believed that Tangun actually existed and that the historical proof of his existence had been spitefully destroyed by the Japanese during their brutal occupation of the country from 1910 to 1945. Shortly before his death in 1994, Kim ordered an archeological expedition to find the tomb of Tangun in order to prove his hunch. Miraculously, some months later, DPRK archeologists managed to do just that. Conveniently, it was found on Pyongyang's outskirts.

Besides the obvious propaganda value of locating the birthplace of Korean civilization near the capital of the DPRK, squaring the chronology proved problematic. While the conventional dating of the kingdom's founding is 2333 BC, DPRK historians insist that the bones discovered dated back to at least 3000 BC. If true, this would make Korea one of the oldest civilizations on record. This unlikelihood is presented as fact in the DPRK. During a visit to the Korean History Museum on Kim Il Sung Square, a guide once asked my group if we could name the five major ancient civilizations. We awkwardly stumbled through a list of the Mesopotamians, the Egyptians, the Mayans, the Hans in China... When we weren't able to finish to her satisfaction, she granted us the correct answer: the Taedong River civilization of King Tangun. But of course!

In most mainstream historical accounts, Pyongyang hadn't amounted to much until AD 427, when it was made the capital of the Koguryo Dynasty, one of the Three Kingdoms of Korea. The Koguryo—which would later morph into the Koryo, giving rise to the English word "Korea"—became one of the more powerful actors in the struggle for control of the Korean peninsula, and the next two hundred years might very well have been Pyongyang's heyday. It enjoyed a level of prosperity and vitality that it has struggled to regain ever since. For this reason, North Korean historians tend to favor this period of the peninsula's lengthy history over others, as it was one of the uncontestable moments when the northern half, and Pyongyang in particular, reigned supreme. (In South Korea, the Silla Dynasty, another of the Three Kingdoms, which had its capital in Seoul, is similarly revered by nationalist-minded scholars and activists.)

Alas, Pyongyang's good fortune was not to last. Beginning in the late 500s, a series of Chinese attacks against the Koguryo rulers centered on Pyongyang, taking advantage of factionalism and territorial spats that were tearing apart the Koguryo's ruling circle. Finally, in 645, the Silla Dynasty in the south teamed up with the Tang Dynasty of China to lay siege to the Koguryo capital. This would be its downfall. By 688, the city of willows had devolved into a city of weeds.

★

After a long period of instability, the Koryo Dynasty was established by King Taejo in 918. The city was given yet another name—Sogyong, or "Western Capital." That qualifying *Western* is key for understanding the city's provincial status during the period; the actual capital of the Koryo Dynasty, on the border with modern-day South Korea, was Kaesong.

During the Koryo reign, Confucianism was imported from China, together with its civil service exams and doctrine of morality that would come to serve as the foundation for much of Korean law and customs over the coming centuries. At the same time, this gave rise to a deep-seated resentment among Buddhists, who felt that Korea had become weakened under the influence of Confucian ideals. One Buddhist monk, Myo O, left Kaesong with his followers in an attempt to establish an independent rival state in Sogyong/Pyongyang. The rebellion was quickly crushed, but it wasn't the region's only tumult in those years. As a less guarded secondary capital, Sogyong/Pyongyang would be the target of numerous foreign invasions. The kingdom was under constant siege from the Mongols, the Khitans of Manchuria, and the Chinese, and the city would suffer heavily from the violence of these attempted coups.

In 1392, the Koryo would fall to the Joseon Dynasty, which would endure for five centuries, making it the longest period of Confucian rule in Korea's history. The capital shifted from Kaesong to Seoul, and Pyongyang was made a provincial capital—not quite a backwater, but still not the center of the action. The far more impressive cultural developments were under way in Seoul under King Sejong, whose accomplishments include the creation of the unique Korean alphabet—known as Hangul in the south and everywhere else in the world, though in the North called Chosongul. Choson, after the Joseon Dynasty, is the name North Koreans use when referring to their country.

No kingdom, it turns out, could protect the conspicuous peninsula for long; its geographically strategic importance simply couldn't be ignored. The Japanese made their first bids on Korea in the 1590s, the beginning of a centuries-long struggle. Much of Korea was ravaged in what DPRK historians would come to term the Imjin Patriotic War. The city was taken by the Japanese in 1592. The Joseon army was notoriously weak. King Sejong begged for assistance from the Ming court in China. It responded by sending some thirty thousand troops from Manchuria in an offensive that succeeded in regaining the city in the following year's Siege of Pyongyang. (History has an ironic way of repeating itself. In the Korean War, Kim Il Sung would similarly be forced to call upon China for assistance once the Americans landed in the South, and Mao would respond by sending in two hundred thousand troops on October 25, 1950, which would quickly enable the communists to retake Pyongyang.)

But in the subsequent century, several more attacks—alternately by the Japanese and Manchu tribesmen—would see the city completely destroyed. Seemingly each time Pyongyang was rebuilt, violent tragedy would strike again. These invasions left Koreans with a deep-seated suspicion of foreigners—a tendency that endures to this day, particularly in the North. During the latter years of the Joseon Dynasty in the nineteenth century, Korea attempted to cut itself off from the world as a protective measure as much as possible, earning the moniker "Hermit Kingdom," which is still frequently applied to the North. Its sole diplomatic relations were with China, of which Korea was essentially a client kingdom.

That didn't stop other nations from trying to force Korea open to trade. One of the more riotous manifestations of Korea's resistance to these endeavors occurred in Pyongyang in 1866, when an American merchant marine vessel, the *General Sherman,* was attacked by locals who killed all crew members onboard. If you visit the Korean History Museum on Kim Il Sung Square today, you will be shown a painting depicting the attack, which has been interpreted as an organized rebellion against foreign imperial forces and which the North Koreans claim was led by Kim Ung Woo, the great-grandfather of Kim Il Sung—although there exists no historical evidence to back up either claim.

Although North Koreans prefer to emphasize the supposed purity and originality of their culture, foreign influence has made its mark on the evolution of Korea since the twelfth century. The Chinese introduced Confucianism, and many supposedly indigenous customs actually evolved during the more recent Japanese occupation. By the time of the *General Sherman* incident, another outside influence, one that would have long-lasting consequences, had already laid its roots deep in Korean soil. Koreans' spiritual life, up to this time, had been dominated by a mixture of Buddhist and Confucian belief as well as widespread Shamanist practice. In 1603, a Korean diplomat named Yi Gwang Jeong returned to the kingdom from Beijing carrying a curious collection of books by Matteo Ricci, a Jesuit missionary to China. The spread of Christianity made the Joseon imperial authorities nervous. They viewed the religion as a subversive threat to their rule. Crackdowns were harsh and frequent; many were martyred. The persecution of Christians culminated in 1866, when eight thousand Catholics throughout Korea were killed in a massive uprising that also saw the death of a number of foreign missionaries.

As Korea began to tentatively crack its door to foreigners in the late nineteenth century, Christianity was increasingly tolerated and Pyongyang became the missionary base for Korea. By 1880, the city was a veritable holy land, home to more than one hundred churches and more Protestant missionaries than any other city in Asia. Up until the Korean War, the northern half of the peninsula boasted more Christians than the southern half. Communist rule would put an end to all that, forcing Christians to flee south. Today, 30 percent of the population of South Korea claims adherence to the faith, making it by far the most successful missionary endeavor ever accomplished in East Asia.

By 1890, Pyongyang boasted some forty thousand inhabitants. If the growing population implied a stability that had been so lacking in the past, new trouble was brewing. Look at a map and the vulnerable position of Korea is immediately obvious. Sandwiched between China and Japan, Korea became an increasing point of contention in the mounting tensions between the two great Asian powers. War was inevitable, and Korea was literally in the middle of it.

Pyongyang was the scene of a major land battle between the two powers in 1894 that completely decimated the city. The clash would end with the Qing Dynasty forced to sign an agreement acknowledging the total independence of Korea—but that independence was won at a harsh price. Weeds once more replaced willows, and many surviving inhabitants would perish in the following year as a result of plague.

Korean authorities were able to reestablish political control in 1897 under the official name of the Korean Empire, based in Seoul. Pyongyang had been rebuilt and would serve as the capital of the newly demarcated South Pyeongan province until 1946. Once again, peace would not last. In 1904, war broke out between two feuding empires, Russia and Japan, each of which held imperial ambitions for Korea and Manchuria. Japan occupied Pyongyang. Although the war would only last a year, it was long enough to give the Japanese useful insight into the city's infrastructure. In 1910, they commenced their occupation of all of Korea—an occupation that would endure until 1945.

✪

The Japanese occupation is really where the modern history of North Korea begins. By most accounts, it was a brutal and ruthless occupation, with Koreans treated as second-class citizens at best, outright slaves at worst. It is a period that haunts the North to the present day; on my first trip to the DPRK in 2012, one of my guides cheerily informed me, "Don't worry. We hate the Japanese much more than we hate you Americans!"

The force of oppression exercised by the Japanese over their Korean colonial subjects was exerted in waves. The first ten years were characterized by the concentration of military force, with all forms of dissent among Koreans ruthlessly crushed. This endured until 1919, when on the first of March a protest against Japanese rule swept the peninsula. In response, the colonial authorities relaxed their iron grip, allowing limited forms of free expression among Koreans, who nonetheless were largely relegated to serve as either feudalist slaves or elite collaborators.

The one bright side of the Japanese occupation—a side the North would certainly never subsequently acknowledge—was sweeping modernization. Urban development, economic expansion, and forms of mass media and entertainment that hadn't existed previously spread under Japanese rule. Pyongyang was built up into an industrial center. Since the north is largely mountainous, much of the peninsula's industry would be installed and developed there—a factor that would greatly benefit the infrastructure and economy of North Korea in the first years of the peninsula's division, while the south, with its fertile plains, was given over to agriculture.

As Japan's entry in the Second World War neared, harsh measures were reintroduced, with Koreans forced into working at Japanese factories and serving on the front line in battle. In 1939, with Japan becoming increasingly fascist, Koreans even had to take Japanese names. Tens of thousands of Korean women were made to work as "comfort women," sex slaves for Japanese soldiers. Still, the Japanese could take credit, for better or worse, for leading Korea into the twentieth century; by the time the occupation ended with Japan's surrender at the end of World War II, Korea was the second-most developed nation in all of Asia—next to Japan itself.

Kim Il Sung was born in Pyongyang two years into the occupation but wouldn't spend much time there until 1945, when he returned to his native city and was shortly thereafter installed as leader by the Soviets of the newly created Democratic People's Republic of Korea. From hence, the city would be granted yet another name. The capital of willows and weeds was now the "Capital of the Revolution": a title it enjoys to this day.

FOUR

JULY 23, 2016. It is mostly Western tourists on Air Koryo flight 152 from Beijing. A handful of elites returning home from business and study trips abroad. The tourists riffle through their complimentary copies of *The Pyongyang Times* and the glossy *Korea Today,* published by Pyongyang's Foreign Languages Publishing House; the Koreans onboard peruse the day's *Rodong Sinmun.* After takeoff, monitors come down to display the in-flight entertainment, a concert of the Moranbong Band, the country's hottest girl group. Red-uniformed stewardesses make their way down the aisle offering drinks and the notorious Air Koryo burger that only the hungriest of passengers will dare touch. Crossing the border into Korean air space, triumphant trumpets sound and the head stewardess delivers a short breathless revolutionary lecture over the intercom. After ninety minutes, we begin our descent over the denuded hills surrounding Pyongyang's Sosan Airport.

Since my last visit, the airport has undergone a major renovation; it now looks like an actual airport, replete with terminals, gates, security, and check-in areas rather than the large single warehouse of a room that was the airport's previous form. Like many things in the new North Korea, all appears "normal" on the surface, though upon closer inspection, the only plane on the tarmac is ours. Planes are now connected to jet bridges—previously one walked down the steps onto the tarmac and into the building. Once inside, the airport is largely desolate, save for the staff—very few flights land in or depart Pyongyang these days. Still, everything is impressively gleaming. That new airport smell!

First stop is passport control. A prestige posting for the young soldiers on duty in immaculately pressed uniforms. Once your passport and visa—issued on a separate flimsy sheet of paper with photo pasted in, handed to Alexandre and me at the airport in Beijing by Alek—have been inspected, you breeze past to the luggage carousel. This is where the chaos begins. The country is under international sanctions, so that means every North Korean on the flight has brought back boxes and bags full of electronics, cosmetics, and food for selling, trading, gifting, bribing, or personal consumption. It takes nearly an hour for our luggage to finally come through.

Then there's customs, a process that has become much more rigid since Kim Jong Un recently increased the crackdown on foreign media entering the country. On my previous visits, I breezed through. Now, each and every passenger's bags are inspected, and we are instructed while standing in line to remove our phone and tablets, computers, and books for inspection.

Simon had warned me the day before about the new procedure. I spent most of last night after dinner cleaning my hard drives, deleting all the South Korean movies and ebooks about North Korea I had amassed over the years. On Koryo's last trip, the customs officer had been clicking through the video files on one tourist's iPad and randomly opened a file that turned out to be gay porn. Oops. The iPad was confiscated but returned to Simon the next day, via the North Korean guide, with the file deleted.

The result of this rigorous inspection ritual is a painfully slow-moving line. We stand there bored, chatting idly with a North Korean student returning from a year abroad at a university in Bangkok, trying to make sense of the swarm around us. A couple of elites push their luggage cart, piled high with Gucci valiserie, to the front of the line, where the soldier standing guard nods and lets them through.

When it's my turn, the middle-aged officers erupt in laughter. I'm spending a month here, so my arms are weighed down with a stack of books, iPad, laptop, mobile phone... They have their task cut out for them. One soldier grabs the book on top of my pile and attempts to read the English title aloud: "Landyscabies opuh Comooneezehmuh." "Communism," I correct him. He looks back at me skeptically. Another grabs my laptop, opens the lid, turns it on, and then holds it upside down toward the light as though expecting something to come tumbling out of it. "How much cost-uh?" he asks me. I'm confused. "How much cost-uh computer US dollar?" he clarifies. "Oh, uh... five hundred bucks," I say. He nods, satisfied, clearly more interested in the value of the object than what it might contain.

Another soldier appears and grabs my iPad, flips it open, and demands I enter the password. At the exact same moment, another comes and orders me to open my suitcase. Unsure whose call to answer first, I flail between them.

Yet another materializes to ask if I've brought any magazines or books into the country. Well, yes, but your comrades have already taken them away somewhere, I try to explain in a combination of mime and dumbspeak. He demands I go find them, while the soldier who has asked me to open my suitcase starts yelling at me that I still haven't opened it and I'm holding up the line.

With my luggage now strewn across the floor in a confused pile and an equally confused mob of passengers, soldiers, and civilians milling about, I spy a group of soldiers standing before a metal examination table on the side inspecting my books with a laser light. I go to retrieve them, but on the way, I am stopped by a female soldier who inquires where my electronic devices are, a question to which I had assumed *she* might hold the answer; forbidden from moving forward to regain my books, I retreat back to my luggage.

Just as I start to suspect I won't be going anywhere for the rest of the day, a man around my age in khakis and Rolex watch, a typically manicured *donju*, busts into the security zone from the waiting area outside, takes one look at me and my stack of books, and emits an enormous belly laugh. He cracks a joke in the direction of the customs officers and soldiers that gets them all laughing and then says "Come on, Travis," helps me gather up my belongings, and smoothly escorts me into the arrivals zone, where Alek and Alexandre are waiting alongside our two guides, Min and Roe. Comrade Kim slaps me on the back. "Welcome to Korea!"

As a foreign tourist to North Korea, one of the first things that happens once you meet your two mandatory guides in the waiting lounge is that they take your passport away. Ostensibly a practical measure—it is your guides, after all, who will be responsible for you for the duration of your stay. But it's also symbolic: You are not a citizen of the country. You are not entitled to the freedoms—limited though they may be—of a DPRK citizen. You are a guest—not of any one person or particular entity, but of the country, as a monolithic whole. For that is exactly how North Koreans are taught to think of themselves in the presence of foreigners: the omniscient first person plural.

Usually, tourists are given a stiff introductory speech in the van on the way into the city, featuring such fun facts and figures as the longitudinal and latitudinal coordinates of the Korean peninsula and the population size of the two Koreas. But since we've all been here before, these formalities are put aside in favor of casual chatter as we all get to know each other.

Min, a small but corpulent clear-complexioned woman of twenty-six, is asking Alek in nearly unaccented English about his girlfriend, who accompanied him on his last trip to the country. It was Min who first introduced Alek to her boss, Comrade Kim, who's up riding shotgun next to our young driver, on that fateful trip in 2013 that led to the formation of Tongil Tours. Min will be our lead guide. Roe, the junior guide, is actually Min's senior in age; I ask him how old, and he gives me a knowing smile and laughs. "The same age as you," he says. "But you look much younger!" Roe smiles throughout much of the journey back to the hotel. When his face relaxes to its usual expression, it is one of pensive anxiety. An expression that seems to give away more about his insecurities than he himself would ever care to.

Min is shy around Alexandre and me at first, but she turns out to be much chattier than Roe. Roe gives away very little about himself, other than that he's not a native Pyongyangite. He comes from the coastal city of Wonsan, where we plan to visit at the end of the trip. Since he doesn't hail from Pyongyang and he's in a lower position than a woman ten years his junior at the Korean State Travel Company, I suspect that he's of slightly lower *Songbun*. Songbun is the official class system, unacknowledged by the government but widely known. It's completely political, tied to your family's history; you're born into it and can never rise above it—though do something wrong and you can readily fall. That his father was able to get him to the capital, where he studied at the Pyongyang University of Foreign Studies prior to taking his present position, means that his family isn't the lowest of the low; no one from the hostile class would ever be permitted to resettle in Pyongyang and given the opportunity to interact with foreigners. It reveals a certain ambition on the part of his family—that they were able to get themselves, or at least their son, to Pyongyang during the blackest period of the country's history, the famine years of the 1990s. And Roe did it without ever even serving in the military, which means he doesn't suffer from the permanent sunburn that most North Korean men, such as our young driver, wear, a sign of having been drafted for manual labor outdoors. He knows how to get out of things—how to remain in the shade. Maybe that's why he looks worried all the time. Eventually, I come to realize that he is probably just very bored. He's one of sixty tour guides at the Korean State Travel Company. It's a cushy job—which, in North Korea, means very little to do. Since there is so little tourism to the country, it involves showing up at the office every day, sitting around, and figuring out new ways to kill time.

My airport savior is up in the front cracking jokes and snickering, in a perpetual state of amusement. "And you!" Comrade Kim laughs, turning around to shake his finger at me in mock reprimand. "You are the first American ever to study in our country. Very brave man!"

Our driver, Hwa, laughs, though he can't understand English. He has the cherubic looks of the perpetual innocent, all smiles and sweetness. The van will be our chief mode of transport for the next month. We're on our way to the Sosan Hotel. Although we're technically here as students, we're not permitted to stay in the dorms—Alek and Comrade Kim are working on that for future trips. Instead, we're staying in the larger of the two hotels in west Pyongyang's designated sports village, built for the occasion of the 1989 World Festival of Youth and Students, intended as a communist alternative to the Summer Olympics, which, to Pyongyang's chagrin, had taken place in Seoul the year prior.

On the way, we drive past the Arch of Triumph, the first stop for most tourists in Pyongyang. Erected on the spot where Kim Il Sung met a crowd of cheering Koreans in August 1945 to mark the end of Japanese colonial oppression and the start of a new era, the monument bears a strong resemblance to its Parisian namesake, though Pyongyang's is eleven meters higher—which the guides never tire of pointing out.

Stalin's influence can be felt everywhere in Pyongyang. Especially in structures like these. Towering neoclassical facades fronting vast areas of monumental empty space. The individual is meant to feel tiny and insignificant when confronted with such colossal architecture. As with many of the landmark monuments punctuating the Pyongyang skyline, the Arch was unveiled in 1982 on the occasion of Kim Il Sung's seventieth birthday. A showcase piece of what some historians have come to call "succession architecture," a series of projects Kim Jong Il initiated in lavish honor of his father.

Today, aficionados of Soviet Realist architecture, upon seeing the city for the first time, are often struck by its beauty. Expecting to be confronted with a montage of gray monolithic prefab apartment blocks arranged along pompously widened boulevards, the sort of soul-deadening concrete jungle synonymous with other Stalinist cities, what they find stretched before them is instead a highly varied arrangement of muted pastel rectangles. It is not a wild, Latinate geometry, to be sure, but a tasteful and restrained sea of blocks awash in shadings of light peach, turquoise, lavender, rose, golden amber, canary, ochre, and mint among the whites and grays. Photographed in black-and-white, parts of the city still look like East Berlin. It's amazing what a coat of paint can do.

Pyongyang has its fair share of monuments. But the majority of structures comprising the cityscape are residential apartment blocks. Pyongyang was all but obliterated by its enemies in a bombing campaign that took place during the Korean War in 1952. By the end of it, only three buildings erected by the Japanese would remain intact. Still, even as the war waged, as official biographies would have it, Kim Il Sung had his mind on the postwar urban development of Pyongyang. In 1951, he supposedly even called upon an architect, as planes buzzed overhead and the blare of anti-aircraft guns reverberated, to discuss his vision for a rebuilt capital. The city was to be the DPRK's most emblematic work of propaganda art, replete with wide boulevards, huge squares, tall and imposing monuments—in fact, much like the model of city he had seen in the Soviet Union built under the image of his mentor Stalin, of which East Berlin came to serve as an icon. A city made of white concrete, sparkling clean and devoid of traffic jams. The very epicenter of the Korean People's Paradise.

With Pyongyang in ruins, the signing of the armistice was hardly an excuse to relax after a brutal three-year war. Kim took a cue from the Stakhavonite movement in the Soviet Union, whereby model workers were rewarded and celebritized, inspiring others to outdo them. Using language he imagined would appeal to the exhausted but still-militarized populace, Kim fashioned the need for a quick rebuilding of Pyongyang into a nationwide "battle." He enlisted the services of everyone he could get—not just soldiers but university students and office workers as well—to keep the construction sites in operation twenty-four hours a day.

The result of this frenzied work effort was what an employee of the Pyongyang Architecture Institute characterized as the country's first "miracle": the "Pyongyang Speed" campaign, where by the end of the 1950s, a family-sized apartment could be constructed in thirty minutes. The city was on its way to becoming the elite dwelling place that it is today. If you ask an average North Korean living anywhere else in the country what their dream is, most will answer: "To see Pyongyang in my lifetime."

✪

We cruise through the city streets. Although it's Saturday, there's a steady flow of traffic and a lot more taxicabs than I ever recall seeing before. After dropping Comrade Kim off at his office on the willowed banks of the Potong River, we make our way to the hotel. Situated on an incline overlooking a football stadium and the surrounding palaces devoted to tae kwon do and gymnastics, the Sosan's towering, thirty-floor, salmon-colored presence unmistakably connotes *hotel* in international functionalist lingo. The building underwent renovation last year for the seventieth anniversary of the founding of the Workers' Party, and the empty lobby is grand and palatial, much like the other Pyongyang hotels I've stayed at in the past. In place of the usual souvenir shop, there is an outlet vending sportswear and gear.

As we wait for Min and Roe to check us in, I'm reminded by the row of international clocks posted above the reception desk that my watch is off by thirty minutes—yet another change from my visit to the country just two years ago. On August 15, 2015, the seventieth anniversary of Korea's liberation from Japan, the North officially set its clocks back thirty minutes, creating its own time zone. This was to revert to the time the country kept before the occupation. But this modification can also be seen as yet a further notch in North Korea's idiosyncratic manufacture of time; rather than referring to the birth of Christ as their way of marking the years, North Korea marks the first year, Juche 1, as 1912, which saw the birth of Kim Il Sung. So here we are in Juche 105, 6:46 p.m.: thirty minutes behind South Korea, thirty minutes ahead of Beijing. One thousand nine hundred eleven years behind the rest of the world.

My room is on the twenty-eighth floor, across from Alek and Alexandre, who are sharing to cut down on costs. We drop our bags off. I'm grateful to find that the renovations weren't restricted to the lobby. My room has two brand-new queen-sized beds and glittering made-in-China furnishings, a big closet, a balcony overlooking the city—and a leaking air conditioner. So much for the renovation work. I don't have much time to take it all in, however. The comrades want us to come down for dinner.

Min had frowned when Alek told her in the van that we wanted to make some changes to the itinerary. So Alexandre suggested we offer to take them out for pizza that night to help smooth things over. Min and Roe smiled at the idea. Things are going well.

They're eager to show us the newly opened Mirae Scientists' Street, where there is also a new Italian restaurant. The street occupies six lanes between the Taedong River and the main railway station. Replete with the snazziest new apartment buildings—with their strange but endearing blend of postmodern skyrise and retro-futuristic seventies housing block—it's an architecture you can't really see anywhere else. The street, which is meant to house scientists and institutes from the Kim Hwak University of Technology, is the city's latest showpiece. Here we are in the twenty-first century, it seems to say: we've finally made it.

Inside the restaurant, we order pizzas for the table. Driver Hwa eyes the strange bread with bloodred sauce and white goo suspiciously. He has never seen or tasted pizza before. We cut a slice and put it on his plate, encouraging him. He picks up a pair of metal chopsticks and pokes at it before digging in for his first bite. He smiles. Not bad!

We order beers and soju. Since Alexandre's not drinking, there's more for the rest of us. Min chatters away idly. "Ahh, sometimes I really miss Cuba," she says absentmindedly.

What?! Cuba? I was just there!

"I lived there for eight years," she tells me.

Eight years? I'm shocked. It's rare to meet a North Korean who's even traveled, let alone lived, abroad. Especially one so young. "So were your parents diplomats?" I ask.

She shakes her head no and then looks down embarrassed. Too much information, too soon.

Suddenly, music comes blasting through the PA system, the triumphant opening bars to "Dash Towards the Future," the latest Moranbong Band hit. Our waitresses step in front of the karaoke machine with wireless microphones in hand and fall into a synchronized dance routine as they sing the opening bars.

> *In this proud era we reached our youth*
> *There is nothing we cannot achieve*
> *Dash towards the future—a new century is calling*

My country—a strong and prosperous fatherland,
Let's cultivate it into a paradise!

The North Korean guests at the tables surrounding us clap their hands to the rhythm, drunkenly elated.

After dinner, I suggest we finish the night off with our own round of karaoke at the Taedonggang Diplomatic Club. With its somewhat deceptive name, the club was built in 1972 to host diplomatic relations of a very specific sort—meetings between North and South Korean nationals. When the frequency of such acts of diplomacy dwindled and showed no signs of increasing, it was time to turn the building into a restaurant and recreational facility for foreigners and their hard currency. It is located in the vicinity of the Taedong River and the diplomatic quarter; it is not, however, the exclusive domain of diplomats—all foreigners, whether they be tourists, diplomatic staff, NGO workers, or students like us, are permitted to use its facilities, which now include several restaurants, an indoor swimming pool, karaoke rooms, and bars. The Diplomatic Club also functions as a sort of continuing education center, with foreign residents able to take classes here in the Korean language, painting, calligraphy, swimming, and tae kwon do.

Mostly, however, in a city all but devoid of nightlife options in the conventional sense, the Diplomatic Club serves as a haven for drunken debauchery. On an earlier trip to the country, one of my guides, an older woman who had lived abroad in the 1980s as an employee at the DPRK Embassy in Vienna, was hopped up to get down to "Dancing Queen" the moment she checked that the door to our private karaoke salle was tightly secured. Throughout the course of the night, she proved herself to be familiar with ABBA's entire repertoire. Even more astounding, she smoked several cigarettes. It's common for men to smoke in the DPRK (it is believed that the country statistically has the highest rate of smoking-related deaths in the world) but it is *verboten* for women to partake—in public, at least. North Koreans of both sexes, however, love to drink, much like their Southern counterparts, and it is among the few activities that know no restrictions here.

Oddly enough, tonight I've been delegated to give a tour of the premises. Neither Min nor Roe has been here before, nor have Alek and Alexandre. Even though it's Saturday night, the place is eerily deserted. We make our way down the dimly lit marble corridor into the karaoke bar. Two waitresses chat with a single customer, a middle-aged man from Nepal.

Alexandre and Alek take advantage of the empty room to impress our hosts with their extensive repertoire of DPRK pop songs. A waitress turns on the karaoke machine, and Alexandre bursts into a rendition of "Whistle." A love song, highly unusual for North Korea, it stems from the late 1980s and early 1990s, reflecting somewhat of a relaxation from the heavy ideological content that infuses most cultural expression. The era could hardly be recognizable as a perestroika—the DPRK leadership watched the transformations under way in China and the Soviet Union with a combination of shock and dread—but it was also during this period that Kim Jong Il was at the height of his obsession with modernizing his country's film industry.

Up until the late 1980s, romance had never been a big theme of DPRK films, music, or literature. The only time the word "love" was meant to be uttered was in reference to the Leader, the Nation, the Revolution. "People love love," Kim Jong Il reportedly complained. "We must show it on the screen!" What followed from this directive was a set of films featuring story lines in which attractive citizens would fall in love with one another for their selfless patriotism and devotion to the revolution. In literature, the "Hidden Heroes" movement of the period turned its fictional narratives away from the exploits of Kim Il Sung and his guerilla fighters and toward everyday characters like factory workers and farmers. Accompanying this wave was a spate of love songs, of which "Whisper" is the most famous and catchy. Its lyrics boast almost no political referents whatsoever. Today, the release of such a song would be unthinkable.

Alexandre strikes up a conversation with the Nepalese guy. He's been living here now for seven years, working for a children's charity, one of many NGOs stationed in Pyongyang. Alexandre asks him where all the action is—after all, it's 11 p.m. on a Saturday night, and this is the Diplo Club; surely some of his fellow expats are eager to let loose? He tells us that the happening spot right now is the Friendship Club. "But I don't think your guides will let you go there," he warns us.

Mr. Shakya has a wife and kids back home in Nepal. Why has he willingly chosen to remain in Pyongyang for so long? He likes it here, he insists. He's gotten used to it. Take the Diplomatic Club. He's something of a regular. He comes several times a week to take painting lessons from a local artist. Before that, he took Korean classes here. He speaks with the staff fluently, knows all the songs. They're clearly on flirtatious terms. It would never come to anything. Relations between Koreans and foreigners are strictly forbidden. But at one point, I catch him trying to fondle one of the waitresses. She brushes his hand away quickly, startled by the presence of strangers in the room.

FIVE

COMRADE KIM IS back at home. It's been a productive day. He managed to secure a deal with a Chinese supplier he met in Beijing last week to import luxury skin care products from France. They will be big sellers among female elites. Then he picked up the foreign students from the airport, he tells his wife. He hasn't had a chance yet to return to Alek with his revised proposal for importing Australian beef. But it's on his to-do list. He has a month, after all.

He helps his daughter with her English homework. Then they settle down in the living room in front of the nightly TV news while his wife cooks dinner in the adjoining kitchen. As the twenty-five-minute broadcast commences, Kim begins to doze. It consists almost entirely of footage of Marshal Kim Jong Un, cheery symphonic music in the background, the newscaster's ecstatic voice narrating his exploits in a quivering alto.

The Marshal inspecting a fish-food factory operated by a unit of the Korean People's Army. The Marshal guiding a military drill for ballistic rocket fire. The Ninth Congress of the Kim Il Sung Socialist Youth League taking place in the presence of Marshal Kim Jong Un. The Marshal visiting the Taedong River Pig Farm. The Marshal swamped in a crowd of admiring, sobbing female soldiers. The Marshal monitoring the satellite launch that took place earlier this year.

The images flash before the faces of father and daughter, who sit next to each other on the sofa. Midway through, Kum Hui and her father are deeply immersed in games on their Koryolink phones.

The Marshal inspects a mine. The Marshal tours an ostrich farm started by his father in an effort to relieve the country's perennial food shortage. At each visit, he dispenses valuable advice on every aspect of the operation, advice that is written down and memorized in turn by the managers, relayed subsequently to employees, and enacted accordingly. The newscaster reads, verbatim, every single thing that the Marshal says at each of these inspections. The content is often banal—"this is good, that is bad"—but its banality is overwritten by the newscaster's melodramatic delivery, which imbues every phrase with a Wagneresque gravitas.

After the news, a musical program. The lyrics to the country's latest anthems scroll across the screen, karaoke-style, allowing everyone to learn them at home—important because you could theoretically be drafted at any moment to participate in some event where you're expected to sing in chorus. As Comrade Kim dozes, little Kum Hui sings along to the latest hits: "Our Marshal," "We Cannot Live Without You," "Our Destiny and Future Entrusted to You," "We Will Follow You Only," "Revolutionary Armed Forces Upholds Leadership of the Marshal Only."

No commercials in a socialist country. In lieu, inspiring quotes from Kim Il Sung, Kim Jong Il, and Kim Jong Un fill the screen for a few moments at each transition.

As the Kim family sits down to eat, a movie comes on. Tonight they're showing a classic that Comrade Kim and his wife remember from their adolescence: 1986's *A Traffic Controller on the Crossroads*. A great flick about the correct socialist way to cross the street. The sexy uniformed traffic girls are a famous part of Pyongyang civic life. Rumored to have been personally selected by the Supreme Leadership on the basis of their outward appearance, they demonstrate that traffic lights aren't necessary when you have a beautiful and racially pure Korean socialist signaling when to stop and go.

Comrade Kim switches off the film, which no one was watching. In the player, he inserts a pirated copy of *Zootopia* he bought today at a DVD stall. The family resumes their meal in silence, eyes glued to the screen. When it finishes, Mrs. Kim takes Kum Hui off to bed. Comrade Kim switches back to Korean Central Television to catch the tail end of another news show, this one focusing on the Marshal's more recent peregrinations. This one is without much live action. Instead, the anchor reads from the script she holds in her hands, describing in evocative detail the Marshal's steps across the country in building a victorious socialist revolution. This is followed by the nightly "Report by the Unification and Peace Committee," in which the broadcaster deploys a colorful range of crass and insulting words berating the United States and South Korea for their continual division of the Korean peninsula and the enemies' latest provocations against the North. Finally, the weather forecast for the coming days flashes across the screen. Bright, sunny days ahead for Pyongyang. The screen goes blank as the nightly broadcast comes to an end. By then, Comrade Kim is already snoring.

SIX

IT'S MIDNIGHT BY the time we arrive back at the hotel tipsy from karaoke. We say good night to our guides, who make their way up in the elevators. As the three of us are about to get on, we're intercepted by a tousled Chinese business-man who's even more wasted than we are (save for teetotaling Alexandre, bien sûr). "Who are you? Never see you before here...Come, have drink in bar." The three of us exchange glances. "Why not?" answers our non-drinker.

In the enclosed lobby bar, the businessman introduces himself to us as Simon. He's excited to hear we're here to study. "I want my daughter to study at uni-versity here, too. But she doesn't want," he says sadly. He orders several bot-tles of the local Taedong beer, the waitress pouring it into glasses for us. Simon addresses us in a combination of Mandarin and English, relying more on his native language the further he slips into inebriation. He oversees a jointly owned gold mine on the outskirts of Wonsan. As with other ostensibly socialist coun-tries like Cuba, foreigners aren't allowed to own businesses or property in North Korea. They can, however, join up with local partners—guys like Comrade Kim—if the investment and expertise look attractive enough.

"I have invested *a lot* in this country," Simon whispers to us. He looks around suspiciously. He qualifies all of his assertions with retractions. Hotels are among the few places in the country where foreigners might speak freely among them-selves. For this reason, it is widely believed that they are bugged—as they always were in the Soviet Union.

This theory has its detractors. English Simon from Koryo, who's been to the country more than anyone, dismisses it. "They have more than a thousand rooms at the Yanggakdo Hotel alone," he says. "Why would they bother listen-ing in on every one?"

Mere tourists, he argues, offer little intrigue to the regime. It's only their money anyone's interested in.

"Nonono," says Chinese Simon in a low voice. "Must be careful. All rooms here...microphones. *All.*"

Mark, Simon's young assistant, walks into the bar. He's from Qingdao but studied in South Korea and speaks the language fluently; he often serves as an interpreter for his boss and their North Korean partners.

"It's true," Mark says in flawless English as he takes his first sip of beer. "I even found a tiny one in our office in Wonsan, hidden in the light fixture. You know the Tonmyong Hotel? The entire eighth floor, that's ours."

Still, it seems more plausible to me that the North Koreans would bug their joint venture partners than they would an ordinary tourist...Then again, isn't Alek the business partner of Comrade Kim?

Simon gets progressively drunker, and his paranoia seems to increase, swinging pendulum-like with his desire to communicate openly and directly. "Watch what you say, they are listening, listening," he intones in Mandarinized singsong before singing the praises of Kim Jong Un and denouncing democracy and free-market capitalism.

When he braves to discuss politics under his breath, he says that Kim Jong Un is surrounded by too many old men. That's what's hampering progress here. The coterie the young Marshal inherited from Kim Jong Il is burdened with too many hardline idealists. This, Simon implies, is the logic behind the recent purges that the upper echelons had been rumored to be undergoing of late, the most well-reported one being the execution of Kim Jong Un's uncle, Jang Song Thaek, previously believed to be the number two man in Pyongyang and one of the young leader's top advisers. But when I ask Simon if he thinks Kim might be yearning to go in the direction of Mao's reformist successor Deng Xiaoping in China, he simply nods in the affirmative before reverting back to his incantations of *Watch what you say, Kim Jong Un great, capitalism bad.*

"It's the first time I've met any American here," Mark says with a note of concern in his voice.

"I've been before, many times," I say, lighting a cigarette, voice slurred with liquid confidence. "I know...how to conduct myself. There aren't going to be any problems."

"Yes, but...it's really not a good time for Americans to be here."

"Great danger, great danger," Simon adds to his chant litany.

"You need to be careful. More careful than those guys." He nods toward my compadres across the table.

Simon hands me his card. "You have any problem, you call me. I *know people* here. Any problem you have, I take care." He points to himself authoritatively.

I nod and thank him.

As we're leaving, Mark makes us promise to have drinks again the following night. The Sosan isn't exactly a happening place, unlike the hotel bars in the city center. Finally, people his own age to hang out with. As part of his job, sometimes he has to spend months at a time here, no internet, no way to contact his girlfriend back home, his sole human contact being his boss and assorted older North Korean businessmen and bureaucrats. We tell him sure, then make our way up to the twenty-eighth floor, our home for the next month.

On my balcony, I stare out at the dark city below, with a good notion of what it will all look like when I open my curtains to morning in a few hours. Kim Jong Il used to like to say, "We must envelop our urban environment in a dense fog, to prevent our enemies from learning anything about us." It would be a dramatic exaggeration to imply that the morning mist somehow forms the essence of my experience of Pyongyang. But it is also true that what comes to us when we think of cities we've visited is often an abstract panoply of associations. The people you've met over drinks. The scenes you take in while waiting to cross the street. The aroma of simmering food drifting out of restaurants. The mist that enshrouds you as you're looking out your hotel window.

How a place makes you *feel*. A place like this in particular. Where you are bound to spend each day on a roller coaster, alternately charmed, intrigued, disgusted, amused, terrified—often all of these at once.

There is a great divide between the city Pyongyang yearns to be and the city that it is. There's a painting from 2012, the year I first visited, not long after Kim Jong Il's death and Kim Jong Un's ascension: *Night in Pyongyang* by Kim Myong Un. It depicts the capital aglow, a myriad of colored lights bouncing off the surface of the Taedong River to further illuminate the bright nocturnal city. When I first saw the painting, I read it as not so much a distorted misrepresentation but a depiction of an ideal state of things, an ideal city, that had yet to be attained.

So much has changed in four years. The city below me is not as dark as it used to be. With projects like the shimmering Mirae Scientists Street, Pyongyang is at least making strides toward closing that gap between the ideal and the real. *Life* is what takes place in that gap: that quagmire of glittering contradictions and blatant hypocrisies, mind-numbing sloganeering and the thrill of whispered secrets, horrific threats and wishful thinking. Confused as this mess appears, and the mess of emotions it provokes, this is a city I have somehow come to care about in all its fucked-upness—even though the better I have come to know it, the less I am able to understand it. And the less of a grasp I have on it, the more it fascinates me. The city of a people long struggling against defeat. The city shaped by the dreams of one man and his progeny.

PART TWO

"WORLD'S WORST COUNTRY"

SEVEN

THE NEXT MORNING, as the hotel waitress places before Alek, Alexandre, and me cups of instant coffee, we are joined by Simon in the mammoth empty breakfast hall. He remains strangely silent for the duration of breakfast, even though he is clearly listening with intense interest to everything we say, as though still trying to figure us out. It occurs to me that maybe his foreign language skills aren't so acute in the dull light of sobriety. But his silence is nevertheless curious, considering how chatty he'd been the night before. Perhaps his decision to remain silent betrays a fear that he has said too much already. Indeed, in the coming weeks, we'll spot him several more times, both at the hotel and around town, but he'll never make an effort to speak to us again. More usually, he'll do his best to keep a distance.

It is one of the anomalous traditions or rules of North Korean travel that you never eat breakfast with your guides. Maybe it's because, in Pyongyang especially, the perpetually empty hotels have been built with so many restaurants that they have to come up with reasons to use them. Or maybe it's to restrict the Koreans from taking part in the lavish buffet offerings of Chinese, Korean, and Western food items that the foreigners are treated to. Anyway, after dining in the Hochparterre, we walk down the stairs to meet Min and Roe in the lobby.

Min is still confused as to what to do with the day's itinerary we no longer want to follow. It's the standard tourist schlock we've all done: interesting for first-timers but boring for repeat offenders, as every museum and historical site is guided with the same venerational spiel about its significance to the life narrative of Kim Il Sung and/or Kim Jong Il. Today we were meant to visit the Tower of the Juche Idea, which each of us has done two or three times. Yesterday, Min's face had a look of confused, mild panic when Alek told her in the car that we wanted to make some minor adjustments to the itinerary. Since each site has its own guide, all arrangements have to be made well in advance, and for certain places, advance permission must first be granted. Spontaneity is all but impossible in the DPRK.

As Min waffles, Alexandre suggests we first journey to Mansu Hill to lay flowers at the Grand Monument—the statues of the leaders. At that, Min perks up, relieved. "Yes, let's do that," she agrees. "And afterward, why don't we go to the new water park? You can have some fun before class starts tomorrow. Did you bring your bathing suits?"

★

In order to understand anything about North Korea—past, present, or future— one must have a good understanding of Kim Jong Un's grandfather, Kim Il Sung. But in order to gain that understanding, one must comb through an absurdly reverential state-sanctioned hagiography whose supposed truths consist of wild exaggeration when not blatant fabrication. Add to that challenge the outlandish rumors and obfuscations that have been generated outside the country—often by foreign media and government agencies—over the years, many taking the form of sensationalized and unsubstantiated reports of events that no one has bothered (or been able) to confirm or contest, as though the "world's worst country" isn't deserving of the dignity of truth.

North Korea's ultra-nationalist ideology, shocking and incomprehensible though it may appear today, is rooted in the country's unique postcolonial situation. At the Cairo Conference in 1943, Winston Churchill, Chiang Kai-shek, and Franklin Roosevelt together decided that after Japan's defeat, the country should lose all of the colonies it had gained by force, including Korea. Simultaneously, toward the end of the Second World War, the Soviets promised their American allies to contribute to the Pacific front following the defeat of Nazi Germany. In Korea, the Soviets swiftly gained so much ground that the US government began to worry they might soon control the entire peninsula. Pressed for time, on August 8, 1945, two young officers—Dean Rusk and Charles Bonesteel, neither of whom had ever been to Korea or knew anything about the country—were handed a map of the peninsula ripped out of a *National Geographic* article. They had thirty minutes to divide it. The officers made their mark across the thirty-eighth parallel, a line that nearly perfectly bisected the peninsula, the benefit being that Seoul fell in the proposed US-controlled southern half. To the surprise of the Americans, the Soviets immediately accepted the proposal—likely out of a more or less equal state of ignorance. Korea's fate was thus sealed by two antagonistic powers that knew nearly nothing about it.

If it was the Japanese occupation that spurred the burning desire for independence and the subsequent foundation of the Democratic People's Republic of Korea, it was Comrade Kim Il Sung, according to official mythology, who led the guerilla armed resistance that fought the occupiers off Korean soil and returned the nation to its people. This is not quite accurate, though neither is the overly simplified claim that Kim was immediately installed as leader of North Korea by Stalin. One of the ironies of Korea's division is that there were no communists in North Korea at the time of division. Seoul was the capital of Korea's fledgling communist movement, which had largely been dispersed by the Japanese, so that most Korean communists were in either Manchuria or the Soviet Union at the time of liberation. The reality is that Kim Il Sung was one of many men in Korea who had been imported into the North by the Soviets. At first, he was given a rather modest role: Minister of Defense. While the particulars of his rise have been made cloudy by the obfuscations and veiled maneuvers of Cold War history, Kim's brisk and all but accidental elevation to the top of the ladder within a month of his landing in Wonsan—which he may not have even anticipated, let alone desired—can be attributed to the Soviet military authorities and advisers on the ground in Pyongyang, who were the ones really running the show up to at least 1949.

Driving to Mansu Hill takes you into the heart of downtown Pyongyang, through the new luxury high-rise apartment cluster—including one building that appears to be a near-replica of New York's Trump Plaza—that expats have sardonically dubbed "Dubai." As we pull off the main stretch, our route takes us past the imposing marble brutalism of the Mansudae Assembly Hall, where the rubber-stamp parliament congregates once a year. Foreign guests arrive at a side parking lot, where a flower vendor sits in a small hut. We buy a bouquet and then begin the procession up the small sidewalk to patriotic music piped in on hidden speakers, setting the somber mood for what is, in essence, a mourning ritual undertaken by millions of Koreans each year. The surrounding park is immaculately maintained by "volunteer" citizens, its blades of grass cut with scissors; the approach to the statues is empty today, save for a lone teenage boy in a Young Pioneer scarf sweeping the steps with a twig broom.

Mansu Hill is, without a doubt, the centerpiece of Pyongyang—geographically, politically, spiritually. In 1972, in honor of his father's sixtieth birthday—the most important in Confucianism's tradition of filial reverence—Kim Jong Il had a seventy-two-foot bronze statue of the Great Leader erected at the crest of the hill, overlooking all of Pyongyang. (Five years later, the statue was enriched with gold leaf. But the plating was soon stripped to its original bronze after a state visit by Deng Xiaoping, who, upon seeing it, expressed concern over how Chinese aid money was being spent.) Since then, it has become a custom for Koreans to pay homage by laying flowers at the foot of the statue and bowing.

A week before my first visit to the country in 2012, Kim Jong Un had attended an unveiling ceremony at Mansu Hill, where a revised version of his grandfather's likeness had been installed alongside a second statue: one of his recently deceased father, Kim Jong Il. The original statue of Kim Il Sung presented to the world a younger portrayal of the Great Leader, with an open trench coat revealing the Mao suit that he wore early on, his right arm outstretched to the heavens and the stern, determined expression on his face denoting unwavering commitment. The revised statue replaces the Mao suit with the formal suit and tie he would don in later years, the rugged revolutionary having been transformed into the respectable world leader, and presents a warm smile on his face, with a pair of spectacles completing the grandfatherly image of the Eternal President. His son, the Dear Leader Kim Jong Il, stands next to him, an equally warm smile animating his features—a smile, it must be said, virtually absent from all official photographic documentation—as he stares out over the horizon of the country he and his father ruled for more than half a century. The statues are works of epic kitsch, laughably repulsive with their cartoonishly blocky shapes approximating the two men's girthy stature, loud and tacky with their bronze pseudo-sheen.

Still, you would be foolish to laugh here. This, after all, is the most sacred site in all of North Korea. It is here where you are told, prior to your arrival—and again by your guides, who will likely be staring over your shoulder as you raise your camera—that the entirety of the sculptures, from head to foot, must be captured in any photographs taken; close-ups of any details of the leaders' bodies are strictly forbidden. The icons are backgrounded with one of North Korea's most famous mosaics, by Pak Po Sik and Mun Ki Song, rendering in beige, white, and gray Lake Chon, the volcanic waterbody nestled in the caldera atop Mount Paekdu, considered to be the most sacred mountain in all of Korea by northerners and southerners alike. The mosaic encompasses some two hundred thirty feet of the back wall of the Korean Revolution Museum, whose contents tell the story of the country from its founding to the present day.

"Travis. Can you remove your sunglasses, please?" Min asks.

Fuck. I've already made a gaffe, and it's only our second day. The sunglasses—of course. I quickly snatch them off my head and return my arms to the sides of my body, staring unblinking ahead at the two daunting figures before me.

Why Kim Il Sung? What did the Soviets see in him?

Documents from the Soviet archives imply that they had few, if any, real plans for North Korea following the Second World War. It was an afterthought. They were improvising. They may have even considered letting the Americans take control of the entire peninsula at one point, so vague was their interest—though Korea does share a border with Russia, so that was one reason not to let that happen. Same reason why China today has no real interest in a South Korean–led reunification: nobody wants American troops at their border.

In such murky environs, where disinterest runs high, unusual events tend to unfold. Kim caught the attention of the Pyongyang-based Soviet advisers early on. Had he arrived in Pyongyang a few weeks later, it's probable that his name would have been lost to history. Clearly, he was seen as a good tactical intermediary between Moscow and the local populace. After all, he had spent the past two decades in exile in the Soviet Union and spoke passable Russian—even though, with his eighth-grade education, he was by no stretch of the imagination a great intellectual; many of his Soviet counterparts found his comprehension of the teachings of Marx and Lenin to be embarrassingly paltry. Still, great thinkers weren't required or even particularly desired in the Soviet Bloc in those years. Obedience was the quality most sought after. And Kim had kept his distance from the clique of professional revolutionaries and apparatchiks that Stalin had so grown to despise, a factor that increased his worth in the Generalissimo's eyes. What's more, he had actually been born in Pyongyang, which is where the new capital was, and was famous among many Koreans for his guerilla exploits against the Japanese—though these exploits would soon come to be so exaggerated and distorted in the official propaganda as to appear unrecognizable to anyone with an intimate knowledge of Kim's actual activities prior to his return to Korea on that hot autumn day in 1945. Kim, it was decided, would make the perfect puppet.

He was born in the present-day Pyongyang district of Manyongdae in 1912 on the same day the *Titanic* went down, April 15—perhaps that's one of the reasons why *Titanic* would later become one of his son's favorite films. (A North Korean remake produced at Kim Jong Il's behest would later tank—or, if you prefer, sink—on the international festival circuit.) His birth name, the name he was known by until he changed it in the 1930s, was Kim Song Ju. National myth ascribes his background to the poor oppressed peasantry, though in actuality his family was moderately well-to-do by the standards of the day, with a schoolteacher father deeply ensconced in the Presbyterian church. Like many families, the Kims resented the Japanese occupation of the country and moved to Manchuria, a hotbed of the anti-Japanese movement where two million Koreans resided.

In 1932, when the Japanese launched a military offensive in the region to further extend their colony, resistance was fierce. Among those to respond to the attacks was twenty-year-old Kim, who organized his first guerilla unit. Though his middle-class background would have set him on course to become a clerk or businessman, Kim, angered by injustice and emboldened by revolutionary fervor, would make a name for himself in a major battle when his ragtag unit managed to save the life of Chinese commander Shih Chung-hung. From that moment on, Kim became a confidant of prominent Chinese officers active in the region's battlefront.

The rebellion was soon quashed, and the Japanese puppet state of Manchukuo came into existence—though resistance continued, led by the local Chinese Communist Party, which, despite its name, consisted largely of Koreans opposed to the Japanese colonizers. Koreans like Kim and his cohorts. By 1936, the resistance had fomented into a formidable Sino-Korean army, with Kim commanding the third division. He would spend much of the last half of the 1930s in combat.

Far from being the single force fighting off the Japanese that North Korean propaganda eulogizes him as, Kim's was but one of a number of scrappy units staging random attacks on the Japanese with wavering success. Subsequent exaggerations aside, his activities were brave and heroic, and his leadership role was clear enough for the Japanese to issue a bounty for his head. After a devastating defeat in 1940, Kim and his surviving comrades were no longer safe in Manchuria. They had little choice but to flee to safety in the Soviet Union. There, the Korean guerrillas were enlisted in the Red Army, undergoing training for the next few years in anticipation of the Soviet war with Japan; Kim became a major. But when that battle finally erupted in the final days of the Second World War in 1945, victory came so quick that Kim's unit didn't even get a chance to fight—though that didn't stop North Korea from claiming that victory as Kim's alone.

For the official history of the period that followed, you can visit the Workers' Party Foundation Museum in central Pyongyang, not far from the Koryo Hotel. Housed in what is touted to be Kim Il Sung's office in the first years following the liberation from Japan, the modest two-story structure, constructed in the early 1920s, is a rare surviving example of colonial architecture. Blocky and imposing, the building sports a small domed rooftop, a minor riff on the Tokyo Imperial Diet building's central tower. The ground-floor exhibit tells the story of the creation of the Workers' Party, the country's ruling political faction, while the second floor preserves the president's offices and a meeting hall, which contains, astonishingly, busts of Marx, Engels, Lenin, and Stalin—images of whom have been deleted elsewhere in the propaganda stream. Here you will learn that, practically the moment he vacated the womb, Kim Il Sung was already at work on the blueprints for the Korean Workers' Party. (In actuality, the first Korean Communist Party was founded secretly in 1925 in Seoul—many miles away from the teenage Kim, who would have no feasible means of knowing of its existence—and was dissolved within three years as a result of infighting and pressure from the Japanese colonial overlords.)

You are taught that Kim's original Juche doctrine was always at the heart of the Workers' Party ideology. Another blatant fabrication. The concept of "Juche" wasn't introduced into the North Korean lingo until the 1950s, only to be later significantly expounded upon, by neither Kim nor his son but by Hwang Jang Yop, the North Korean state's official ideologue, in the 1970s and 1980s. Another thing your guide at the Workers' Party Foundation Museum will neglect to mention—because, in all probability, she is unaware of it herself—is that Kim was actually a member of the *Chinese* Communist Party throughout his time in Manchuria.

The official foundation of the Workers' Party of North Korea is dated to October 10, 1945. In actuality, that date marked the foundation of the North Korean Bureau of the Communist Party of Korea, a Soviet organization—the founding of the independent Workers' Party didn't take place until a year later—though these details matter little, as Kim Il Sung, though not nominally the head of either party or organization at this point, was very much the man at the top from February 1946, less than six months after his return to the homeland.

"The following year," enthuses your guide, "a democratic reform took place. It only took one year to complete!"

This "democratic reform" consisted of many of the processes that will be well familiar to students of communist regimes. Land reform was instituted, albeit in a less bloody fashion than in neighboring China, with many former landowners opting to simply flee to the South, where some were given prize positions in Syngman Rhee's US-backed police state. The country's main industries, for which the Japanese laid the groundwork, were nationalized. Christians were hunted down and killed or expelled, many fleeing to the South.

All this took place with little resistance among the people, unused to participatory politics after having been ruled as colonial subjects, caught up in the dream and promise of independence. Nor did many protest the Soviets' involvement with their early state, as the Soviets were deemed allies, having sided with the Koreans against the despised Japanese. North Korea's foundational ideological platform was essentially more anti-Japanese than it was pro-Soviet. As historian Bruce Cumings has pointed out, the beginning of the official state narrative is always the terrible suffering endured by the Korean people under the spiteful and inherently evil Japanese, followed by the anti-Japanese insurgency led by Kim Il Sung. "It is drummed into the brains of everyone in the country," writes Cumings, "by an elderly elite that believes anyone younger than they cannot possibly know what it meant to fight Japan in the 1930s or the United States in the 1950s."

For the first time, Koreans could feel what it meant to be part of a sovereign nation in the modern world with their own language, history, culture—and, now, their very own government. The first congress of the Workers' Party took place on August 28–30, 1946. This could be regarded as the authentic foundation of the Party, the moment when all the disparate communist-affiliated parties then active in North Korea merged into one. There were four main groups of Korean Communists imported into the North by the Soviets: a faction that had been exiled in China; the Soviet Koreans; the South Korean communists from Seoul; and, finally, Kim Il Sung's gang of guerilla fighters. Over time, members of all three rival factions would raise objections to the emerging cult of personality surrounding Kim and to his mismanagement of the economy. Consequentially, all three factions would be violently purged till there was no one left but Kim's former guerilla comrades, giving rise to the monolithic ideological system of fanaticism surrounding the Kim family.

With the Workers' Party in place, the Democratic People's Republic of Korea was formally declared on September 9, 1948. This put an end to the provisional government; Soviet troops and administrators left the country, ceding all power to the Workers' Party. Any mention of Soviet presence in the early days of the DPRK is conspicuously absent from the exhibition at the museum. Like Kim's membership in the Chinese Communist Party, all references to foreign influence have been deleted from official history. No factional intrigue or infighting is noted. What's left, much like in every other such historical museum, is a dull celebration of the brilliant mastermind who singlehandedly did everything: Kim Il Sung.

By 1949, Kim had already taken on the title of *suryong,* a term taken from the Koguryo Dynasty, that golden period when Pyongyang was at the center of all things Korean, which meant "Great Leader"—a shocking and bold heresy in the Soviet World, where only Stalin was deemed worthy of such a title—but also a clear indication of the new direction North Korea would be taking now that the reins were no longer in the hands of the Soviets: a socialist country in name, a monarchical despot in appearance.

★

To say that the Soviets came to regret their selection of Kim Il Sung to lead the country would be something of an understatement. While the foundations of the North Korean experiment, which has now endured for more than seven decades, were certainly Stalinist, the DPRK would go in an even more extreme direction under Kim's leadership, diverging far from the path prescribed by its Soviet benefactor, which it has now far outlasted. Why? For one thing, it could be that Kim's relations with Stalin and the Soviets were not as rosy as history has simplified them into being.

In the end, they underestimated Kim's cunning, for sure. But the Soviets also seemed to lack an understanding of how communism was viewed in Asia. Just as democracy has been practiced in a different way in countries like South Korea, Japan, and Taiwan than it has in the United States, Asian communism has similarly taken different forms. Soviet communism's idealistic roots were in a utopian aspiration toward socioeconomic equality, its internationalism ("Workers of the world unite!") justifying the Soviets' quasi-imperialist expansion. Asian communists like Mao Zedong, Ho Chi Minh, and Kim Il Sung were first and foremost *nationalists;* they viewed communism as a way of emancipating their backward countries from colonial enslavement. A vehicle that would accelerate them into the twentieth century, modernizing and joining the developed world while attaining the national sovereignty they so burningly desired. Nowhere was this more the case than in North Korea.

Kim's nationalism must have been further incensed by Stalin's harsh treatment of Soviet Koreans. During the Great Purge of the 1930s, Stalin had ordered every Korean Comintern agent to be rounded up and shot while simultaneously deporting hundreds of thousands of Soviet Korean citizens to Kazakhstan and Uzbekistan in a stunning act of ethnic cleansing, on the racist pretext that it was impossible to tell them apart from the Japanese enemy.

But Kim was still fully dependent on Stalin up until the Korean War. It is often said that the biggest lie propagated by the DPRK—and the most sacred one, as the entire legitimacy of the country's continual existence is predicated upon an unwavering belief in it—is that the Korean War was started by the US-backed South. Even some leftist South Koreans subscribed to this idea until the Soviet Union itself fell and its archives opened up to reveal a trove of official documents, including correspondence between Stalin and Kim Il Sung, with the North Korean leader imploring his benefactor's permission and support in launching a general invasion, nay, "liberation" of the southern half of the peninsula.

Whether the North was *provoked* into attacking is another matter. Syngman

Rhee issued many incendiary statements at the time announcing his clear intention to send his soldiers into the northern half of the peninsula, confidently assuring the international media that the process of rescuing the country from the communists would only take a few days. In June 1950, just weeks before the North launched its invasion, soldiers peered through binoculars across the thirty-eighth parallel to find prominent US government and military figures on official visits peering back at them—all the more reason to suppose that an attack was in the works. What's more, the civil war—which is what the Korean War, as it has become known to history, actually was (something that is seemingly forgotten at times by historians)—had more or less already erupted in the South in the late 1940s, with violent leftist uprisings against Rhee's oppressive police apparatus, which was widely despised. (This does not mean, however, that South Koreans necessarily preferred communist rule, Kim Il Sung–style. Nor has the South Korean government's claim that these rebellions were supported by the North ever been substantiated.) In a sense, one can say that it matters very little who started the Korean War; it would have broken out regardless, within a matter of weeks or days from that morning of June 24, 1950, when North Korean troops crossed the thirty-eighth.

Stalin was reluctant to give his assent to a general invasion. This would mean, effectively, declaring war on the United States, the world's sole nuclear superpower at the time, with the memory of Hiroshima still fresh. North Korea was a newly established third-rate client state of the USSR, about which Stalin cared very little. The Soviets well understood the North Koreans' nationalist zeal and were increasingly put off by it, as reports from the Soviet Embassy back home to Moscow make clear. Stalin said no to Kim repeatedly. He was far too shrewd to allow a bunch of ultra-nationalist zealots to get him into a deadly war. It would have been suicide.

What changed Stalin's mind in the end is that the world began to change. In 1949, the Chinese Communists declared victory in their civil war that had erupted not long after China's victory against Japan. Under Mao, the biggest country in the world—and a neighbor of both North Korea and the Soviet

Union—was now united beneath the red banner. And, inside Stalin's own kingdom, the Soviets had managed to successfully test their very own nuclear device.
Then there were the intelligence reports that suggested to Stalin that the United
States had no real strategic interest or long-term plans for the situation unfolding
on the Korean peninsula. Perhaps they cared even less than the Soviets about
the runty divided country. They were not likely, Stalin now believed, to respond
to the North's "liberation" of the South—just as, at various moments in the
not-so-distant past, Stalin himself had considered letting the entire peninsula
go to the Americans. With Kim continuing to rattle at the Soviets' door, Stalin
finally gave the nod of approval.

Kim had assured Stalin that the war would be won within three days. Here,
he was relying on his own (no doubt ideologically tainted) intelligence reports
that described the Korean people in the South as suffering under a brutal military dictator whom they resented and assuming that the peasants, upon seeing the Korean People's Army, would immediately throw down their sickles and
pick up guns to join the armed revolution against their oppressors.

The first part of that report might have been true. But the mass uprising
that Kim entertained in his vision of "liberation" never came to fruition. The
three-day battle he envisioned stretched out into a three-year-long civil war. The
North, in its mangled rewriting of history, has insisted it was somehow both a
war of liberation and a war instigated by the United States. It is officially known
as the "Victorious Fatherland Liberation War." The name poses more than one
challenge to the rational mind. If the DPRK was merely defending itself against
an attack by a foreign enemy, how could this be a war of "liberation"? And in
what way was this *war of liberation* "victorious" when the end result was not the
liberation of the bottom half of the peninsula but the same division that stood at
the war's beginning?

At first, the North *was* poised to win. When the United States-led UN
surprised Kim and Stalin by joining the war in September 1950, the North's
advance south had been so successful that it was in control of some 95 percent of
the peninsula. The Korean People's Army overwhelmed the Republic of Korea's
(ROK, South Korea's official name) in terms of strength, as most of its fighters
had fought alongside the communists in the recent Chinese civil war. If the US
had not gotten involved, the war would have been over at that point, with the
entire peninsula under the Kim Il Sung dynasty.

Indeed, the US's entry caught Kim Il Sung by surprise. But this was the height
of the red-baiting McCarthy era in the United States, and the UN-backed US

entry into what would become known as the "Forgotten War" was a prelude to the US's subsequent catastrophic attempt to "prevent the spread of Communism" that would be seen in Vietnam. Within a matter of weeks, UN forces—composed mostly of US and South Korean troops—were able to completely reverse the onslaught. The North Korean leadership had to vacate Pyongyang and retreat to the Chinese border. Kim, in a panic, begged Mao to send People's Liberation Army soldiers. Mao, recalling the Koreans' assistance in the Chinese civil war in 1947, quickly acceded, only informing Stalin afterward, much to the Generalissimo's surprise. Kim Il Sung was humiliatingly sidelined by Chinese Commander Peng Dehuai, who had little respect for the North Korean leader and the mess he had made. Within two weeks, the Sino-Korean defense was able to fight enemy troops back over the thirty-eighth parallel—though the Chinese made it clear that they did not intend to go any farther south. Nevertheless, by the end of November, the North was able to retake Seoul. (While the Chinese assistance has not been completely erased from subsequent domestic propaganda, it has certainly been minimized.)

General Douglas MacArthur, who was leading the UN command at the time, reacted to the Chinese entry into the war by ordering the entirety of the upper half of the peninsula, from the thirty-eighth parallel up to the Yalu River that marked the border with China, to be turned into a wasteland. The Americans decimated much of North Korea in aerial bombing raids, committing innumerable war crimes along the way by bombing dams that resulted in mass flooding of civilian infrastructure and depleting drinking water reserves while raining napalm upon the population. Through these brutal attacks, the allied lines below Seoul were able to regain force. In early April, the UN army retook Seoul, and shortly thereafter, American ground forces were able to cross the thirty-eighth parallel once again—though they didn't get very far beyond it. At this point, roughly a year after the war had officially started, fighting stabilized at the thirty-eighth, though World War I–style trench warfare would continue for another two years, up until the 1953 ceasefire agreement, which left the border demarcating North and South almost exactly where it had been before. The war, which left millions of Korean, Chinese, and American soldiers and Korean civilians dead or wounded, was in the end a pointless tragedy. In a further absurdity, no peace treaty was ever signed. The two Koreas remain in a perpetual state of war.

★

Today, you can visit the hundred-sixty-mile-long Demilitarized Zone (DMZ)—something of a misnomer since it's probably the most heavily militarized borderland in the world, with legions of soldiers and minefields surrounding either side—at the Joint Security Area of Panmunjom, a truce village where North and South Korean soldiers stand face-to-face between two small blue houses meant to contain diplomatic exchanges between the DPRK and ROK governments. Your experience of the Joint Security Area will be markedly different depending on which side you're visiting from. From the South, it must be done on a package tour, typically departing from Seoul, and is conducted with an air of high drama and deep paranoia, with participants rigorously briefed and made to sign a waiver acknowledging the possibility of injury or death as a result of enemy action. (At the end of the trip, you are handed back the waiver to keep as a "souvenir.") One wrong move by a tourist, the South worries, could reignite the decades-long stalemate. US soldiers, stationed at the base alongside their South Korean allies, inform you not to point or wave at the North Korean soldiers standing opposite the dividing line (though there was only one on the day I visited, standing at the distant entrance to Panmungak, the main North Korean building)—the fear being that a waving tourist might be photographed by the North Koreans, only to have that wave transformed via the magic of Photoshop into an extended middle finger, which could then be used in yet another propaganda offensive against the South. Tourists are ordered to stand in a neat line staring straight forward at the North Korean side, frown on the face and arms stuck to the sides, only to raise them to take photographs once the signal is given.

Visiting from the North is almost comically relaxed by comparison. Of course, there are fewer tourists—you will usually be completely alone, save for the other members of your group—and even fewer visible soldiers. The bus leaves you at a souvenir shop in Panmunjom, where, after doing your shopping, you are introduced to the single soldier who will be your guide and protector. He calmly accompanies you to the DPRK Peace Museum, which is in a reconstructed house that must resemble what the homes in Panmunjom looked like when it was a functional village and is where the Armistice Agreement was signed on July 27, 1953. Here, the soldier-guide somberly narrates the events leading up to and concluding that day. It's the North Korean version of the war—namely, the country's victimhood, having been led into a war it never wanted to fight by the US aggressors, and its subsequent victory over them. Finally, you are led to the Joint Security Area—where you are free to laugh, wave, or point at the South Korean side all you want.

On my three visits to the DMZ on the North Korean side, I have never seen a single soldier standing on the ROK side. In fact, except for the smattering of soldiers standing guard on the Northern half of the border in bulky brown Korean People's Army uniforms—I can only imagine the envy they must feel when confronted by the stylish uniforms worn by their brethren from the South, with their ankle-high trousers, dark-lensed sunglasses, and black-and-white helmets—there was no human presence at the border. I found this surprising, as documentaries on the Korean conflict are always sure to include scenes shot at this precise location with the enemy soldiers standing face-to-face, dramatically illustrating the peninsula's ongoing divide. Such a scene that led then-President Bill Clinton to deem the DMZ "the scariest place on Earth." While the world was arguably a slightly less scary place back then than it is now, the only distressing thing nowadays is the barbed rhetoric spat forth on both sides.

Once I asked my North Korean guide why there never seemed to be any soldiers standing on the ROK side of the divide. "They only come out when there are tourists," she said with a smile. "And it is the same on our side. When you leave, the soldiers will go away."

Visiting from Seoul, I noticed North Korean items like bottles of soju for sale in the souvenir shop. And once on the North side, I spied a soldier drinking from a can of that favorite imperialist beverage, Coca-Cola, all of which leads me to suspect that the two sides have managed to find a way to engage in some covert friendly trade. What was once a sensitive site where talks between the two sides might take place, eventually leading to a reconciliation—if not full reunification, then at least a peace treaty—has become a tourist site with the passage of time.

The survival of all political systems relies, to greater and lesser extents, on the notion of a common enemy. This becomes solidified in the formation of national identity. In the United States in the past century, it has been "communists," followed more recently by "radical Islamists." In the left-wing dictatorships of the Second World during the Cold War era, the notion of an internal enemy—a citizen who looks like me and you but is actually an enemy agent who has infiltrated the system to poison it ideologically from within—is one of the foundational myths of the paranoid totalitarian national psyche and a charge that virtually anyone could stand accused of at any time. It is utilized as a tool for exercising total control over a populace, in the name of *protection*—those governments allegedly of and for the People: that abstract mass that is said to comprise, in North Korean lingo, a "single-minded unity."

With the exception of Kim Il Sung and his fellow Manchurian guerrillas, the founders of the North Korean state were by and large university-educated men and women whose intellectual formation could be traced to the canonical texts of socialism. Most had spent a good portion of their early lives abroad and were thus prone to combining a reasonable level of nationalist sentiment with a cosmopolitan worldview.

Following Nikita Khrushchev's denunciation of Stalin in 1956, the Soviet Bloc launched campaigns against cults of personality, and many of these countries' leaders who had opportunistically modeled themselves on the Generalissimo now found themselves ousted from power in popular campaigns. This emboldened factions of the Workers' Party, including the Soviet Koreans as well as the Yanan (Sino-Korean) faction, to stand up against Kim Il Sung's increasingly despotic rule. These rival factions denounced and attempted to oust Kim from power in 1956, in what would come to be known as the August Incident.

Kim had read the signs and knew what was coming—he had also been summoned to Moscow and given a dressing-down by Khrushchev—and it was during that trip that his enemies at home planned the onslaught against him. It would take place at the already-scheduled Second Plenary Session of the Third Central Committee.

The Great Leader had much to worry about. Prior to that moment, the Manchurian faction composed of himself and his guerilla comrades was relatively weak in its quantitative representation in the Politburo. What's more, the Soviet and Yanan factions each had secured support from their respective powerful sponsors, countries that the comparatively weak DPRK still depended on financially, politically, and militarily. The signs of a coup were ominous.

Upon his return from Moscow, Kim wasted no time. He invented a pretext to postpone the upcoming session for a month, giving him enough time to orchestrate a response and ensure the emergence of an army of loyalists within the Central Committee through a combination of intimidation, blackmail, and bribery. When the session finally took place and the combative factions commenced airing their grievances against the *Suryong*—for, among other charges, the foment of a cult of personality, the creation of a police state, the concentration of both state and party in his own hands, and the emphasis on the development of heavy industry that had resulted in mass starvation in rural areas among the largely peasant-farmer populace—they were booed by the majority of Central Committee members.

The Chinese- and Soviet-backed factions of the North Korean political establishment were subsequently purged over the course of the next two years. Those replacing them in the most prominent positions of power were selected from the former guerillas who had fought alongside Kim in his Manchuria days and tested sycophants. These men would oversee the development of the North Korean system as it has come to be today. Rather than the committed intellectuals of firm Marxist-Leninist pedigree, the new political elite comprised coarse, rugged ex-fighters who could scarcely boast an elementary school education, many of whom were functionally illiterate, whose worldview—in stark contrast to the cosmopolitanism of their forebears—represented the plight of the simple peasant. Rather than regarding this as detrimental and shameful, the ideologues and intelligentsia of the DPRK would come to embrace this kind of simplicity as a redolent quality of the innocence and childlike goodness and purity supposedly endemic to all Koreans as a race. Emotionalism and jingoistic patriotism came to replace the sophistications of dialectical materialism and rational discourse— hence the continual intellectual impoverishment that persists in North Korea to this day.

In the wider communist world, the late 1950s also saw another major drama play out in the form of the Sino-Soviet split. Already, the two red superpowers enacted very different forms of communism. As the Soviet Union became comparatively permissive and liberal after Stalin's demise, Maoist China was all about endless ideological mobilization and self-sacrifice to the cause and blind devotion to the great leader. North Korea, being a pre-modernized East Asian country where deference to authority was an inherent part of the Confucian tradition, was culturally much closer to China than it was to the USSR and shared similar nationalist aspirations. In developing its own unique brand of socialism, Kim's DPRK borrowed heavily from the Maoist side while shunning the relatively permissive culture of the post-Stalin Soviet Union; despite his shaky relationship with Stalin, the Generalissimo remained Kim Il Sung's role model, and elements of Stalinism would be retained throughout his reign.

In one respect, at least, Kim's cunning would far surpass that of his mentor.

As the relations between China and the Soviet Union worsened over the years, rather than taking sides, North Korea would exploit the division between superpowers for all it was worth. Kim's tactic was to play the two off each other, ingratiating himself so as to reap aid from both countries while fully taking the side of neither. Domestically, the DPRK distanced itself from both China and the Soviet Union in the development of its own ultra-nationalist ideology that would come to be known as Juche.

The new elite had neither the intellect nor the experience to lead a fledgling country. They did, however, have the one attribute that had, in the wake of the August Incident, emerged as the single most important one in a country where all forms of political opposition had just been annihilated: an unbending obedience and loyalty to the Great Leader.

When we finish bowing, I slide my sunglasses back over my eyes and retreat to inspect my favorite detail on Mansu Hill: the two sculptural groups on either side of the statues. One represents the armed struggle against the Japanese that led to the foundation of the country, while the second means to evoke the triumphant building of socialism, replete with a soldier trampling an American flag. These works, in contrast with the Kim statues, have been rendered in painstaking detail, and though they may belong to the much spat-upon Socialist Realist canon, there is something compelling in the evocations of persistence, hope, and anger etched into the faces of the soldiers, workers, and peasants who make up these relief-like groupings, a naturalness in their arrangement clearly connoting struggle, and a fluid grace in the individual bodies forming the whole.

What, precisely, are those Kim deifications smiling at? Turning your back to them to stare out at the same monumental vastness—made all the more dramatic by the steepness of the stairs one must climb to reach the statues from the street down below—one leg of the major downtown Pyongyang urban axis, extending across the Taedong River, becomes apparent. What the Kims are smiling at and regarding is not only the idyllic sight of the capital surrounding them but one monument in particular situated on the other side of the Taedong River.

If your vision is not good, you might need binoculars to fully appreciate it, as it is fronted with a vast green park exceeding one hundred sixty thousand square feet. It culminates in a slightly smaller plaza, where rallies and mass dances are held, and, finally, the monument itself. The three emblems making up the core body of the Workers' Party Monument were built with granite blocks. The hammer stands for the worker, the brush for the intellectual (North Korea's unique contribution to the iconography of international socialism, with "intellectual" here being something of a catchphrase to include all white-collar officials), and the sickle connoting the farmer. The tripartite symbol is ringed by an outer belt, also made in granite, with a bronze inscription running across that reads, "The organizers of the victory of the Korean people and the leader of the Workers' Party of Korea!" As with much monumental architecture and sculpture in the DPRK, its construction is loaded with numerological significance. In the case of the belt, for instance, it is made of 216 blocks and consists of an inner diameter of 42 meters: the birthday of Kim Jong Il, 2/16/1942. Beneath the monument, the circular foundation contains a seventy-meter-long relief—meant to represent seventy years of the Workers' Party, including its dubious foundation as the Down-With-Imperialism Union, the organization that fourteen-year-old Kim Il Sung is said to have founded in Manchuria. As a stunning filler, two red flag-shaped apartment buildings have been erected on either side of the monument, crowned with the slogan "Ever Victorious" in Korean. This is one of the more recent works of monumental sculpture in Pyongyang, having been unveiled in 1995 to mark the fifty-year anniversary of the Party's founding.

As you turn back to face the Kims, a short path to the right of the Mansu Hill Grand Monument takes you to the Chollima statue—which overlooks, among other things, the Party Founding Museum; yet another line in the axial web that forms the Pyongyang city center. The Chollima is a winged horse that plays a prominent role in East Asian mythology—it is said to fly so swiftly and so elegantly that no mere mortal could ever mount it.

The statue was erected in 1961 in celebration of the Chollima Movement of three years prior. In that period of purges and increasing nationalization, Kim Il Sung again took a page from the book of Stalin. Here, to the dismay of the rival factions who had deigned to express their outrage at Kim's intent on the development of heavy industry to the detriment of the starving peasants who made up the majority of the population, Kim rebranded Stalin's Stakhanovite movement with a Korean face.

The Chollima Movement pushed industrial workers to achieve wildly ambitious overproduction targets by working double shifts—on a low-protein diet, no less—and mobilizing students and office workers to "volunteer" their time in helping the nation to meet these goals. Despite the hyperbole surrounding the results of this push in the official history, the Chollima Movement resulted in an excess of poor-quality products, churned out at top-notch speed by a completely unskilled workforce and an exhausted, burnt-out populace. The term "Chollima Speed" has assumed a permanent place in North Korean lingo and has set an unfortunate precedent in an economy in which speed and quantity are privileged over endurance and quality. In 2014, a recently completed apartment building in the capital collapsed, killing several residents, thanks to the slipshod construction and round-the-clock labor resulting from a campaign initiated by the latest Kim: "Korea Speed."

EIGHT

AFTER OUR MORNING at the empty monument, we go in search of people. Sunday is the official day off granted to North Koreans and, as it is stifling, the Munsu Water Park, opened to great pomp in November 2013, is packed with elated Pyongyangites eager to cool off.

In its splendor, size, and sheer quantity of amenities, Munsu Water Park would be the envy of any ten-year-old in the world. Arriving, we are greeted in the lobby with a wax statue of Kim Jong Il in his trademark khaki suit, high heels, and pompadour standing with a wide grin before a panoramic painting of a sandy beach shore. We complete the ritual of bowing to this unintentional comedic atrocity. Stifling a grin, I slowly raise my camera to take a photograph. Roe quickly waves his hand in front of me. "No photos, no photos." At least someone is sensitive enough to perceive the camp value of this aesthetic eyesore.

Encompassing a palatial thirty-seven acres, the park contains countless indoor and outdoor slides of varied size and design, including a steep free fall where you race to the bottom on a raft while the waiting crowds below cheer you on. The outdoor pools are ringed by a lazy river with a gentle current that allows you to float or swim along, making for a cinematic people-watching extravaganza. Roe negotiates our entrance at the ticket desk before leading us into the changing room. The moment we walk in, the pungent stench of unwashed ass attacks my nostrils. Despite all the outward signs of luxury abounding in Pyongyang these days, toilet paper is still a rarity in most parts of the country, as is hot water, factors that tend to take their toll on personal hygiene. I try not to breathe as I quickly remove my clothes, stash them in my locker, put on my bathing suit, and head to the shower room.

After showering off, we head to the swimming pool. A man trails after us, buck naked, thinking he's heading back to the changing rooms. He's clearly lost in some daze of introspection because it's not until he's walked out into the middle of the packed water park and everyone has turned to look at him that he suddenly realizes where he is, turns around, and darts back into the shower room.

"Maybe he's looking for a wife," jokes Alexandre. Roe doubles up with laughter. It's clearly the funniest thing he's seen for a long while.

The three of us are the only foreigners in the entire place, providing a bonus sideshow for the giggling masses. If you're foreign, getting stared at constantly wherever you go is the norm in North Korea. You learn to ignore it, though you never quite get used to it. Everyone stares, but very few are willing to interact beyond that. One of the questions I am most often asked by people interested in my travels to North Korea is whether I am allowed to speak with "ordinary people." While locals are discouraged from and often fearful of doing so, what most often prevents that from happening is shyness or, more usually, a lack of fluency in a language besides Korean.

Alek, who doesn't swim, retreats with Min and Roe to grab a snack at one of the park's fast-food restaurants, leaving Alexandre and me to explore on our own. In the massive dry sauna—which, health and safety measures be damned, also includes a small baby pool, with mothers and their toddlers splashing about— we stare through the open window at one of the indoor pools.

"You see that guy over there?" Alexandre points to an older gentleman walking around the edge of the pool with his arms held behind his back. He has his bathing suit on but isn't wet and doesn't appear to be interacting with any friends or family members; rather, he's just walking back and forth, casually observing the scenery. "There are guys like that everywhere. You begin to notice after a while. I've been watching him all day. Look, he's not swimming or doing anything. His job is to just watch people and report."

"Maybe not everyone," I whisper. "Maybe just one person or family."

"You're right. He might not even be *bowibu*."

The *bowibu*, or State Security Department, is the most dreaded branch of the police. They're the ones tasked with investigating crimes of a political nature, the ones who might cart you and your family away in the middle of the night without advance warning.

For all we know, he could be.

For all we know, he could also be someone's private security. There are rich people everywhere. "Do you know how much it costs to get in here?" Alexandre asks.

I don't, but I know it's pocket change for us and several times the official monthly salary for average North Koreans. And the park is jam-packed. Some would have been given admission tickets from their work units as rewards. But certainly not all. Earlier, waiting in line to take our turn on a waterslide, we were bypassed by a family accompanied by a lifeguard. Obviously, they had paid extra for VIP service so as to avoid the pain of standing in line all day with the proles.

That morning in the van on the way to Mansu Hill, Alek had asked for permission to post photos and videos of me on the website he is developing for Tongil Tours. It would be key, publicity-wise, in attracting more numbers for next year's tour, he said. I had consented unthinkingly.

"Are you sure you want to do that?" Alexandre asks me, now that Alek is out of earshot.

I reply that I honestly hadn't given it much thought.

Alexandre's eyes dart about. He obviously has something on his mind. But the sauna is packed with people. Who knows who's listening in? With a nod, we mutually agree to find a safer area to continue our conversation.

We walk outside to one of the wading pools. The roar of an artificial waterfall drowns out our voices.

"I told Alek that I didn't want my face to appear in any of the photos," Alexandre says. "I've been to this country now many times. And under…different contexts. But I'm a discreet guy. And I don't want to give the wrong impression."

"What do you mean? Give who the wrong impression?"

Alexandre's eyes go back and forth again, making sure no one is near. "That I'm…endorsing any of this. I mean, I don't like the regime," he says.

He does have reason for concern. There are foreigners who are apologists of the DPRK system. On my first trip to Pyongyang in 2012, I spotted a stout Spaniard sitting two rows in front of me on the plane, frothing at the mouth as he pointed to a picture of Kim Jong Il in *The Pyongyang Times* and raving to the poor sob seated next to him. A feeling of dread and fear welled up in my stomach. I recognized him from *Friends of Kim*, a 2006 documentary about a tour of North Korea organized by the Korean Friendship Association (KFA), a pro-DPRK outfit that claims to have members around the world.

This was Alejandro Cao de Benós de Les y Pérez, the chairman of KFA. Over the years, Alejandro has presented himself as the official Western spokesman of the DPRK government, wildly exaggerating claims of his ties to the country, even boasting of titles that the government never actually bestowed upon him, as a means of luring foreign guests on trips he organizes to the DPRK. Among Alejandro's boasts, he has said that he has been conferred honorary citizenship and a DPRK passport. "Impossible," scoffed my Korean guide when I asked her about it on my first trip to the country in 2012. Nevertheless, gullible tourists who are unaware of his exaggerations and outright lies are often persuaded in the mistaken belief that this is the only way one may visit North Korea or that KFA will be able to provide them with *special access* to sites that ordinary tourists are unable to visit.

In *Friends of Kim,* this "special access" amounts to a pro-DPRK propaganda parade that his group members are forced to march in beneath the reunification monument on Tongil Street. Most disturbing about the documentary, however, are the myriad displays of behavior that could perhaps best be described as sociopathic. More zealous in his devotion to the regime's politics than even the most fervent North Korean propagandist, Alejandro goes so far as to break into the hotel room of a journalist on the trip to destroy his camera and laptop in the paranoid belief that he might be preparing to report unsympathetic views of the DPRK in his subsequent dispatch—much to the embarrassment of the North Korean guides on the trip. Other delegates on KFA trips have reported that whenever anyone challenges him or otherwise ignites his very short fuse, Alejandro has threatened to have them deported or else report them to his "contacts" in the state security apparatus.

Despite his boasts of insiderdom, I've never met a North Korean who actually likes Alejandro or shows much appreciation for the work he does on behalf of their country. The DPRK's political system is, after all, an ethnically closed system in its ideology, not intended for foreign consumption—this is why foreign tourists need not worry about being "brainwashed" or "converted." Any North Korean will tell you that their political system is designed by Koreans and for Koreans only. Surprisingly, this seems to have eluded Alejandro, as he constantly speaks about the country in the first person plural, as though he himself were a part of the Korean masses—something that clearly aggravates actual DPR Koreans, who, owing to the traumas of their colonial past, are militantly against the idea of *any* outside force speaking on their behalf. On a more profound level, when they see these propaganda antics being parroted by an outsider, it must make them realize how ridiculous and fanatical their entire system looks.

Behind Alexandre's fear of being used for propaganda purposes, does his refusal belie his trust in Alek? Now that I think of it, Alek has a tendency to withdraw when, in our whispered conversations, Alexandre and I become either too critical of the politics of the DPRK or too gossipy in our speculations on the private lives or beliefs of our hosts. A professional distance, I suppose.

Certainly Alek is no Alejandro. He is in the difficult position of playing a dual role—as both organizer of the trip and student participant—which makes him both one of us and, in a sense, not.

All Western tour operators to the DPRK find themselves in a similar predicament. They are, after all, peddling a product that many find indefensible. Like Koryo Tours, Alek and Tongil Tours emphasize the importance of person-to-person engagement over the negative repercussions of isolation that international diplomacy overwhelmingly imposes on the country. Such policies, he argues, only adversely affect the North Korean people—who already suffer enough owing to the policies of their government. In conversation, Alek can become quite passionate in his advocacy of the need for what he calls a *nuanced* understanding of North Korea.

Neither Alexandre nor I would deny that Alek is right on this point. But there are moments when his passion seems to lead him toward an empathetic identification with our hosts, revealing what I can only describe as a willful naïveté. And naïveté, whether willed or not, can be dangerous. There are limits to every kind of engagement.

But there is something more going on between Alek and Alexandre—an exchange of knowing glances here, a whispered conversation there. Now that Alexandre and I are alone beneath the waterfall, I ask him if I'm missing out on something. His face turns sheepish.

"Okay, I'm sorry, I wanted to tell you this earlier, but I didn't want the guides to hear. Even though they probably *know*—I'm sure they are given a file before we come, where they can see everything, but still..." Alexandre trails off.

"So what is it? What's up?"

"Two years ago, my university did an exchange program. It was highly unofficial, it was not announced anywhere—France is participating in the sanctions, so if word ever got out, it would have caused a huge scandal. But anyway, it happened. Some North Korean students came to my university in France, and I was one of ten students who came here, to study at Kim Il Sung University."

I'm stunned. I had never heard of *any* foreigners studying here before us. I thought we were the first. I ask him how long he was here.

"It was just one month," he says, "like us on this trip. But the difference is I was on a *student* visa. I got to live in the dorms, and because I wasn't on a tourist visa, I didn't have guides. I could walk around anywhere I wanted to go. One day, I just decided to go for a walk, and I traipsed through the entire city for five hours."

"Did anyone try to stop you?" I ask, incredulous and a little envious.

"No. They could have—lots of people were looking at me funny—but no one did. They didn't say a word...So now, you can imagine why this trip is so hard for me, having to be accompanied by *them* everywhere we go. When I was here before, I could go almost anywhere alone. But for now, doing this program with Alek is the only way I could find to come back."

"And you haven't told Min yet?"

"No."

"But surely, they *must* know. It's not something you can really keep secret around here."

"Maybe," says Alexandre. He looks down shyly. "But for the moment, I just want to be a bit discreet."

It seems strange. Then again, everything is a bit strange here. Not just the place but the people—and not just the local people but the tourists who willingly choose to come here. And especially, it follows, the ones like us—the moths who keep flocking back to the flame, overtaken by the mystery.

Back at the hotel that night, odd thoughts cloud my thinking. Alexandre's insistence on discretion, his unwillingness to be completely open with our guides—it makes me wonder whether he has an overarching agenda in being here that he doesn't want anyone, including Alek and me, to know. Is he really here independently? An international man of mystery?

Maybe I'm being paranoid.

For this place, it's not unusual to drift into that thoughtsphere. It's something you easily get locked into, that you begin to notice, even in places as benign as the water park. An undercurrent of paranoia is woven into the fabric of daily life. I notice it but wonder if the Koreans are aware of it as well or if they have grown completely immune to it. When I was in Havana last year, the artist Tania Bruguera told me that Cubans currently live under a condition she deems Fear 2.0, where you have two or three generations who are simply born with fear already encoded in their DNA. (More recently, in her book *The Future Is History: How Totalitarianism Reclaimed Russia*, Masha Gessen tracks the multigenerational evolution of a similar process of fear-encoding that continues to afflict the mass psychology of denizens of the former Soviet Union and their descendants.) Paranoia comes to form the *natural order of things*. It comes encased in the subtlest of details, which you become adept at reading, such as that everyday occurrence, felt most strongly at the water park, where everyone was staring at us but no one wanted to engage for fear of the possible repercussions. No foreigner, after all, is to be trusted. Even Min, who on the surface seems more cosmopolitan and open, given her life experience. Even Min has her limits.

Min: child of intrigue. If it's true that North Koreans often come across as enigmatic figures to foreigners who encounter them, then it is also true that this is usually intentional, and for a complex set of reasons. Cultural differences: in North Korea, there's a general distrust of fellow human beings, a natural consequence of living in what is probably the most heavily monitored society the world has yet known, where anyone is a potential snitch. Everyone has at least one experience of betrayal to provide a fine coating of distrust. When you cannot fully trust your neighbors or extended family, you are not likely to confide very much in a foreigner, especially when you have been taught your entire life that all foreigners are potentially enemy agents.

What you are born into defines who you are. Who you are will define what you are able to do. In the Songbun system, instituted by Kim Il Sung around the time he was conducting those purges against his enemies in the Politburo, your born essence is inescapable. Save for the very few, whose position of high privilege is determined by the helpful things their grandparents or great-grandparents did in Kim Il Sung's glory days, there is no direction to travel in besides straight ahead or else way down. Upward mobility is a possibility for an extremely small minority; with it comes tremendous risks.

Min clearly belongs to some Pyongyang minority of privilege, though it is hard to determine which—there are many gradations within the three categories of *loyal, wavering,* and *hostile* classes. But her parents were at least trusted enough to be selected to go and live in Cuba for eight years, where her mother worked as chef for the DPRK Embassy and her father did business, and that is essentially the world Min was reared in. From the age of ten to eighteen, she went to Cuban schools, spoke Spanish fluently, learned to dance salsa and mambo. Cuba ostensibly operates under a similar socialist system to the DPRK; in actuality, it is much more open. Unlike the DPRK, Cuba does not forbid its citizens from watching or listening to foreign media. Min grew up listening to Green Day, System of a Down, Madonna, Britney Spears, watching Harry Potter movies— without fear of being punished.

She's been back in Pyongyang now for nearly eight years, but still slips up, lets her guard down constantly when she's around us. Says things without any fear of consequences. She tells us that she wishes she had stayed behind in Havana to finish her university studies and then bites her tongue. She sings "Barbie Girl" at karaoke. She tells us that one of her colleagues at work was recently reprimanded for constantly playing *World of Warcraft* on the clock.

Recklessness or naïveté. Both, perhaps. Part of it is that Min feels protected enough by who she is, who her family is. But it's also that Min is, in a sense, a creature from another world. A creature of circumstance. Not the born revolutionary. Yearning to be more than merely someone's daughter, but what? She wears the badge, she talks the talk, but this is not her natural habitat. She's trying her best to wade through the waters. She is still trying to figure out, after all this time, what it means to be Korean. What it means to be disciplined. What it means to obey.

★

I take the elevator down to the lobby to see if Mark still wants to have that drink. Tonight, he's seated at a table with a tense-looking crowd—Simon and the Korean "colleagues," all in Mao suits and chain-smoking, trapped in some bureaucratic stalemate. Mark gives an awkward wave and then shrugs his shoulders. The scene doesn't look very inviting, so I head back to my room. It probably wouldn't be good to start tomorrow with a hangover anyway.

I'm getting ready for bed when a knock sounds on my door. I open it to find Alexandre standing there in his underwear.

"Sorry, Travis, can I come in for a minute?"

Seeing that I'm also a bit underdressed, we both laugh awkwardly. It doesn't really matter—there aren't any other guests staying on our floor.

"I just wanted to tell you," he whispers, "Alek and I decided that tomorrow, we would all dress nice for the first day of class. You know—to make a good impression."

I smile. For Alexandre, it's all about first impressions—the Korean songs at karaoke, visiting the Mansu Hill to leave flowers. But I've caught up with him. My pressed shirt and new trousers are already laid out for the first day of school.

PART THREE

NORKOREALISM

NINE

OUR CHERUBIC DRIVER Hwa can't be a day over twenty-five, though no one's bothered to ask. He's just gotten out of the military, so he's probably a bit older, since most men are conscripted for ten years in the DPRK. He also worked as a driver for his military service. For someone of lower-middle Song-bun, it's considered a specialized job. Until recently, very few were entitled to the use of vehicles. Even fewer knew how to drive them. At the very least, it's a job that relieves one of having to engage in backbreaking manual labor—though Hwa's dark tan indicates the frequency with which he is called away when there is no delegation to shuttle about. When he's with us, he's always smiling and fully present.

Unlike other drivers I've had, who tend to play a more servile role, always wait-ing behind in the parking lot whenever we're driven to a new site, Hwa accom-panies us and takes a keen interest in whatever activity we're engaged in, whether it's a visit to an aquarium or a museum. Alexandre says it's because we're mainly going to places that tourists don't normally go, and so they are places that Hwa also hasn't seen. I think it's more likely that he hasn't had the opportunity to see much of anything before.

Since it's considered a somewhat vaunted profession in the DPRK, drivers—whether they be truckers or chauffeurs—take their jobs seriously. Each morn-ing, Hwa pulls up in front of the hotel entrance, and the van is spotlessly clean inside and out, no matter the duration of the previous day's road trip and the state we left the vehicle in the night before. Alexandre tells me that he got up early one morning for a walk on the hotel grounds and watched as Hwa dili-gently removed each of the tires from the van and gave them a rigorous inspec-tion, making sure everything was in perfect running order.

Our route takes us the same way every morning, from west to east through the heart of Pyongyang, providing us with a moving panorama of the morning city as it readies itself for the day. Past the scenic Potong River, with the leafy branches of its overgrown willow trees dipping into the placid waters, and the Potonggang Hotel, considered one of Pyongyang's swankier digs—among other amenities, it has the best Japanese restaurant in town and even CNN in all the rooms.

We wind our way through the Changgwang district of central Pyongyang, with its white, dome-shaped ice-skating rink, a retro-futuristic relic that wouldn't look out of place among the space age–style buildings scattered around the Eastern Bloc in the 1970s. Past a wide empty street, blocked off with a mobile metal gate and a guard, a forest of trees obscures the views of the buildings. Though you won't find this area marked on any official map, this is where members of the Central Committee live and work; satellite images show a green park with palatial villas fringed by smaller guardhouses; where trees and hills don't suffice, a row of apartment blocks, likely the dwelling places of slightly lower-ranking cadres, obscures the view. Though no one would ever say so out loud, this is also the likely central Pyongyang office of the number one man in the country.

Cars everywhere. It's morning rush hour, for sure, though never enough traffic to warrant a jam. The vast majority of vehicles these days are taxis. The sheer quantity reveals the burgeoning wealth of the city. In the mornings, they are crammed with people sharing the ride, making for a comfier alternative to Pyongyang's overcrowded buses and trams, where pickpocketing is said to be rampant.

We cross the Taedong River into east Pyongyang. There, on the banks, we are greeted with the glass-windowed facade of the large Ryugyong health and recreational complex, which kind of resembles a middle American corporate office park. It's a series of buildings that include the Golden Lanes bowling alley, a hamburger fast-food joint, an upscale espresso bar popular among expats, indoor and outdoor skating rinks. More recently, a large sauna complex has been opened for the *donju*. It boasts ground-floor shops selling foreign luxury clothing brands, a gym, an indoor swimming pool, and men's and women's saunas crowned with an expensive restaurant and bar. The first time I visited, on my way upstairs to the restaurant, I was greeted with an unusual large framed photograph. In the middle of the frame, what appeared to my eyes was a stout butch lesbian wearing an ugly apron and sullen frown, dangling a dead fish over a frying pan. It took a long squint for me to decipher that it was actually a young Kim

Jong Il with his glasses removed, demonstrating his culinary genius. So unlike the standard propaganda portraits you see of smiling Kim Jong Il everywhere else you look in North Korea, you have to wonder what they had in mind by installing it here. Again, I saw proof that they're aware of the inherent vulnerability of such images; as I raised my phone to take a photo, a guard who had been seated at a desk partially hidden behind a wall in the hallway emerged and ordered me to stop.

As we get deeper into the east part of town, away from all the monuments and the beating heart of the Workers' Party, another Pyongyang reveals itself. The apartment buildings grow increasingly run-down, and as we traverse the depths of the Tongdaewon district, it becomes clear we're in the poor part of town. Tourists are rarely taken farther east beyond the Juche Tower and the recreational facilities of the Ryugyong complex, both of which sit on the eastern banks of the Taedong.

Though there is a part of the east, where Comrade Kim lives, that is up-and-coming—"gentrifying," if such a concept existed here—most of it remains quite poor. This and the neighboring Songyo district were among the only parts of Pyongyang that were actually afflicted by the famine of the 1990s, where some residents starved to death. This is the part of town where Hwa lives.

As we approach Kim Hyong Jik University of Education, apartment buildings give way to single-story shack-like houses reminiscent of the colonial period, surrounded by dirt roads. The university is itself on one of the main avenues, however, its front entrance kept in pristine condition—as one would expect of a school named after Kim Il Sung's father. The gated entrance is manned by a security guard who checks the documents of all who enter. On the stone scaffolding above this entrance, a brass-embossed calligraphied stencil, a facsimile of Kim Il Sung's handwriting, has been installed, preserving yet another profundity for all eternity; Alek translates for me: "Kim Hyong Jik University is a good university."

Pedagogy is the main subject. Future teachers from around the country learn their trade here. Then there is the small Korean for foreigners program in the linguistics department, where international exchange students—predominately Chinese—can complete BA and MA degrees in the language of Choson. The linguistics department is housed in one of the front buildings facing Saesalim Street, before which stretches a soccer field that won't see any use while we're here. School's not in session in the summer months, and anyway, it's too hot to play. The only students around are a handful of Koreans enrolled in remedial classes. Each university has its own uniform; at Kim Hyong Jik, it's blue blazers and red ties, long skirts for the girls and slacks for the guys, with the men also given bulky hats that look like a cross between those worn by navy captains and the traditional communist worker's cap. Whenever a North Korean student passes a professor in the hallway, they are obliged to stop and give them a deep respectful bow—a gesture of courtesy Alek tells us is also practiced in South Korea and one that we quickly learn to adapt.

We walk past the obligatory painting of Kim Jong Il in the entrance corridor, down the unlit hallways to the staircase, and then up to the third floor. We are led into the linguistics department's office—where, like in most offices in North Korea, there is a complete absence of computers or any other electronic equipment, making it reminiscent of an office from an earlier century. The administrator, a kindly, middle-aged woman with a bad perm, introduces us to our three teachers. We smile and make polite bows. It is all very formal and solemn, though with an underlying giddiness on the part of our teachers, who have never taught Western foreigners before.

Mine, Ms. Pak, is in her late thirties—only two years older than me, it turns out. She has a much better perm than her colleague in administration. It's a popular choice among North Korean women of a certain age, though it is growing less fashionable with the underground importation of the latest looks from Seoul. She flashes me a toothy grin and a shy glance from behind her gold-rimmed glasses before leading me down the hallway to our classroom where I will have my choice of the dozen-some wooden desks each day as the only student in the beginner-level class.

TEN

ONE OF THE consequences of Korea's seventy-year-plus division has been the evolution of distinctions between the ways Korean is spoken on either side of the thirty-eighth parallel. Accents vary throughout the peninsula, but North Koreans in general stand out for speaking in a way that often comes across as rural, prollish, rough, and lowbred to Southerners, especially in Seoul. North Koreans seem to implicitly agree—as South Korean television dramas and films began to spread on the black market, young North Koreans could suddenly be heard imitating the posh accents of their brethren in the South.

At the same time, the Korean spoken in Choson tends to be much more stiff, with the formal polite style—a style in the South that is usually only deployed in the military or when addressing a large crowd—being the favored mode of address in everyday life. This endows the North Korean version of the language with a quaint, charming sound to South Korean ears—as though the entire country were "a small village undisturbed by time," as one writer put it. This formality is undercut with frequent eruptions of the profane, however. Even in official propaganda, when speaking of politicians from enemy nations like South Korea or the United States, it is not uncommon for newscasters or print media to refer to them as bastards, bitches, and whores. (Or worse. In one editorial, President Obama was said to resemble "a monkey in an African jungle.")

English-speaking students who wish to learn Korean in the South benefit from the frequent adaptation of words from their mother tongue. In their push for ethnic purity, North Koreans have attempted to keep their language pure. As a result, they have different words for many everyday things, which tends to cause some confusion when North Korean defectors arrive in the South.

Learning a new language typically begins with the task of basic pronunciation.

In the case of Korean, this coincides with the learning of the Korean alphabet: Hangul, as it is known in the South; Chosongul in the North. Prior to its invention by King Sejong, Korean was written using complex Chinese characters. As a result, most Koreans were effectively illiterate. When Sejong introduced his script in 1443, he asserted that a clever person could master it in one hour, an idiot in ten days. I'm about to find out where I fall on the King's IQ test.

Unlike Chinese, with its complex pictographic system consisting of thousands of strokes that must be memorized, as they do not correspond to sounds, Korean's series of horizontal and vertical sticks and circles forming a total of twenty-eight letters—seventeen consonants and eleven vowels—is completely phonetic. The King's conception was equal parts cosmological, phonological, and anatomical; the vowels are meant as configurations of three primary sounds that represent the three primal elements of the universe—sky, earth, and human—while the form of each consonant resembles the shape of the mouth and/or tongue as it pronounces the letter. As such, what Sejong accomplished is nothing less than a writing of the corporeal—an alignment of the body with the earth and the cosmos.

Chosongul's graceful phoneticism culminates in the stacking of these letter sounds atop one another in order of pronunciation to form syllables. As daunting as it appears to foreigners and the otherwise illiterate, the systematic ingenuity of Chosongul is that within hours of mastering each letter's pronunciation, you can theoretically read any Korean text aloud without even understanding its meaning.

My first task, then, is to learn this alphabet and its corresponding sounds, starting with the vowels. Which sounds easy enough—were this Spanish or Italian, it could be accomplished in less than five minutes. But Korean's vowels, in part because there are so many of them, pose an immediate challenge to nonnative speakers. For one thing, the differences between many of the sounds are subtle to American or European ears, though quite distinct to Koreans. What's more, many of these vowel sounds are actually diphthongs, vowel chains pronounced in rapid-fire succession. At the same time, this is made somewhat easier by the way Chosongul is written, with the letter meant to illustrate the position of the lips or the tongue when it is being pronounced, which Ms. Pak demonstrates by pointing to her mouth and the letter as it is written on the whiteboard.

My first day gives me a glance into "the *real* North Korea" that foreign journalists are always bemoaning they never get to see. There's no electricity in any of the public areas—surprisingly, even the mural of Kim Jong Il at the entrance is shrouded in darkness. My classroom has electricity, but it's patchy, to say the least. Besides the whiteboard, above which the requisite portraits of Kim Il Sung and Kim Jong Il smile down at the students, Ms. Pak's other main teaching apparatus is a flat-screen television upon which she will flash words and bits of the alphabet that she points at for me to repeat. In the middle of the first lesson, the power goes off. Without missing a beat, Ms. Pak moves to the whiteboard and commences writing the lost vowels.

The task proves difficult enough to warrant the entire first day's lesson spent on reading and repeating each vowel sound. At the end of class, Ms. Pak suggests I make a video of her repeating the vowels on my phone so that I can practice pronunciation as part of tonight's homework. I'm no cinematographer, but I manage to arrange the shot so that I capture both the written letters as I've penned them in my notebook and Ms. Pak's face as she points to each inscription and pronounces it. At the end, there is some agreement between Ms. Pak and me that I have gotten it halfway right. Or at least right enough so that tomorrow I can look forward to the next daunting task: consonants.

After class, I meet Comrade Kim, who's shown up unexpectedly, pacing the dark hallway. "Well, how was it?" he asks anxiously.

I dutifully ejaculate the eleven vowel sounds I've learned. Comrade Kim claps his hands and repeats them with me before erupting in laughter.

"You are very lucky," he says, suddenly turning serious. "When I was arranging the course, the administrator from the department told me that Ms. Pak is *the best teacher for beginners* in Korea. She has *fifteen years'* experience!"

I nod dumbly at the number, my head still spinning with vowels.

"*All* foreign students who want to learn Korean in our country have her for a teacher."

Wow, I think. Not only is she the best in Korea; she's also the only!

On the wall, a long poster illustrates each accomplishment of the Chollima Movement, a poster I will study each day on my fifteen-minute study break while sipping a can of iced coffee purchased from the deserted canteen next to my classroom.

"I will learn Korean at Chollima Speed!" I declare with a smile.

Comrade Kim laughs hysterically and then shoots me a somewhat despairing look, the same one younger people will give to their elders when they're trying cluelessly and desperately to sound "cool." "Nowadays, it's 'Mallima Speed,'" he corrects me.

"Did you also study at this university?" I ask him.

Kim laughs at the notion condescendingly. "No, I went to the University of Foreign Studies," he replies. That's also where Min and Roe both went—the second-most prestigious university in North Korea besides Kim Il Sung University. "Actually, I studied many different things! At the university, my major was Southeast Asian languages: Thai, Lao, Malay, Vietnamese. But I also studied Chinese and English. Then I did a degree in business..."

"You must have studied for many years then."

"Noooo," he replies modestly. "I actually spent many years working overseas. In Vietnam, mostly. At the Korean Embassy. But also...as businessman."

This dual role might sound improbable coming from any other country in the world. But for North Korea, it is one of the main tasks of its embassies: generating hard currency for the regime.

"Oh, and some Italian, too! I forgot to mention." Comrade Kim laughs at this for no real reason. I laugh, too. It's that kind of infectious laughter. The same laughter I was greeted with at the airport, the laughter that got him through the security barricade and that rescued me and my stack of books. The laughter of someone important enough to relax, to laugh his way through life.

ELEVEN

THE MANSUDAE GRAND Monument, with its sculptures of the smiling Kims extending across the Taedong River to the Workers' Party Monument, forms one leg of the axis of central Pyongyang. The second axis, also extending from the Mansudae Assembly Hall, stretches from Kim Il Sung Square across the river to the Tower of the Juche Idea. Actually, when seen on a map, the shape formed is less of a dual axis than a half circle—a metaphoric extension of Kim's outstretched arms, embracing the entirety of Choson.

But it is the wide expanse of Kim Il Sung Square that is most recognizable to the outside world. Where military parades, rife with displays of missiles and goose-stepping soldiers that form the mass media's stock footage of North Korea, are held. Standing on the square, you can observe the rows of numbers that have been painted onto the pavement, a testament to the frequent assemblies held here.

On the opposite side of the Taedong River, where the axis terminates, is the Tower of the Juche Idea. Kim Jong Il gave it to his father as a seventieth birthday gift in 1982. It was constructed at Chollima Speed: thirty-five days. The tower's body consists of 25,550 blocks—one for each day of Kim Il Sung's life up to that point. It is crowned with a cherry-red flame that, like the Grand Monument, is kept lit throughout the night, regardless of electricity shortages elsewhere in the capital. When it is open, visitors can take an elevator up for a panoramic view of Pyongyang. Positioned at the top of the steps on the riverbank leading up to the tower, another bronze statue has been installed with three figures representing the worker, the peasant, and the intellectual—a theme that never grows old.

The square is dominated by the Grand People's Study House, from whose balcony the country's leaders can be seen monitoring those parades. It is one of two prominent examples of North Korea's unique style of architecture, the other being the Pyongyang Grand Theatre: a combination of late Stalinist brutalism and traditional rural Koreana. Both buildings are composed of columnar support structures that fit Soviet architecture's penchant for using neoclassical dynamics to suggest ideals of state power, though they are crowned with the curvaceous flow found in traditional Korean thatched rooftops. Korean head, Socialist body.

The Grand People's Study House, being the more gargantuan structure, is more eye-catching in its elaborateness, consisting of a whole series of sloping roofs, implying a miniature village, in the dashing and elegant syncopation of its ten stories. It was also unveiled on the Great Leader's birthday, April 15, 1982—though it could be said that this was his present to the people. Lest they forget, there is a massive granite statue of him to greet them at the entrance. Consisting of a hundred rooms and a hundred thousand square meters, the building was erected at a cost of one billion dollars and is the place where Pyongyangites from all walks of life—not just students—come to do research or read. The library is said to contain some thirty million titles across a vast array of subjects, from Western classics by the Greeks up through Shakespeare and the Russian greats of the nineteenth century, to a multilingual selection of journals recording the latest research in science, mathematics, and technology, plus special rooms dedicated to the works of Kim Il Sung and Kim Jong Il and, now, Kim Jong Un. When foreigners visit, the librarian is always sure to show off the library's prized copy of *Gone with the Wind*—one of the few American novels the leadership has deemed worthy for the public to read, perhaps unsurprising, given the triumphant victory of the righteous North over the oppressive slave states of the South in the American Civil War that forms the novel's backdrop—a favorite in North Korea.

I recall my visit here in 2012, when I was introduced to the philosopher-in-residence, a wizened official in a windowless room, where, my guide informed us, students can ask any question and he will give "the correct answer." Seated before a desk, he shuffled through some yellowing handwritten papers as my group stood before him awkwardly. "Does anyone have any questions for Mister Philosopher?" the guide asked. *Can you clarify, once and for all, whether the Juche idea had its origins in classical Marxist theory?* I nearly asked. But I choked. To his relief, no one else could think of anything to ask either. On the way out, I'm sure I heard our guide apologize for waking him.

The Grand People's Study House is surrounded on either side by the Ministry of Culture and Ministry of Foreign Affairs. Bisecting the square is Sungni, formerly known as Stalin Street. On the other side, two venerable cultural institutions, the Korean Art Gallery and Korean History Museum, face off.

After digesting our first day of lessons over lunch, we drop Comrade Kim off at the office and head to the square for a visit to the art gallery—though, first, I insist on a stop at the Viennese coffeehouse behind the history museum for a much-needed espresso. This was one of the first coffee shops to open in Pyongyang, a joint venture with the Austrian company Helmut Sachers that opened in 2011. A shot of espresso costs more than an average North Korean's monthly salary—around three dollars. The coffee shop is empty, save for the barista, an extremely attractive young woman in her early twenties, which fits the profile of every employee I've ever seen at this coffee shop. Men are never employed in the service industry.

After we down our coffee, we head outside, where the barista is fawning over two baby squirrels in a small cage she caught on a recent excursion to the mountains. One is running in a miniature wheel that's been constructed out of the remnants of a plastic bottle. The other is munching on a piece of apple. Min squeals with delight and takes out her phone to make a video as the little squirrel runs and the wheel turns round and round and round.

TWELVE

THE KOREAN ART Gallery is home to the largest art collection in the DPRK, consisting mostly of paintings but also a few sculptural works. Upon arrival, I am instantly recognized by Ms. Kwak Song A, who is waiting outside for us in her trademark pink *joseon-ot,* that traditional floor-length Korean dress that looks like it was stitched together from a particularly gaudy silk curtain. In a culture that prizes modesty, it does the trick, completely masking the curves and shape of the wearer's body.

I had met Ms. Kwak on my previous visits to the gallery. She's the main tour guide, trained as an art historian. When I asked her about her theoretical work, she informed me that one of her winning contributions to the field, published in the nation's art history journal, was a paper on the necessity of having guides in the art museums. Her thesis? "The guides must provide people with the *correct* revolutionary interpretation of each painting, or else they will be lost."

The Korean Art Gallery plays host to temporary exhibitions in addition to the revolving display from its permanent collection. Now, there are two shows on, both consisting of recent paintings by the country's most prestigious artists. The first, presented in the main reception corridor, features seven large oil paintings by artists from the Mansudae Art Studio commemorating the recent Seventh Workers' Party Congress. Although the rules of the Workers' Party dictate that a congress be held every seven years, the previous one took place in 1980, when Kim Il Sung officially announced Kim Jong Il as his successor. This year's congress saw Kim Jong Un elected as chairman of the Workers' Party, an event that surprised no one. Although the congress had taken place a couple months before, it still hovers in the air everywhere we go.

All of the paintings, Ms. Kwak tells us, have been personally approved by

Marshal Kim Jong Un. Four of them are landscapes depicting Mount Paekdu in the wintertime. Since most artists working nowadays are too young to have had any direct knowledge of the harsh climate in those environs that Kim Il Sung endured during the years he spent fighting off the Japanese, a group of them were sent there on a field trip in the depths of winter. This punishing experience would supposedly aid the artists in the act of creation. Each was permitted to choose their unique perspective and angle; one, presumably hoping to escape the clichés that have inevitably enveloped this endlessly explored subject, chose to depict the forest surrounding the holy mountain, where Kim Il Sung and his comrades hid out. On the opposite wall, the three remaining paintings making up the exhibition would be no anomaly to those familiar with the tropes of Socialist Realist painting: workers at happy toil in the factories, celebrations of quotas being exceeded—the usual inflations of the communist banal.

In the hallway leading to the permanent collection, a second series of oil paintings make up the National Exhibition, held once a year. Of the thousand-plus paintings submitted, only around a dozen are selected. The rest of the paintings go into the museum's permanent collection. Among this year's winning works: *Girl Mother,* a 2016 painting by Ri Yung Un executed in a colorful bombastic cartoon realism. A young woman, around twenty years of age, is depicted in traditional university dress in a field, surrounded by laughing children in the red scarves of the Young Pioneers. She is one of North Korea's latest stars of propaganda, Chang Jong A, instantly recognizable. A national hero, the university student was recently given the title "Girl Mother" by the Marshal for her selfless task of raising orphaned children while still practically a child herself.

The main collection is arranged chronologically, commencing with reproductions of Koryo Dynasty–era tomb murals. The reproductions are kept behind glass and appear rather sad, dusty, faded—most were made during the Korean War in haste in order to document what very well might have been lost as a result of the destructive bombing by the Americans. One of the highlights features the excavated walls of an imperial tomb outside of modern-day Nampo on the west coast, a UNESCO World Heritage site.

Traditional Korean paintings were done with ink on silk or rice paper. In the twentieth century, these classic techniques would morph into one of North Korea's sole indigenous art forms, Chosonhwa. "Hwa" means painting; "Choson," of course, the land of morning calm, the official name of North Korea—how North Koreans refer to *all* of Korea—with South Korea ("Hanguk," as it is called in the South) being referred to as "southern Choson." In the early days of the Republic, Kim Il Sung would encourage artists and writers to study the works of the Soviet and Chinese Socialist Realists for inspiration in making their own work. But by 1960, during the so-called Chollima era, Kim Il Sung was preoccupied with the task of separating his nation from the sphere of Soviet and Chinese influence—through his purges behind the scenes and the promotion of Korean ultra-nationalism on the forefront. Naturally, the arts—which have always been the central disseminator of propaganda in the DPRK—had to follow.

In 1961, at the Fourth Party Congress, strict guidelines were introduced in the cultural realm. Artistic freedom and personal style, as they are venerated in the bourgeois West, were discouraged. Rules for *correct* form and content—again: Korean mind, Socialist body—were brought to the table. The earliest painter to take his cue from the new policy was Kim Young Jun, who is credited as the inventor of Chosonhwa in 1967. True to the new aesthetic doctrine, Chosonhwa used traditional materials—ink, rice paper—and techniques, but its subject matter was contemporary, reflecting the ideals of socialist North Korea. In essence, despite propagandistic claims that this is a pure Korean invention, the roots of Chosonhwa reflect North Korea's specific postcolonial situation: it is a fusion of traditional Japanese Nihonga painting, the dominant form during the years of the occupation, with Soviet socialist realism. Much like the political system itself, that unusual panoply of what came before—Japanese imperialism with its emperor worship, and the Soviet Union of Stalin's era. It seemed to do the trick. Chosonhwa effectively formed the aesthetic foundation of every North Korean fine art form to come.

One could never reasonably expect art to be exempt from the monolithic ideological system that Kim Il Sung developed in those post-purge years. But the significant role that the arts would come to play in the promulgation of North Korean domestic propaganda was synonymous with the rise of the man who engineered it: his son, Kim Jong Il.

By the end of the 1960s, Kim Il Sung was experiencing further bouts of strife within the upper echelons. It culminated in the 1967 purge of the so-called Kapsan faction led by Pak Gum Chol. The Kapsan Operations Committee was an underground organization that had provided logistical and intelligence support during the occupation for anti-Japanese guerilla fighters and, in particular,

Kim Il Sung's militia. Pak and his cohorts felt slighted by the rapid expansion of the Kim Il Sung personality cult and the rewriting of history that had completely omitted their own courageous efforts in attributing the liberation of the peninsula to the Great Leader alone.

Suffice it to say that their machinations did not get very far. Pak was soon expelled from the Workers' Party, exiled from Pyongyang, and forced to work in a rural factory, while the rest of his cohorts were arrested and tried on the usual trumped-up conspiratorial charges.

Then, in 1968, an armed coup was attempted to remove Kim Il Sung from power. It was masterminded by the Minister of National Security at the time, Kim O Bong, who was subsequently purged and replaced by General Choi Hyon. Jang Jin Sung, the pseudonymous writer who would emerge as Kim Jong Il's favorite poet in the 1990s and later defected to the South, would attribute the genesis of Kim Jong Il's hereditary succession to General Choi. Of course, filial succession was unheard-of, taboo in the communist world—such an idea would have immediately struck the Soviets or Chinese as a remnant of monarchical imperialism. But Choi was deeply conservative, his values ensconced in the traditional Korean neo-Confucian view that power should be transferred from a father to his eldest son. It was Choi's advocacy that launched Kim Jong Il's rise—while serving to simultaneously distance the DPRK from the mainstreams of communism in China and the Soviet Union. We can imagine, after all the internal threats and purges of the past two decades, that Kim Il Sung would be easily persuaded by now to "keep it in the family." Jong Il, for his part, played his role in the solidifying the Monolithic Ideological System when he was elected in 1969 at the age of twenty-seven to join the Organization and Guidance Department (OGD), the most powerful organ in the North Korean government, which has direct access to the leader himself.

At the time Kim Jong Il was given his first prominent position, Kim Il Sung's ironclad rule was through the *government* of the DPRK, which possessed all the ruling powers—*not* the Workers' Party. The OGD was merely an instrument of the Workers' Party, which was, at the time, just one of many bureaucratic institutions in the country. In a cunning ploy that would unravel slowly over the course of the next decade, Kim Jong Il would elevate the authority of the OGD by argu-ing that North Korean society needed the Party to play a stronger role in uphold-ing the command and ruling stature of the Great Leader Kim Il Sung. Eventually, the power to appoint personnel was shifted away from the government and to the OGD, run by Kim Jong Il. Among its activities, the OGD was tasked with carrying out surveillance on all of the Great Leader's supposed internal enemies. This surveillance became so rampant that it culminated in Kim Il Sung himself essentially falling under surveillance by the OGD. By that point, Kim Jong Il and his cohorts in the OGD had taken over all the prominent positions, transforming the Workers' Party into the most prominent political organ in the DPRK. From 1980, it was no longer Kim Il Sung's government that actually ran things but the Workers' Party under Kim Jong Il, whose own deification soon commenced. Kim Il Sung was still officially the "Great Leader" to North Koreans and the outside world. But in actuality, all of the real power lay with the son. In this dual struc-ture, Kim Il Sung's men, who were by now of advanced age, were given the most prestigious titles—but that's all they were: titles. They wielded very little power. The real power was held by men in the OGD: Kim Jong Il's men.

This is why there is so much mystique behind the political structure of the Hermit Kingdom—why so few outsiders are able to understand it. It has its roots in Kim Jong Il's division of powers, which enabled his usurpation of the throne. His pruning would culminate shortly after his father's death in 1994, with the purging of all his father's loyalists, banning them and their progeny from Work-ers' Party membership, and the banishment of several thousand prominent fam-ilies from Pyongyang. Clearly, a new sort of loyalty was now required.

Walking or driving through the streets of Pyongyang, it becomes quickly appar-ent that the DPRK has more public art than any other country in the world. In place of the visual pollution of advertising that clutters so many cities in the twenty-first century, the Pyongyang streets are filled with colorful posters, murals, and mosaics—all made by hand, extolling the virtues of leader, party, country. The art we see and the cultural system attached to it tell us a lot about how the nation functions, how it views itself, and how art serves the ongoing project of engineering the ideal citizen and society.

But who makes all this stuff? What is it like to be an artist in North Korea?

Certainly the classical model of artists nurturing their private visions solitarily in their studios, churning out works to be sold through the commercial gallery system, does not exist here. The very notion would likely be regarded as classically bourgeois, reactionary, capitalistic. Art, rather, has more *utilitarian* value than it does in the West and other places: that of propaganda. It is meant to educate, to uphold the system's values, through conveying clear and easily legible messages, not to titillate or provoke contemplation through ambiguity. As Kim Jong Il wrote in one of his numberless treatises on aesthetics: "There is no such thing as pure art disconnected from the lives of the people."

If you're lucky, you get discovered early on. Talented children in all of the visual and performing arts are scouted across the country on a yearly basis. The good ones might end up at their local schoolchildren's palace, where their talents are nurtured in after-school lessons; the very best are sent to Pyongyang for the country's most rigorous art training. (Thanks to Kim Jong Il's obsession with the arts, talent is one of the few means by which a person might overcome poor Songbun—though this is by no means guaranteed.) The *crème de la crème* will attend the grandiose Manyongdae Schoolchildren's Palace, renovated with bright, marbleized splendor in 2015, with departments for virtually every field in the arts, sciences, and athletics. Here, tourists and foreign dignitaries are customarily taken on tours to witness classes and rehearsals, culminating in spectacular performances where the country's brightest little singers, dancers, acrobats, musicians, and actors showcase their craft with stunning perfection.

Post-secondary school, after training for five years at one of the nation's art academies, performers will be taken on at any number of theaters or bands, while visual artists will typically go on to employment at one of the art studios, the most venerated of which is Mansudae, which boasts around a thousand visual artists and four thousand assistants and administrative staff. Mansudae is where the huge statues of the Kims on Mansu Hill—and the hundreds of others elsewhere in the country—were produced. All of Pyongyang's murals and mosaics are rendered here. And it is where, in the department of oil painting, the vast majority of the works showcased in the Korean Art Gallery on Kim Il Sung Square were painted.

Once employed at an art studio, artists are given free rein to paint or sculpt anything they want. They have a monthly quantitative quota to fill, but subject matter and content are up to them. By that point, they are trusted, as they have already undergone the lifelong ideological training that is guaranteed to result in only *correct* images. Occasionally—or often, depending on the department and medium—a commission will come in that will require the talents of one artist (in the case of, say, an oil painting or small tapestry) or up to an entire department (for monumental sculptures or mosaics).

Successful artists work their way up the reward system. The highest commendation is People's Artist, the second highest Merited Artist. There are only a couple hundred artists awarded with such designations. Most live in Pyongyang and are gifted with luxury housing for their families in a new high-rise facing the Taedong River and extra rations. The most successful might even win the Kim Il Sung Prize.

So artists live relatively charmed existences in the DPRK. They might be granted inspiration trips to idyllic locales in the countryside or, rarer, sojourn abroad. Artists work at their studios from Monday to Friday; on Saturdays, like everyone else, they are required to attend study sessions, where the theoretical writings of Kim Il Sung and Kim Jong Il might be taught—a further extension of the Juche aesthetics they absorb during their studies at the art academy. Upon retirement, they may join the Songhwa Art Studio in Pyongyang, which holds its own exhibitions of members' work.

There is, however, no star system among artists and writers like there is in the West. Rather, there are famous works. North Koreans, when asked about their favorite novels, can recite vivid plot summaries but most often won't be able to tell you the author's name. In art, the most iconographic painting is undoubtedly Chung Young Man's *Evening Glow at Kangsun Steelworks*. The sky is alive with that fiery dawn glow, smoke spewing snakishly out of the factory towers above the glistening river. Never mind the content; Chung's painting can be admired for color alone. Standing in front of the painting, Ms. Kwak tells us the story behind its creation: that its theme was suggested to the artist by Kim Jong Il personally. Full of inspiration, Chung set out for Nampo in search of scenes to paint. When he happened to catch a glimpse of the factory at the waning hour, he recalled the General's advice and dutifully brought out his paints and a blank canvas and set to work.

Really, the whole city can be treated as one gigantic art museum. Look at the subways: the veins of the city. The stations one extended gallery. Each designed by a different artist meditating upon a theme based on the station's name: Red Star, Glory, Revolution, Liberation.

The palatial architecture, with its marble pillars and arches and extravagant chandeliers, will be familiar to anyone who's taken a subway in Moscow. But it is the colorful mosaics, made collectively by the Mansudae Art Studio, that are worth dwelling on as you await your train's arrival. At Prosperity Station, there's *The Great Leader Kim Il Sung Among Workers* stretching across the rear wall, with the middle-aged maestro marching against the smoking factory chimneys of a golden sunset, his open trench coat flapping in the wind, as a dozen happy, smiling blue- and white-collar workers follow close on his trail. The murals of Construction Station dramatize the rebuilding of Pyongyang after the war, while Glory Station's centerpiece is the spiritual birthplace of the Korean nation, Mount Paekdu, the birthplace, according to propaganda, of Kim Jong Il. Outside the country, it is known that his actual birthplace was a Siberian army camp, where his father was in exile.

In the West, Kim Jong Il has long been mocked as an emblem of high camp with his pompadour hairdo, fur-collared jacket, oversize designer shades, and long-hemmed pants obscuring those custom-made pointy high heels he wore to obscure his challenged verticality. In a West where not so long ago, racist, late colonial Dr. No caricatures were evoked to propagandize an evil Asian other—and arguably still filter into our characterizations of the Chinese and North Koreans—Kim Jong Il seemed to fit the part. A wizened gook Liberace with blood on his fingers and world domination on the brain.

Defectors often claim that Kim Jong Il in actuality enjoyed far less popular support than his father. Others nevertheless express admiration for what they characterize as his artistic genius. Even though he never made any art himself, his wizardry behind the entire North Korean culture industry is well known. Those who knew him personally have said that he had the personality of a temperamental artist rather than a politician. Simultaneous with his role at the OGD, Jong Il was also given another position: head of the Propaganda and Agitation Department (PAD).

There's a good reason why Kim Il Sung allowed his son to wrest power away from his hands: he didn't notice it happening. As head of the PAD, Jong Il accelerated the expansion of his father's personality cult in a full-on artistic assault. The elder Kim was in turn bedazzled by the city being erected around him—the city *of* him. Everywhere he went, he would see his likeness projected. Even when he himself did not appear in a painting or sculpture or film, it was made clear, through a dedicatory plaque, speech, or text, that the monumental work was indeed *about* him. Inspired by him. A promulgation of his greatness.

Clearly, Jong Il recognized early on his father's weakness for flattery. His role at the PAD allowed him to indulge that weakness to a distracting degree. In philosophy, Jong Il adapted the nascent idea of Juche, or Subject Thought, as one commentator has translated it, only to recenter it upon the idea of the Suryong, the Great Leader. "Man is the master of all things": this is how the Juche idea is often summarized, leading to the erroneous belief that Juche is some sort of crudely sloganified existentialism. But actually, the Juche doctrine states quite clearly that all people are in need of a Great Leader for guidance. And in Korea, that Great Leader could only be one man.

Under Kim Jong Il, Juche thought morphed into Kimilsungism, wherein the Great Leader guides the Party—which by 1973 had come to mean Kim Jong Il himself—and the Party then guides the people. Anyone seen to challenge the post-Kapsan purge ideology of Kimilsungism was a reactionary. This was a charge that nobody wanted to risk. By then, the justice system was well known by all inhabitants of the DPRK: if you are *accused* of a political crime, that means you are guilty. The punishment can range from banishment from Pyongyang, if you are lucky enough to live there in the first place; to "being sent to the mountains," the local patois for imprisonment in the hellish environs of labor and reeducation camps, from which many never emerge; to public execution in front of your fellow citizens. In most cases, punishment would be applied not only to you but to your family extending into three generations. In 1973, the Ministry of State Security was created to oversee this system: the dreaded *bowibu* as it has come to be known in North Korea, a massive surveillance and political police organ that reported directly to Kim Jong Il of the OGD.

Thus, the monolithic ideological system that Kim Il Sung created was solidified under Kim Jong Il, who came to be known as the "Dear Leader." The cultification of Kim Il Sung—in politics, philosophy, art and culture, and everyday life—was deployed as a weapon to further Kim Jong Il's own powers, to the extent that they eventually overcame his father's, even while his father remained the *de facto* ruler until his death in 1994.

THIRTEEN

WALKING THROUGH THE empty halls of the Korean Art Gallery, I discover a richer history of modern art, beyond all the Girl Mothers and Kims. It is rooted in the first decades of the North Korean state. In the corridor behind the main hall where temporary exhibitions take place, a number of small oil paintings dating from the 1940s and 1950s have been installed. Paintings refreshingly unideological: images of a different time, a different place. Among them are the landscapes of Mun Hak Su, a South Korean artist who fled to the North before the war and remained there until his death in 1988. His paintings show the clear influence of Delacroix, though Ms. Kwak denies this when I bring it up. "All Korean," she insists.

Finally, we are taken to the third floor of the museum, normally off-limits to foreign visitors. Here, we find in reverse chronology a whole suite of paintings that further flesh out the DPRK's art history up to the present day. We walk to the back rooms to begin our tour in the 1950s and 1960s, an era of greater artistic freedom compared to today. While there certainly isn't any abstract expressionism on display, there is at least more variety in the individual styles, veering between Soviet socialist realism and French impressionism. *Love,* a painting from 1961 centered on two young girls fishing from a boat, is an idyllic landscape study that could have been copied from Degas or Seurat were it not for the Korean faces. Again, I mention this possible influence to Ms. Kwak, who shakes her head in response. "Nonono—all Korean. Pure." Patently untrue—as art historical scholarship in the South has documented, a number of Korean artists during the colonial period went to study in Japan, where French academicism was en vogue.

All the same, by the early 1960s, the Kim Il Sung cult in the fine arts had already begun to emerge. And in the 1970s and 1980s, coinciding with Kim Jong Il's rise to power, the paintings become increasingly didactic and limited in both style and subject matter. A classic example of the era's kitsch would be Ri Dong Hui's clunky rendering of two peasant women, their facial expressions overcome with dumb joy, as they tend to pigs by a river in a springtime rural landscape with a large mountain in the background.

Everywhere you go, mountains. Ninety percent of the country is mountainous, and these daunting formations are deployed as an easy metaphor for the majesty and natural endurance of the political system. The mountain that can be neither moved nor destroyed.

Though there is also the city. A 1988 oil painting by Sun Gon Chan depicts two young women on bikes, delivering morning copies of the *Rodong Sinmun*. They make their way down the slippery path of Changgwang Street, the twin towers of the Koryo Hotel shining in the background. The colorful reflection on the rain-stained street implies that the sun has broken through, stormy weather is out of the way, as are the two young women, who happily ride toward the bright socialist utopia beneath the virginal sky.

Of all the art forms, Kim Jong Il loved cinema best. He never personally directed any films—at least none bear his name in the credits—but he was by all means the executive producer, the man who ran the state's cinema industry for the entirety of his adult life. From 1965's *The Path of Awakening* onward, Jong Il was on the set of every film shot in the country nearly once a day to give on-the-spot guidance. And while he forbade his citizens from watching foreign media, Kim himself had a personal library of more than fifteen thousand films.

Some in his inner circle would later claim that Jong Il's love of celluloid may have clouded his perception of reality. According to one confidant, he believed that the exploits of James Bond were virtual docudramas, lightly fictionalized accounts of real-world international espionage affairs. Appropriately, beginning in the 1970s, Jong Il engaged in a number of his own 007 hijinks. He sent his agents to Japan, where they kidnapped a number of random citizens and brought them to the DPRK to train spies in Japanese language and customs.

North Korean agents made a number of assassination attempts on the leaders of South Korea. Most notoriously, Jong Il arranged to have his favorite South Korean filmmaker, Shin Sang Ok, and his former wife, the actress Choi Eun Hee, kidnapped and brought to the North, where he forced them to make films in an effort to garner international attention for North Korean cinema.

The plan didn't work. After making seven films in the North for Kim— including a hilariously bad remake of *Godzilla,* 1985's *Pulgasari*—Shin and Choi managed to escape from their minders while visiting a film festival in Vienna and made it safely to the American Embassy.

Pulgasari aside, the films Shin and Choi made in the North brought Kim Jong Il the attention he was seeking from international critics. But whatever contribution they made was not to outlast their stay. DPRK cinema, while of limited interest to diehard researchers of the culture, proves to be an endurance test for everyone else. When ideology is forced to reign over every other impulse, style suffers. Not to mention plot. And character...After all, no Korean can ever be depicted as truly evil. That limits the potential for conflict, which is the place where plot holds its audience's attention captive. And when there is a lack of believable human emotion, tons of sentiment must be employed as filler material. Hence the emotional, melodramatic style of acting that dominates in these films, wherein characters are constantly bursting into tears when they're not unnaturally smiling or laughing at innocent nothings, boastfully asserting their happiness and great fortune to have been born in the Korean People's Paradise. Illustrations of Ideal People, flawless Heroes of the Revolution that are meant to be emulated in real life. Films that are less meant to entertain than to impart "lessons" to the audience. Lessons that can be contained in pithy one-sentence summations to be uttered aloud in study sessions following the film's viewing.

What the development of Juche aesthetics under Kim Jong Il entailed was an intense delimiting of subject matter. A micromanager to the most obsessive degree, Kim Jong Il personally issued the decrees. Everything painted, filmed, sculpted, or written must include a "seed," an ideological nugget of glorification of the Suryong and the state he founded. Eventually, Jong Il himself would come to be included as the second subject of glorification in this illustrious canon—a move that, whether he initiated it himself or not, he apparently never protested. This even extends to academia, where every paper, on no matter what subject, be it mathematics or zoology, must begin with a quote from one of the Kims.

Among the countless books Jong Il is said to have written—one defector claims they were taught that he wrote fifteen hundred books during his three years of study at Kim Il Sung University alone—are a number of treatises on art, literature, cinema, and aesthetics. Translations of these works are available for sale at bookshops in every hotel lobby and at the Foreign Languages Bookshop off Kim Il Sung Square, which stocks exclusively books by and about Kim Il Sung, Kim Jong Il, and Kim Jong Un, with a few other titles by North Korean authors thrown in. North Koreans themselves apparently don't read any of the texts authored by the Kims unless they are forced to—for example, nearly everyone must memorize the annual New Year's Day address for recitation at their Saturday study sessions. But if you ask your tour guide for recommendations on which book by the Great Leader you should read, the typical response you get is "all of them." The reason why becomes clear when you crack open several titles at random and begin to read: the contents are all more or less the same redundancies repeated with minor variation ad nauseam. In actuality, and particularly in primary and secondary school, it is the *biographies* of the leaders that form the propagandistic foundation of North Korean education.

The illegibility of so much of the theory is reflected in artistic practice. Part of the bizarreness of the personality cult, to outsider eyes, is how kitsch it all appears. To my North Korean hosts, it is all just art with a capital *A*: the visual cacophony of the city that constantly surrounds them, wherever they may go. I feel a certain degree of guilt for the further degrees of sublimity and cynicism I am able to read into the visual culture of Pyongyang whenever I am there.

What first appears as perverse spectacle, however, soon becomes accepted as the humdrum quotidian. When I look at this art—the paintings, the films, the performances—and the closed aesthetic system from which it emerges, I can't help but see a distance from the Soviet style of socialist realism that it is so often dismissed as by outsiders. The North has fostered its *own* realism. A realism no less distant from the real than socialist realism was in the Soviet Union, but still distinct from that iconography. It's a realism that extends into daily life in ways that other totalitarian aesthetic systems could only dream of.

Norkorealism might have roots that can be traced back to Stalin's Soviet Union and imperial Japan. But its greatest accomplishment is the creation of its own version of time. And it's an ongoing process. The Juche calendar to replace the Gregorian; the setting of the clocks back thirty minutes; the lack of *urgency* in everyday life; that painting style that never quite evolves; the homilification of the banal, inscribed across every available surface. On my first visit to the country in 2012, I felt that the DPRK remains perpetually stuck somewhere in the middle of the twentieth century. Now I realize that the system's production of time is welded to an oblivious stance toward all those aspects of the modern world that do not concern it.

FOURTEEN

WHEN WE FINISH our tour of the museum, much of our own time is eaten up with Alexandre's quest to buy an Arirang smart phone. He has been wanting one of these geek DPRK souvenirs for a long time but didn't manage to buy one on his last stay here. Foreigners residing in the country can also buy service on the local Koryolink network—albeit on a separate network that only allows you to call other foreigners in the country; you are blocked from dialing any Korean numbers. Unlike Koreans, you can even buy an expensive data package that allows you to connect to the internet; their smartphones likewise are barred from dialing foreign numbers and connect only to the country's internal Intranet.

We spend what's left of the afternoon at the international communications center by the Potong River trying to get this all arranged. As in most socialist countries I've lived or traveled in, such procedures require endless hours of bureaucratic hassle. In a moment of impatience, I confront Alexandre. What's the point of buying service? We're going to be here for a month, the only people we can call are each other, and we're going to be together the entire time. It's absurd!

"I'm very sorry, Travis. But for me, it's necessary." He winks at me. Later, when we're out of earshot of our guides, Alexandre will explain that he wants to call a contact of his working in the recently established French consular service. This, Alexandre reasons, will help us cement our big plan for Saturday night: to visit the diplomatic compound, which has its very own nightclub.

★

For dinner, we visit a newly opened restaurant below the Kwangbok Shopping Center. We dine on my favorite local dish, *Pyongyang naengmyon*: thin, brown chewy buckwheat noodles in an ice-cold radishy broth piled high with sliced meat, fiery kimchi, cucumber, and spices. For more flavor, stir in a spoonful of mustard and a few squirts of vinegar. Sip the broth to see if you've got it right, and then grab your metal chopsticks and dig in.

"What the hell were you doing in class today? Learning to make animal noises?" Alexandre snorts over his noodles. "Sorry, Travis. But the door was open, and it was, um, rather loud."

"It was indeed carnal," Alek adds.

"I know, I know! I have to learn vowels. What can you do?"

Well, you *could* close the door—but that's not something likely to happen. Particularly when there's only one student and that student happens to be an American bastard.

"How would you rate your teacher? Is he doing a good job?" Alek asks Alexandre, performing quality control.

"Yes, he's good…but he can't speak English. Or French, of course. So he can't explain new words."

"You've gotta get the Korean-English app. It comes on the phone."

"I was checking. It's not on there."

"What about you, Travis? How's Ms. Pak?"

I pull out my phone to show him the video I made of Ms. Pak performing the vowels. I press play and start repeating Ms. Pak's intonations, replicating the "animal noises." Alek and Alexandre laugh. This gets Min's attention—she wants in on the joke, so she gets up from her place at the table to join us. Like most young Pyongyangites, she's obsessed with snapping photos and making videos on her phone to share with her friends. In the split second before she arrives over my shoulder, Alexandre shoots me a look from the corner of his eye. I immediately realize I'm fucked. I attempt to zoom in on Ms. Pak's face, but it's too late. For there, in the upper-left-hand corner of the video, is my mistake: a cut-off quarter of the Kim Jong Il portrait above the whiteboard.

Min sees through my lame volte-face immediately. "Could you scroll back, please? To the full image?"

I have no choice but to follow her directive.

"Can you delete this video?" she asks. Her voice has this curiously flat, affectless, unemotional monotone that I've never heard before. It unnerves me.

"I'm really sorry," I say, sputtering. "I didn't mean to do it. It...it's just for studying. I didn't even realize it had happened until now. I promise not to share it with anyone."

"Please delete it tonight after you've finished studying." She sits back down at her place at the table and resumes eating.

★

I hadn't noticed the gaffe before. But neither had Ms. Pak. She had even asked to see the video after I filmed it, but that was more out of vanity to see how she looked. I wonder if North Koreans themselves are forced to be so vigilant about accidentally capturing fragments of the Kims' likenesses. Since they appear virtually everywhere, it must happen all the time.

When we're alone back at the Sosan after dinner, Alexandre whispers in the elevator that I should just back up the video on my laptop and delete it from my phone. I know, I tell him. Of course I had already thought of that.

"I'm such a fucking idiot." I sigh, grabbing my forehead.

"Don't say that," Alexandre whispers sternly. "You didn't do anything wrong. *She's* the one who's wrong. You were just doing your work. Things like this are going to happen all the time. We can't let them get to us, or else we'll start to believe in it ourselves. We have to remind ourselves constantly so we don't lose our minds: It's *them* who are fucked up. Not us."

PART FOUR

US AND THEM

FIFTEEN

THREE DAYS INTO it, those clusters of letters have been put together to form actual words I can now pronounce. Class is ending, so Ms. Pak suggests we make another video for tonight's review session. As I take out my phone, the lady with the perm walks in to the classroom, surveys the scene, and whispers something to Ms. Pak.

"Mister Travis," Ms. Pak says in her halting English. "Video...look." I show them the video I just made. This time I made sure to shoot from a wider angle so that the portraits of father and son wouldn't be cut off. There they are in full, their toothy smiles beaming over Ms. Pak's head as she dutifully repeats each Korean word written on the board.

The two women study the video closely and exchange whispered commentary. Ms. Pak then walks to the front of the classroom and gestures below the portraits.

"No Mister Kim Il Sung Mister Kim Jong Il," she says.

I get it. I show the administrator that I'm deleting the file. Smile. Happy?

Obviously Min tattled. I hope it won her lots of points.

It is the last time Ms. Pak or her boss will mention it. I go on to make lots of videos and take photos each day. In a small gesture of rebellion, I deliberately make sure I get the portraits in each frame. After all, as long as they appear in their smiling entirety, there's no rule against it.

✪

After class, we make another coffee run. This time we try the coffee shop at the Pyongyang Hotel. Alek says it's considered the best—and most expensive—in town.

"Alek! I forgot to tell you the news," Min says on the ride over. "I got a promotion in June. Now I'm Senior Tour Guide. Just one step below Comrade Kim!"

We congratulate her. I ask her what exactly the promotion entails, besides the rise in rank. It's one of those questions she doesn't like to answer.

"You get to...do more stuff. People, uh, *respect* you more..." She trails off.

"Ahh, so you get to boss people around now!" Alexandre prods.

She laughs. "Yes! It's true!" She slaps her fist in her palm, mock menacingly.

Roe stares out the window glumly.

✪

In the West, they're called millennials; in North Korea, they're known as the *Jangmadang* ("Market Grounds") generation. They came of age during the Arduous March—those years in the mid-to-late 1990s following Kim Il Sung's death, when economic collapse, spurred by the demise of the Soviet Union, combined with environmental disaster to cause the largest famine in the country's history. The public food distribution system that North Koreans had by and large been dependent on until then broke down. Informal markets sprang up everywhere throughout the country. Markets that all citizens now rely upon, to greater and lesser degrees. Nowadays, you can acquire just about anything you want in North Korea, provided you have the hard currency to pay for it. Far from being cut off from the rest of the world, the markets have put North Koreans directly in the middle of it. Daily provisions, pharmaceuticals, luxury items are bought and exchanged. But not only. Just as everywhere else in the twenty-first century, information is the most valuable commodity. At the markets, whispered gossip and hearsay flow relatively freely—tidbits much juicier than anything printed in the *Rodong Sinmun* or dramatically intoned on the nightly news. In providing North Koreans with a degree of autonomy, the markets have driven a wedge between the people and the government. Especially the twenty-somethings of the Jangmadang generation—people of Min's age—who have never known a moment in time when the government provided anything for them. Who still hold childhood memories of the dead and dying in the streets.

Shopping is Min's favorite activity. Besides eating. She takes a subversive delight in all forms of consumption. She also takes an intense interest in all our consumption habits and goes to great lengths to accommodate all of them. It is rare that we go into a shop where she herself doesn't wind up buying something.

What her "promotion" means—what all such promotions these days mean—is an increase in independence granted to pursue business ventures outside of tourism. With all the bad news circulating since Warmbier's detention, the numbers have taken a dive. But thanks to the new rules that have been adapted as a result of the ground-up swelling of the market economy since the 1990s, it is not something that Comrade Kim and his managerial colleagues need fret about. There are other ways of earning money as a state enterprise. You can do virtually anything. For Min, it is medicine and luxury French cosmetics. Tough, because of the sanctions, but not undoable. Especially when you have access to foreign visitors or else can make trips outside the country yourself. Just one day before we arrived, Min had returned from a trip to Uganda, where she had been a guest at the DPRK Embassy in Kampala.

The coffee shop at the Pyongyang Hotel has a separate entrance outside next to the lobby. It is actually a built-on rooftop addition to the hotel. You take the elevator up to the second floor—or the stairs, when the electricity's out—and enter into a rather sumptuous space that wouldn't look out of place in a middle-class neighborhood in any Western city. Here, the furnishings represent the height of glamour: wood paneling, Japanese-style silk-embossed folding screens that can be moved to surround a table when a couple desires more privacy, and a spiral staircase leading to a glassed-in rooftop terrace boasting views of the Pyongyang Grand Theatre across the street, with its excellent mural of Kim Il Sung's mother in *joseon-ot* wielding a pistol. The Moranbong Band's summer hit "Dash Towards the Future" lulls through the background speakers, a danceable pop anthem extolling this great era of the Workers' Party. Behind the counter, a beautiful young barista operates the gleaming gilded silver espresso machine. She was sent to China last summer where she learned the craft and takes a quiet pleasure in demonstrating her expertise. After I put in my order for an americano, she points to the selection of beans on display from across Africa and Latin America and asks me which I prefer. Alek, who has a sweet tooth, is surprised to find his favorite South Korean dessert concoction on the menu: a pile of shaved ice topped with cream and strawberries and gooey syrup.

Alexandre, whose teetotaldom apparently extends to caffeine, watches as the preparations are made, clearly more interested in the barista than the goods on offer.

"Get a dessert!" urges Alek. "This is good shit, man!"

Alexandre looks skeptical. "I thought I told you, Alek. Ice: not a good idea."

Alek contemplates this as he watches the machine spew out tiny frosty bits. "I'm sure they make it with filtered water." A tremor of hope in his voice.

While we await our order—with the single employee behind the counter, it's not exactly Starbucks-paced service—I break away from the group to sneak downstairs to the hotel lobby. The Pyongyang Hotel is one of the older accommodation facilities in the capital, and it shows. The lobby looks like it hasn't been upgraded since the 1970s.

Anyway, I'm not here to inquire about a room. It is, rather, the first time in my life I've gone looking for a lawyer.

Michael Hay, a practicing lawman from England, is said to reside here in the Pyongyang Hotel. One of those shadowy figures of expat lore I've been longing to meet. His firm largely represents foreign companies looking to do business in the DPRK, offering advice and protection in the event anything goes askew. Legend has it that he even sued the DPRK government in local courts once over a copyright infringement case on behalf of a client—and won. The other legend has it that he likes to drink, so I'm going to offer to buy him a couple to see what stories might flow forth.

"Is Mister Michael in?" The front desk receptionist appears startled to see a foreigner standing before him unaccompanied. He picks up the phone and dials. No answer.

"Thanks anyway."

I decide to go up and check for myself. Min is also interested in meeting the guy, since she's now doing business herself—he could be a strategic partner for her. And he must have contacts...but I want to meet with him first, to gauge the likelihood of setting up a meeting. And I want to hear the stories he likely wouldn't tell in front of her.

I make my way up the stairwell, shrouded by leotard-clad teenagers stretching their legs on its banister in preparation for the evening's dance performance. "Zainichi Koreans," as they're called, are Korean residents of Japan affiliated with Chongryon, a pro-DPRK organization. Many of them send their sons and daughters here in the summer for a few weeks to explore their cultural roots in the fatherland. For some reason, they always stay at the Pyongyang Hotel— perhaps to keep them isolated, since so few other guests ever stay here.

On the second floor, I find a door marked *Hay, Kalb, and Associates,* surrounded by regular hotel rooms. I knock three times. I guess that the room inside is a simple suite, fitted with an official-looking desk, a bedroom off to the side. But I'm not destined to find out; nobody's answering. Mister Michael is on vacation.

Later, I will come to find out that just the week prior, he had left the country for good.

Back in the coffee shop, a well-heeled couple has taken two of the empty seats. They speak discreetly over steaming cups, the man vaping from an electronic cigarette. Min stands immersed before an illustrated display on the wall that explains, in English, where the coffee we're about to drink comes from, how it is harvested, its history, its health benefits. "The coffee is expensive here," she remarks. "How much is a cup of coffee in Germany?"

I tell her it averages now between 1.80 and 2.20 in euros. In Italy, you can get an espresso for only eighty cents, I add. She considers this information and then turns toward me, a new idea lighting up her face. "I think I will open a coffee shop," she says. "A coffee shop that is affordable, that ordinary people can go to. Because at these prices, only rich people can afford to drink coffee."

It is an original idea, and one that she is determined to not let go of. She takes a pad and pen out of her bag and begins feverishly making notes. By the time we finally get our order and make our way to a table in the adjoining restaurant, Min has her phone to her ear and is heading down the hallway for some privacy.

"The dictionary app," says Alexandre. "I need to get it, Alek. Seriously. I couldn't understand any of the teacher's explanations in the lesson today."

"Now it is very difficult," Roe comments, settling in next to us, and then laughs at the inevitability. The black humor of totalitarianism.

"I don't get it. I bought the phone. Why can't I just get the language software?"

"It came on mine when I got the Koryolink phone. But that was a couple years ago," says Alek.

"The situation has changed now," Roe notes. Meaning: the rules have changed. He shrugs. He is used to it: the arbitrariness of the system. Not worth moaning about; not even worth mentioning. What is, is. He stands up and stretches and then saunters over to Min, who is whispering into her phone in a hidden corner by the bar.

"They don't want foreigners to have any of the local apps now," Alek says. "I guess that includes the dictionary."

Alexandre shrugs. "Then what's the point of even owning this phone?"

"Just to call other foreigners, I guess."

"You know what it is?" Alexandre whispers, now furious. "They don't really want us to learn the language. Why else would they forbid foreigners from using a dictionary? The less we know, the better."

Min suddenly appears before our table. "Everyone finished with your coffee? Let's go!"

"Where are we off to now?"

She leans in for a whisper. "We're going to try and get you the app."

✪

We—they, to be precise—try everything. We go to the Jongbo Electronics Center behind the Ryungyong Hotel, where Min and Roe attempt to bribe the employees into installing the software on Alexandre's phone while we wait outside. To no avail. Then they take us to some upscale shopping district for elites stashed away behind a row of high-rise apartment buildings. Shops hawking high-end electronics, designer-brand clothing smuggled in from China, hidden behind a hotel that only North Koreans can stay at—an area I repeatedly try and fail to locate on my tourist map later that night. That doesn't work, either. At least we're getting to see areas I haven't visited before. The Pandora's box of Pyongyang.

By now, it is dark, around dinnertime. We drive through the streets of the nocturnal city, clueless as to where we're headed—the Koreans won't tell us.

Hwa cruises along a quiet, narrow stretch of the river Potong. No one's out on any dates on this balmy night—too hot for summer love. We pull down a narrow alleyway. Hwa cuts off the headlights. In the front seat, Min and Roe look around nervously. There's a bar at the end of the alleyway that seems to be jumping with people, but nobody's milling around outside, and the soldiers manning the security booth in front of the apartment house at the end of the alleyway have nodded off. The lone streetlamp flickers out, leaving us in the pitch black.

Detectives on a stakeout. Min picks up her phone, utters a few words into the receiver. A man emerges out of the darkness. Min hops out of the car to meet him. He hands her a bag. Min climbs back into the car; the guy remains outside, pacing back and forth in the darkness. Roe looks around nervously as Min takes the object out of the bag: it is a tablet, the locally made Samjiyon brand. She switches it on, scrolls across the screen. "Shit," she says in English. The app's not on there.

Min hops out, hands the bag back to the guy. We drive off.

"That was my brother," she says, once we're a safe distance down the road.

"You collect things here," says Alexandre, ranting. " 'Look at this: I have this fucking medal, saying what a good worker I am. How much value I have. And you know what? If I work hard, say the right things in front of the right people, next month they're gonna give me an even bigger fucking medal.' "

It's after midnight now, and we're smoking cigarettes on my balcony, staring out at the dark city below. It's like a moldy blanket, all those streets in west Pyongyang, and hardly any lights, as most of them are turned off after a certain hour. Every once in a while a car goes by and you have to wonder who's in it, who would be out driving around this time of night, where they might be going. You have to have a special license that permits you to drive after dark.

"Min is a good example," Alexandre continues. "When you asked her the other day whether she was a member of the Workers' Party. 'No...but I'm a member of the Socialist Youth League!' Pointing to the gold plating on her Kim Il Sung badge. That's how it works here. The gilding on the badges. The little signs designating reward, status, honor. You *get* stuff. It gives you a sense, not just of belonging, but of acceptance. 'Yeah, I'm part of this thing, I'm ingrained in it, I play my role, they reward me. And next time, I'll get something bigger, better. A watch. A car.' That's what you see. These colonels with their reward Rolexes. The medals, the badges, the insignia weighing down their uniforms. This is who I am: a thing you can hold in the palm of your hand. That can be displayed. And eventually, you reach the level where you get to give these little rewards out yourself. To pull rank. Then you're *really* somebody. Somebody with a capital *S*. Somebody people then *owe* something to. You get to lord it over them.

"This is what keeps the system going. And it's all fake. Fake honor. Because this stuff, these little *trinkets,* they all mean nothing. Take one wrong step, and you lose them all. But that's their dual purpose: presence with the threat of absence. They're there, in your hand, pinned to your collar, your uniform, to remind you that everything you've been given can be taken away, and quite easily—your life along with them."

⭐

Wherever I am in the world, on summer nights, I like to leave my windows open, listen to the sounds of the street as I drift off at night. It puts me in a sexy mood—the amalgamation of languages spoken, the sizzling street food, passing vehicles—all those illicit and mysterious nighttime exchanges. To remain a part of it, the city's soundscape, even as I drift off into the ether. The hutongs of Beijing, where people barbecue until 3 a.m., oblivious to sleep's demands. Old Havana with its wisps of music drifting up from the Malecón…

But in Pyongyang, all is silent come nightfall. And at the Sosan Hotel, they've got us towered up on the twenty-eighth floor, at a suicidal distance from the street. Then there's the nothingness we're surrounded by. Trees, mostly. A perpetually disused golf course. All the empty fields and stadiums making up the sports district. There are no residential complexes here whatsoever. Even where there is, there are no congregations of insomniac nighttime wanderers. Law forbids it, and even if it didn't, nearly everyone collapses in collective exhaustion anyway as a consequence of the eight hours of work and eight hours of study that Kim Il Sung once delineated as the ideal socialist day. They leave behind them a silence that is eerie, chilling in the depths of its pervasiveness.

SIXTEEN

MIN'S CORPULENCE IS something. It is on display, albeit modestly, in an expensive purple polka-dot designer bathing suit, the kind with a sort of frilly belt around the waist. Modesty is insisted upon—especially for women. With her $500 Gucci sunglasses crowning the picture, Min, pale and perfumed, looks like she's stepped out of a high-end resort into this scene of Third World revelry.

We're on the beach in the port city of Nampo, about an hour's bumpy drive from Pyongyang on the peninsula's west coast. It's Sunday and the beach is packed with locals making the most of the day off, getting shitfaced, diving into the sea, singing karaoke, dancing in the sand.

The beachgoers eye the foreign invaders with a mixture of curiosity and astonishment. A local security apparatchik approaches Roe, asks him who he is, who he's with, who these foreigners are. He's never seen Roe around these parts; who is he to bring a foreign delegation here before first securing local permission? Roe gives him a one-sentence answer. The guy and his cronies immediately back off. Min wanders over to ask Roe about the exchange. Roe relays it, and they both crack up. A laugh that says: *These country bumpkins.*

Min wanders among the scrawny sunburnt peasants, casually owning the scene. To be able to afford Min's swimwear ensemble, most of these people would have to sacrifice a decade or more of their earnings. Some of the women don't even have bathing suits, wading into the water with their pants rolled high. Modesty also applies to the male sex; no Speedos here, just swim shorts and boxers for those who can't afford them.

The "Arduous March" that these Jangmadangers and their elders managed to survive is a euphemistic phrase, one of many that the regime has recycled. The first "Arduous March" had nothing to do with famine but rather referred to the freezing winter of 1938–1939 when Kim Il Sung's guerilla resistance movement was very nearly defeated by the Japanese. The second "Arduous March" (1994–1998) that remains the formative experience for most Jangmadangers resulted in the death by starvation of between 240,000 and 3.5 million people, according to a number of unverifiable estimates. (The actual statistics have never been released by the government.) Of those who survived, many remain stunted—whether vertically, intellectually, or both. Many are still afflicted with diseases and health conditions stemming from chronic childhood malnutrition.

Food shortages have been a recurring problem throughout the DPRK's existence. Ever since Kim Il Sung decided to follow his leader Stalin in focusing his economy on the development of heavy industry—a directive that was zealously carried out—the country has experienced a continual degradation of infrastructure and agriculture. The labor-intensive regimen forced upon a populace fed on a protein-diluted diet leaves them chronically exhausted. On the way to Nampo this afternoon, we drove past the West Sea Barrage. This is perhaps the most lavish example of one of Kim Il Sung's vanity projects, a gargantuan dam upon which precious resources were squandered, resulting in the catastrophic environmental devastation that was no small contributing cause of the resulting famine in the 1990s.

Heavy industry versus light industry. Fatness versus emaciation. "It is important to us," a North Korean defector in Seoul once explained to me, "that our leader is fat." A signifier of wealth, of hope. Even though the people might be half-starved, the image of fatness broadcast by the Leader shows the promise of wealth and extravagance. *We will all look like that someday, once socialism has fully triumphed*, it seems to say. And anyway: *We might have it bad, but then other countries must have it much worse.*

Nobody is starving anymore. It is unknowable how many still believe in the propaganda. Probably not many. Even outside of Pyongyang, people have learned that you have to play the capitalism game in order to survive. Here on the beach, people are skinny, but there is food going around. Beer to drink. Most of it might come from China, but the Marshal has made the development of light industry—consumer goods for the masses—a priority, going against the precedent set by his grandfather and followed more or less by his father. Of course, he has little choice in either tolerating these nascent forms of capitalism or investing in consumer goods, housing, infrastructure, and, of late, the environment. It's the very least he can do, since the government he inherited proved not so long ago that it cannot be trusted.

On the shore, a group of teenagers dances furiously, violently, to instrumental techno remixes of the latest Moranbong Band favorites. I study the intense, ice-cold expressions on their faces, the relentlessness of their movement as they flail their limbs about. Roe stares at them and then bursts out laughing. *"Bingdu,"* Alexandre whispers in my ear. A locally produced medical remedy, initially pro-duced by the government for export but now popular among adolescents and adults alike for its curative properties, its ability to diminish hunger and improve concentration and productivity; in the West, it is known as crystal meth.

A group of middle-aged men beckons me over, invites me to drink with them. I accept a swig from the bottle of soju I am offered. A little girl, one of their daughters, is dancing to a Norko synth pop melody blasting from a boom box. As the song arrives at its final kaboom, she lands in a split. The men erupt in cheers and applause and then pull me onto the makeshift dance floor beneath the canopy they've erected. I do my best. The men laugh and cheer me on.

"Which country?" one of them hollers over the music.

His comrades turn toward me in anticipation.

"Germany," I impulsively lie.

They look relieved.

"Germany: good!" one of them concludes. The others shout their agreement.

Our guides let us wander. Min refuses to step foot in the water; Roe occasionally joins us. Alexandre and I swim over to another beach, a short distance down the shore. The locals paddling and floating in the water greet our white faces ecstat-ically, a once-in-a-lifetime chance to interact with foreigners. They ask where we are from. This time, I tell the truth. They smile and greet me warmly. Nobody wants to talk politics today. A crowd gathers as the two of us float up to shore. One young man asks me what it is I do for a living. A writer, I tell him, and a student at Kim Hyong Jik University of Education. I ask him in return what he does. "I am an ordinary worker," he says. A professional photographer makes her way through the crowd, vending her trade. Alexandre waves her over, requests a photograph with our new friends. The photographer looks nervous but finally agrees to take the photo.

We decide to walk back, past makeshift encampments of barbecue and beery karaoke. Alek is deeply engaged in conversation with Min, though his eyes are on a distant beauty dancing with the teenagers across from us. He misses his girl-friend. He's texted her every day on his new phone, but she hasn't replied. Either she's not getting the texts, or else she's pointedly ignoring him. He's beginning to worry he's been forgotten.

The day winds its way toward its sunless halt, and we decide to head back to Pyongyang before darkness attains its apotheosis. Climbing into the van, Alexandre suddenly remembers the photo. "Min, can you find the photographer lady? Or the office where they print the photos? I want to buy one. And here, get one for Travis, too." He hands her two dollars. Roe goes off with her.

We are left to watch the party die down in the parking lot. People stand around, perplexed as to what to do, where to go next. A little boy dances to a bouncy instrumental played from a mobile phone, surrounded by a circle of women who clap and cheer him on. A man in his mid-twenties castigates his girlfriend drunkenly for refusing to get on his motorbike. He hurls insults at her as she stands in a half circle surrounded by her female friends. All of them hang their heads low in submissive shame as the man slurs and wavers.

"Look at that," says Alexandre. "That's the problem with men in this country. Treating women like that. No respect!"

"Come on, guys," says Alek. "We're making it worse for them by standing here watching."

We climb into the van to make our presence scarce. Eventually, the drunk climbs onto his motorbike and rides off into the dying light without her.

Min and Roe return.

"The photo?" asks Alexandre expectantly.

Min mutters something in Korean to Alek.

"The photographer was instructed to delete your photo," Alek translates.

SEVENTEEN

IT'S NOT THAT Kim Jong Il was oblivious to the plight of his people, happy to see them starve. When the Soviet Union, the DPRK's chief financial benefactor, dissolved in 1991, it was clear to both Jong Il and his father that tough times were ahead. From the beginnings of the financial crisis that struck the country in the 1990s and that it has never really recovered from, one of the foreign policy missions undertaken by the regime has been to eventually normalize relations with its number one enemy, the world's greatest military and economic superpower, the United States of America. By closing this long, drawn-out, acrimonious chapter with the US, the North could conclude a peace treaty that would guarantee its sovereignty while also attaining the aid necessary to revitalize its moribund economy and recommence feeding its people.

In reporting on North Korea's development of nuclear weapons and its supposedly irrational hatred of the US, there is one fact that is constantly and universally omitted by the media: that the United States has been threatening the DPRK with nuclear annihilation for decades. Were this fact asserted by any of the hundreds of reporters regularly covering the issue, the North's recent development of nuclear weapons might not seem so irrationally aggressive after all. It is likely, however, that most of these reporters are themselves unaware of the fact. The brain-cleansing properties of propaganda operate, after all, in both directions.

After the Korean War, the US had nuclear warheads installed on the Korean peninsula—in spite of the Armistice Agreement it had signed in 1953 that prohibited the introduction of such weapons. "By the mid-1960s," writes Bruce Cumings, probably the sole American historian who has tried to understand and articulate the DPRK's point of view, "[South] Korean defense strategy [engineered by the US] was pinned on routine plans to use nuclear weapons very early in any new war." Routinely, the US would fly nuclear weapons near the DMZ in training exercises; the threat that one of these helicopters might "accidentally" stray over the DMZ and drop a bomb on Pyongyang was a constant fear. The nuclear weapons were only removed in 1991, after the Gulf War, when then-President George H. W. Bush decided to withdraw all tactical and battlefield nuclear weapons worldwide; this was understood as a conciliatory gesture by the North, since it was obvious that submarines bearing nukes could still arrive on its shores at any moment. What's more, the continual war game exercises conducted each year by US and South Korean troops on the border in plain view of North Korea have, in Cumings's words, "routinely included the introduction to Korea of nuclear-capable aircraft and naval ships of all types, back-pack nukes controlled by mobile units, practice with nuclear cannons, and so on, with many South Korean units working together with the Americans on various nuclear war scenarios." In February 1993, the head of the US Strategic Command announced that the Pentagon would be retargeting strategic nuclear weapons on North Korea. North Korea responded by announcing that it would be pulling out of the Nuclear Nonproliferation Treaty, which states, among other things, that nations with nuclear weapons are not allowed to threaten those without them. It shot a medium-range Rodong-1 missile into the East Sea, the Sea of Japan, in May 1993, spurring a flurry of press reports that the crazed North Koreans were preparing to unleash atomic anarchy.

To quell such concerns, the North Koreans proposed in June–July 1993 to replace their graphite reactor nuclear program—which Pyongyang had long claimed it had to use because no one was willing to help the country's poor power supply with nuclear energy—with US-supplied light water reactors, which would simultaneously make Pyongyang dependent on outside fuel sources. Nothing came of this proposal.

What, it is worth asking, did the DPRK want in return? Two essential things: for the US to cease its threats and to work toward normalizing relations that would solidify a peaceful coexistence, eventually culminating in exchanges on the ambassadorial level.

After a series of back-and-forth talks, shutdowns, provocations, and resumption of negotiations, the US and DPRK finally arrived at a breakthrough that culminated in the 1994 October Framework Agreement. In return for the DPRK freezing its graphite reactors and returning to inspections under the Nuclear Nonproliferation Treaty, the US and a consortium of other nations would supply the DPRK with light water reactors as a means of solving its constant energy problems; financial assistance, including phasing out sanctions against the North that had been in place since the Korean War; and a step-by-step development of diplomatic relations.

Not long after this agreement was signed, control of the US Congress shifted to the Republicans, who were categorically against it. Much foot-dragging and derailment of the US's commitments ensued; with the famine in full swing, many in the US Congress privately grumbled that since the DPRK was bound to collapse at any moment, there was no point for the US to fulfill its obligations. By May 1998, the first light water reactor had still not been constructed. Growing increasingly impatient, the North Koreans threatened that they would resume nuclear research if the US did not fulfill its commitment. The following year, noting that economic sanctions still had not been lifted, the North once again made the same threat.

Credibility is naturally lost when you appear to be lying or deceiving someone about your stated intentions. By the time George W. Bush became president, this loss of credibility was aggravated by a not-so-subtle strain of outright hostility, culminating in his second State of the Union address, given just months after the 9/11 attacks, in which he included North Korea in what he termed the "axis of evil." The hardliners filling the Bush administration purposefully upturned anything the Clinton administration had sought to achieve in its foreign policy, pursuing a course of extreme isolationism that would mar the United States' reputation internationally for the next eight years. North Korean diplomats complained that their new US counterparts, such as Assistant Secretary of State James A. Kelly, were arrogant and evasive in their meetings. Relations between the two countries devolved into open hostility. The US accused the North of harboring a uranium enrichment program; the North denied this and asked the US to provide proof, such as satellite imagery; the US failed to do so, and in all likelihood, this assertion was rooted in the same faulty intelligence that claimed Iraq possessed weapons of mass destruction. The DPRK then went further, proclaiming that, although it did not currently have any nukes, as a sovereign nation, it had the right to possess nuclear weapons as a means of defense—just as the United States had for years.

If a small child is bullied constantly by a teenager three times his size, it is somewhat counterintuitive to react with shock and surprise when that child one day shows up at school wielding a switchblade. In 2003, the DPRK officially withdrew from the Nuclear Nonproliferation Treaty. Two years later, the country announced that it had developed its first nuclear weapons. This is a blade that the North has been openly carrying ever since.

Americans have a troubled relationship with their own history. The truth often comes to us distorted via increasingly nebulous and questionable means of mediation. What we do learn we tend to forget. That is, we tend to *prefer* to forget. Citizens of smaller, less powerful, impoverished nations are less likely to forget the lessons of history; often those lessons are all they have. North Koreans, for certain, have not forgotten theirs. Putting aside the question of *how* these lessons are forced upon them and their own distorted means of transmission, the point is that this *not-forgetting* forms the very essence of North Korean identity.

There is the history of the Korean War, of course, which, through the propaganda machinery, is drummed into the brains of DPRK citizens on a daily, hourly basis. Today, there are, in fact, people still alive who can remember that war, who tell their children and grandchildren about what they experienced. The aerial bombardments that killed millions of civilians. The biological weapons that the United States deployed to sicken, disfigure, maim, and murder North Korean soldiers and innocent civilians. All the daily scenes of horror and carnage that no US civilian has ever had to face directly.

Then there is what we might call a "history of the present," which reminds us that, since 2005, the DPRK has been very open about its nuclear ambitions. That those ambitions are the direct result of another nuclear power, the United States, which has had nuclear weapons in its arsenal for decades and is, in fact, the only country in the world to have used a nuclear weapon in warfare against another nation: a country not so far away from the Korean peninsula. That those ambitions and their resultant implementation are, finally, the result of a foreign policy failure of the United States: the country that *created* North Korea when it drew that line across the thirty-eighth parallel in 1945 and has sought to destroy it ever since.

*

The options that the young, inexperienced Kim Jong Un inherited when he came to power upon the death of his father in late 2011 ranged from bad to worse. Jong Un: age-wise, firmly entrenched in the Jangmadang generation, but in terms of life experience, from a different world entirely. When the troubles began in 1994—both domestically, with the food shortage that would result in famine, and internationally, with the increasingly volatile relations with the United States—Kim Jong Il announced a new policy: *Songun*, or "military-first," which elevated the North's own hard-liners—the army—into the upper echelons of power. These are the men who are most satisfied with the status quo, who do not want things to change, and who have the arms and men at their disposal to make sure nothing will ever change.

With Kim Jong Un's rise, some voices in the Western media cautiously expressed optimism that, given his youth and his early education in Switzerland, the young leader might make moves to "open up" his country, to cleanse its legacy of human rights abuses, to lighten its clampdown on dissent and close its notorious network of prison camps. The naïveté behind such speculations is astounding. There is at least one good reason why the new leader did not undertake such radical measures: the military men surrounding him, his father's men, would never allow any such thing to take place. Had he even voiced such proposals out loud, he would have been deposed of, killed, immediately.

Kim Jong Un may be a tyrant. But he is simultaneously, like all North Koreans, a victim of the system he was born into, a system that he is mostly powerless to change. Unlike his father, he was far too young to have consciously maneuvered his way into power; rather, he was selected, chosen to be his father's successor, and whether he wanted it or not, in such a society that combines filial piety with state terror, one is not allowed much choice in these, or any other, matters. We will probably not know for many years what has been going on behind closed doors in the capital since 2012. What led Jong Un to have his uncle and senior adviser Jang Song Thaek executed in 2013—or even if Jong Un was actually behind the purge. To what extent Jong Un is an autonomous actor, the evil dictator of yore, and to what extent he is the puppet of other, perhaps competing, forces.

What we do know—because it is obvious to anyone who has visited the country and seen it with their own eyes in these years—is that in spite of the sanctions and the country's international pariah status, the effects of economic liberalization have been on display since Kim Jong Un came to power. From the beginning, when he gave his very first speech and asserted that "our people will never have to tighten their belts again," development has been at the core of the new regime's domestic policy.

Today, Pyongyang is living testament to this fact. With ambitious building projects, postmodern and neo-futuristic apartment blocks being erected on entirely new streets in the capital, the city is looking less like a bizarre colorless joke and more and more like a proper East Asian twenty-first-century capital.

Then there are the *donju,* those soldiers in the commercial front: the true pragmatists of contemporary DPRK. Unafraid to flaunt their wealth, they are the living emblems that show us the extent to which capitalism is well and truly alive in this ostensibly socialist land. These new dreamers of North Korea don't have revolution on their minds. Their dreams are wrapped up in business, deals, the attainment and sustenance of personal wealth.

Their existence reveals the inevitable flaw that Kim Il Sung and his cohorts failed to discern when they were designing what to them seemed like their own unique form of socialism: the failure to do away with a class system. While making the surface gesture of doing away with the *economic* class system redolent of capitalism, they instead instituted a *political* class system: that of Songbun. A class system that is just as rife with inequalities as the economic class system of capitalism.

The new dreamers—Jangmadangers like Min, like Comrade Kim—are privileged to have been born into a level of political capital that affords them the ability to attain the economic capital they actually desire. And increasingly, those not born into the necessary classes of political privilege but who are savvy enough can *buy* their way into it—via membership in the Workers' Party and other tokens of prestige and power. The Songbun system is thus diminishing in the evolution of a meritocracy that is but a slightly distorted mirror image of the elitist system at the heart of global neoliberalism.

These dreamers are the ones who will mold this country into something that looks very different from what it has been. They have already started. They are the ones behind the lucrative building projects that are transforming the architecture, layout, and overall image of Pyongyang. Other cities have begun to follow suit.

That the current leader is a peer, age-wise, makes it easier for them to identify with him, revealing a deep generational divide in the landscape. Perhaps they sense the gravity of the *problem* he has inherited. That there are no easy solutions. The recent spate of purges has largely targeted individuals from the older generation—his father's men. Just as Kim Jong Il immediately got rid of *his* father's men.

Beneath the ecstatic declarations of love for the leader espoused by North Koreans publicly, there is, as defectors tell us and as some of us have intuited in our firsthand encounters, a great diversity of opinion unvoiced, unvoiceable. It seems unlikely that Kim Jong Un and the power structure to which he is attached will go away anytime soon. And among the young elites of Pyongyang, there is a sense that they do not want him to. He enables them—and vice versa.

EIGHTEEN

THERE ARE, OF course, more recent events than the Arduous March that have been seared into the Jangmadang generation's collective patchwork of memory. In 2009, the government issued a disastrous currency reform. Citizens had less than a week to exchange their old won notes for the new won. Simultaneously, a draconian limit was placed on the amount of won that could be exchanged by each individual. As a result, many lost the bulk of their savings—particularly those whose wealth had been made trading on the illegal black markets from the Arduous March up till then. So widespread was the discontent, with near-riots erupting in several cities, that Kim Jong Il had to find a fall guy for the disaster. Pak Nam Gi, the country's seventy-seven-year-old finance chief, was blamed for the decision and executed on the charge of attempting to destroy the nation's fragile economy with the reform.

Then there was the *Shimwago,* the "Scrutiny," a new purge that terrorized the entire country. Orchestrated by Kim Jong Il but overseen by his brother-in-law, Jang Song Thaek, it began with Seo Gwan Hui, agricultural secretary of the Workers' Party, who was blamed for the famine. He was accused of being an American spy—a classic charge in show trials throughout the communist world—who had intentionally sabotaged the country's food supply to starve his compatriots. As punishment, he was stoned to death by a whipped-up mob in a Pyongyang stadium in 1997.

The evidence against Seo was scant. During one or two years of the Korean War, there were blank spaces in his identity booklet, carried by all North Koreans to document their peregrinations from year to year. It was during this undocumented period, it was asserted, that Seo was brought to the United States and trained to become a spy.

Naturally, almost everyone who was alive during the war years had blank entries in their identity booklets. The country was plunged into chaos, and it was impossible for any government entity to keep track of people. Any cadre that had been alive during the three years of the Korean War was now a target. The real purpose of the *Shimwago,* actually, was to get rid of all those who had been loyal to Kim Il Sung, rather than Kim Jong Il, in the years following the Great Leader's death. Ironically, as factional infighting took over, the purges even reached into the upper echelons of Kim Jong Il's own OGD, the powerful force field he had developed early on as a tool for wresting power away from his father.

During the three years that the *Shimwago* lasted, around twenty thousand cadres and their families were sent to concentration camps or executed on trumped-up charges. Among the elites in Pyongyang, Jang Song Thaek is still remembered as the main architect of the purge. It was Jang who saw to it that his enemies in the OGD were brutally tortured to death.

Was Jang Song Thaek's subsequent execution under Kim Jong Un plotted by those still alive and in power with revenge on their minds? According to the charges, Jang's purging was attributed to a range of confusing and contradictory factors. Power-hungry factionalist. Corrupt official. Corrupter of the youth. Womanizer. Bribe-accepter.

Nobody knows for sure why Jang was purged. Those who do know won't talk about it. Outsiders speculate that Jang wanted to open the country up to Chinese-style economic reforms, a process that Kim Jong Un ultimately rejected; others have said that it's the exact opposite, that Jang was a hardliner who tried to guide Jong Un away from such liberalization. Still others say that the plotting against him could more likely be attributed to the power of his position, which gave him and his cronies a monopoly on all the lucrative business deals brokered by the regime, blocking the way for other powerful cadres who desired a larger piece of the pie.

These days, everything is about money, and often nakedly so. Money flows, and the direction it goes is up up up. It climbs a ladder, via "loyalty dues," that reaches the big man at the top, his closest family and friends. And in a land that is so heavily sanctioned by the outside world, nearly every means of making money is an illicit enterprise. The whole country begins to resemble a huge underground crime syndicate, operating beneath the blanket of "Socialism" with a rather backward *S*.

But is this system really so corrupt, so separate from our own market-based economics in the twenty-first century, in which literally everything and anything is bought, sold, exchanged at every minute of every hour? Or is this yet another way in which "our" world has once again infringed upon "theirs," forever altering it?

As the Frankfurt School philosophers asserted, it is in capital's nature to expand and expand and expand until it has no place left to go, at which point it will allegedly self-combust. More recently, Slavoj Žižek has pointed to the irreconcilable qualities of capitalism and democracy, noting with typical irony that "authoritarian capitalism" represents a much more sensible compatibility. Žižek attributes the invention of authoritarian capitalism to Singapore's former prime minister Lee Kuan Yew. China was able to adapt it in the 1980s and, in doing so, became a global superpower—while remaining, in name, a communist state; in actuality, it is perhaps the foremost example of what the Slovenian philosopher calls an authoritarian capitalist state.

"Market-based economics has no problem accommodating local religions, cultures, or traditions," writes Žižek. "It is easily reconciled with the primacy of an authoritarian state. No longer wedded to Western cultural values, it is arguably divorced from them; critically reinterpreted, many of the ideas that Westerners hold dear—egalitarianism, fundamental rights, a generous and universal welfare state—can be deployed as weapons against capitalism."

Still, the *donju* are savvy enough to perceive that isolationism, whether imposed from the outside via sanctions or from above in the form of xenophobic ultra-nationalism and the restriction of outside information from entering the country, is not good for business. In the globalized twenty-first century, capital does not respect borders. The *donju* and virtually everyone else interested in making money in North Korea—which is to say everyone—want the doors open. But it is not easy to find trading partners intrigued by the prospect of doing business with what the world regards as a rogue state. A partner willing to risk jail time, devastating fines, and overall ruin in violating sanctions.

Are the sanctions effective? Not in any discernible sense. More than seventy years into it, the time is well past for any mass uprising that would unseat the current regime; rather, citizens are more likely to blame *all* economic woes on the sanctions, giving them one more reason to despise the United States. Each time new sanctions are imposed, the government and the people living under them have sought and found new ways for getting around them. With each passing year, the per capita income continues to rise.

For "us" on the outside, the difficulty with North Korea is that there is no precedent, no preexisting model we might look to politically as a guide for redeploying old strategies. Our politicians lack originality when it comes to creating new solutions. New ideas will not come about until someone is willing to look very hard at what this country, fundamentally and undauntingly, is. North Koreans, of course, realize this, which is why, in spite of all the hardships, they carry themselves with a certain gloat. I keep thinking of a work of calligraphy I saw at the Korean Art Gallery. I was able to read it with my new childlike comprehension of the language; just two words, in elegant script: "Our Way." That way must be understood, and it must be taken seriously. Because, whether anyone likes it or not, it is quite literally the only way forward.

NINETEEN

"WHY DON'T YOU open up a French restaurant in Pyongyang?" Min asks Alexandre as we cruise down the bumpy highway. We drive past peasants at back-bending labor in soppy rice fields on our way back to the city.

We're talking about all the new restaurants that have opened in recent years. Alek is even toying with the idea of publishing a Pyongyang restaurant guide for expats and tourists. Min smells a new business venture in the mix.

"It doesn't cost a lot of money to open up a restaurant in Pyongyang," Min hints.

"Sure. How about a fusion restaurant: Kimchi Baguette, we'll call it."

"Kimchi Baguette!" Min squeals. "I love it!"

"Will you come eat there if I open one?"

"Of course!" Min shouts, excitedly. "Better yet: we could be partners. Let's open a restaurant together!"

"French food is rather expensive to make," Alexandre protests. "It would cost a lot to import all the ingredients..."

Alexandre smiles and stares out the window. A village, comprising a makeshift assortment of three- and four-story apartment buildings, no electricity, followed by a row of dilapidated farm huts.

Min excitedly urges Alexandre on. Exotic cuisines are now all the rage in Pyongyang, she insists. Just last month, a new Italian place opened. And the ingredients won't cost all that much to import. They can be gotten from China.

"Do you think there's really a market here for high-end French cuisine?" asks Alexandre, generally curious.

"That's why you need me," replies Min, with bright confidence. "I know all the right people."

Hwa lays on the horn, and we scream past the sole vehicular traffic on the highway, an old man in tattered army fatigues leading an oxcart piled high with cement bricks.

PART FIVE

THE ATROCITY EXHIBITION

TWENTY

BY OUR SECOND week, a workday routine has been established. In the morning, we saunter down to one of the hotel's three restaurants for a breakfast of toast, eggs, and instant coffee—though we are also free to help ourselves to the more elaborate buffet intended for Chinese guests, replete with sliced bean curd, cucumbers, rice, and porridge. Then down to the lobby, meeting Roe and a constantly late Min for the crosstown commute to Kim Hyong Jik University for two hours of lessons. Afternoons are more eclectic, centered on a list of activities and excursions that Alexandre and I agreed upon with Alek. Given the duration of our stay, some afternoons sightseeing is sidelined by more mundane quotidian tasks, like shopping and laundry. We are kept so busy that we have little time at night for homework. As slow as the time seems to pass here, we are left each night to wonder where it has all gone.

Given Alek's long-term business interests and acquaintanceship with Min and Comrade Kim, who joins us for dinner every few days, we are made to feel less like tourists, more like illustrious guests with a private chauffeur. The longer we stay, the more at home we feel in this strange place; the less strange it feels. At lunch, we slurp our cold noodles and chat with Min and Roe with a relaxed air of conviviality, punctuated by eruptions of laughter. By contrast, on those occasions when other foreign tour groups will appear in the restaurant, their guides and drivers nearly always sit at a separate table, seeming bored with their charges.

Weekends, we usually take day trips outside of Pyongyang. Today's Saturday, so we'll take a drive out to neighboring South Hwanghae Province, which occupies the southwestern corner of the country. Our first stop: rural Sinchon county. Home of the Sinchon Museum of American War Atrocities.

I've been wanting to visit the museum for years, but it is rarely put on group itineraries. It's considered one of the more "sensitive" sites, a polite way of saying that its contents are actually rather incendiary. The Sinchon Museum is intended more for domestic rather than international propaganda purposes; virtually every North Korean visits the museum at least once, on mandatory educational pilgrimages.

After the three-hour ride along the potholed highway through depressed bucolica, our van pulls into the empty parking lot.

"You know what kind of place this is, right?" Min asks, a hint of warning in her voice, as we climb out of our metallic, air-conditioned box on wheels.

Elevated on a royal slope above the parking lot, the museum glistens beneath the scorching late July sun. The guide, in yellow *joseon-ot,* is already making her way down the sidewalk toward us. Above the entrance, a large propaganda slogan has been inscribed in gold lettering. Alek teasingly asks if my Korean is good enough yet to read it. His is: "Do not forget the lesson of blood on the ground of Sinchon." After we exchange greetings with the guide, our tour commences as we make our way up the hill.

Halfway up, we pause before two elevated mounds, familiar to anyone who has visited a Koryo Dynasty–era imperial tomb, such as that of King Kongmin outside of Kaesong. These, however, are not the tombs of an emperor and his wife; one, we are told, contains the remains of one hundred women who died in the slaughter that took place here, the other the remains of one hundred children. To the left of the museum building stand two warehouses, so nondescript that I hadn't noticed them a moment before. These, we are told, are the buildings in which the victims were murdered by the American capitalists.

The museum opened just five years after the Korean War armistice, on March 26, 1958. It was rebuilt in 2015 on the orders of Kim Jong Un, who instructed that it be made "more comfortable" for Korean visitors. Previously, the museum space was located at a greater distance from the warehouses where the victims had been killed; now, they were located side-by-side, presumably to strengthen the dramatic impact of the horrors contained in each of the buildings.

At the time the war broke out, Sinchon was a regional transportation hub and, therefore, a strategic point militarily. To get to Pyongyang or Haeju, the provincial capital, you had to pass through. In the early days of the Korean War, the town was captured by the US military. For the fifty-two days they occupied the area—from October 17 to December 7, 1950, when they were driven out by the advancing Chinese troops—they committed numerous mass murders and atrocities, aimed chiefly at local civilians, that amounted to nothing less than a total holocaust. At least this is the story the museum is here to tell. It has been erected on the locale where many of these crimes against humanity allegedly took place.

The museum is not merely a commemorative site but a vivid, stomach-churning evocation—replete with wax dummies, fake blood, and a piped-in soundscape of screaming children—of the savage butchery and malicious nature that signify American imperialism.

★

We proceed along a chronology of brutality. The US soldiers launched their adventure, our guide relays, by gathering nine hundred local residents into an air raid shelter. Through the air ducts, they poured gasoline and then incinerated the victims. "All of them were innocent civilians. Mostly women and children," she somberly intones.

This was followed by the massacre of October 20, when five hundred twenty people were placed inside yet another air raid shelter, in which the devious Americans had planted dynamite. They locked the doors and detonated it. Our guide takes great relish in elucidating all the gory details. Min takes less delight in interpreting, rendering the English translation in an affectless monotone of a description of human flesh left hanging from the walls of the shelter.

I'm reminded of *Eden Eden Eden,* Pierre Guyotat's anti-novel, with its over-wrought and crude incantations of sadistic violence, rape, and mass mur-der, meant to evoke the horrors of the Algerian War. Indeed, with its lack of

historical contextualization and refutation of any causal factors that might bol-
ster the verisimilitude of what is displayed—even the blurred black-and-white
photographic documentation looks abstract, as though it could have been pulled
from any number of the past century's mass slaughters—the museum, like
Guyotat's book, is a collection of fragments of violence; both works are essentially pornographic.

★

The action shifts to a nearby hot springs resort, commandeered by US soldiers
as a barracks. There, our guide explains, they dragged local women, raped them,
and then threw them into the hot springs and tossed in grenades to "cover up"
their crimes.

Becoming animated, the museum guide bemoans "these American luna-
tics, who tortured women by cutting off their breasts and inserting sticks in
their vaginas." She nearly spits on the floor. "And these Americans preach about
'human rights'! And boast that *they* enjoy the *utmost* of civilizations!"

When not busy raping and murdering women at the hot springs, the soldiers
were occupied with the project of slaughtering an additional twelve hundred
locals. This they accomplished with the help of vicious attack dogs. Or by burning them to death. It is not specified whether these two methods were employed
simultaneously or alternately; it is fruitless to ask, as rationality does not play
much of a role in this type of narrative construction.

Twelve miles north of Sinchon, a bridge was barricaded by the US army. Every
civilian approaching that day hoping to cross was instead murdered.

At another bridge, the soldiers took sadistic pleasure in tying sacks filled with
rocks to the feet of local peasants and tossing them off to drown in the deep river
below. The few who were lucky enough to survive and managed to swim up to
the surface didn't meet a happy end; they were shot at by the evil Yankees above
to ensure not a single survivor was left.

These scenes are enacted by lifelike mannequins—ugly American soldiers
with hooked noses (one can't help but think of the depiction of Jews in Nazi Germany propaganda) and malevolent grins. Others are illustrated in large, mural-
esque wall paintings. Over speakers, a soundtrack of screaming children and
symphonic music. Piles of bodies forming mass graves in grainy photographs.

Every few years, a new mass grave will be discovered in the vicinity, necessitating the museum's constant expansion.

"Some of the skeletons unearthed were scratching the ground, trying to climb to the surface as they suffocated. In one of these mass graves, they found the remains of a nine-month-old fetus in one of the bodies," says the guide. "So you can tell these Americans even killed pregnant women!"

I wonder what's going through Min's mind as she's forced to interpret. Whether she believes all these things, whether she is sickened by them. What kind of detachment her flat, emotionless transcription is rooted in. Surely she has a different relationship to history, to the "history" that is so key in fomenting North Korean national identity, having grown up thousands of miles away.

Alek and Alexandre and I are careful to remain silent, even avoid glancing at one another, throughout the tour. In the past, it has not been unheard-of for tourists to react in anger, even argue with the museum guides, over the veracity of such outlandish claims. This is why tourists are rarely brought here. It is something that has to be requested.

Alek breaks protocol to point out a detail in a particularly gruesome, corpse-strewn photo and begins to whisper something in my ear. Min uncharacteristically reacts in anger, halting her hate-speech translation to remind us "It was *you* who wanted to come here" before huffing off to the next room. Later, when she notices me filming her on my phone as she is interpreting, she asks me to stop.

Understatement has never been considered a virtue in the North Korean propaganda machinery. Overwhelmed by disbelief, I ask the guide to clarify whether *all* of these crimes actually took place here in Sinchon or if this museum is meant to commemorate atrocities that had taken place throughout Korea during the war.

"The museum documents only the crimes that took place here," she responds, before quickly adding, "though *more* atrocities were committed all over Korea."

Of course.

We are led into yet another room with the sound of screaming children at full blast.

"Are schoolchildren also brought to this museum?" I am inspired to ask.

"Yes," replies the guide proudly. "And after seeing the exhibition, the children say, 'The US imperialists are not human. They are wolves.'"

In the hallway, we pass by a large propaganda banner. Alek translates: "Don't forget the US imperialist wolves."

★

As November 1950 drew to a close, the American imperialist wolves realized that the sheep had outnumbered them. They would have to flee as soon as possible, but before they did, they committed a final genocide. To "stop the seeds of communism from growing," they gathered up as many women and children as they could find, separated them in two storehouses, poured in gasoline, and burned them alive. Only three children survived; one, we are told, now works here at the museum. But they were not left orphaned despite the tragedy; they had their new father, the State, the Great Leader Kim Il Sung, to look after them.

As we move on in the display, the exhibition segues from scenes of mass brutality to showcasing acts of barbarity carried out against individuals. In a mannequinized reenactment, a female resistance leader is held down by one US soldier while another drives a nail into her skull. The guide comments, "You can see the atrociousness of the American imperialists, who enjoyed torturing and killing people in an atrocious way while they were here."

A young adolescent, the leader of the communist student union, was murdered "for being a model student," among other transgressions. A "model hero worker" met his end by being torn apart, with each side of his limbs tied to separate oxcarts run in opposite directions. The principal of an elementary school had his head chopped off with a hatchet. Another woman was tied to a tree, had her breasts cut off, and was then burned to death. "It's the exact same way they treated the Indians," our guide notes.

"The United States is still carrying out war exercises in an attempt to invade our country," she continues. Then, with the open-handed gesture with which you are permitted to acknowledge a portrait of one of the leaders—pointing is forbidden—the guide draws our attention to a large photograph of Kim Jong Un, whose wise leadership will prevent that from ever happening.

Nearing the end of the exhibitions, the guide's delivery rises to an emotional peak, her voice quivering wildly:

"We Korean people won't forget the crimes that these animal-like people committed on our land. We will make them pay for all the blood they spilled."

✪

Outside, we make our way down the sidewalk toward the two warehouses. Perched on a hill, we are afforded a glimpse over the town of Sinchon. I attempt to take a photograph of the townscape, but a plainclothes male guard suddenly approaches and demands I lower my camera.

The first storehouse is a replica of the one in which the original genocide-by-fire was alleged to have taken place. Inside, the guide points to air ducts in the ceiling where the gasoline was poured in. The second building is one of the actual warehouses where the children were burned alive. An elderly gentleman with jet-black hair in a khaki worker's uniform appears. I've never seen anyone with dyed hair in North Korea before, but it's hard for me to believe that some-one could make it to that age without a single sprout of gray. Especially consid-ering what he is alleged to have experienced. He is, we are told, one of the three children who survived that day. His speech further embellishes the wickedness committed by the American devils. They passed out cups of water and encour-aged the children to drink, he tells us—but the water turned out to be gasoline. Luckily, he was situated in one of the far corners of the storeroom and passed out early "because of the cold," so his life was spared. "The Americans," he says, "are animals wearing the masks of human beings. Even though time has passed, the flames of anger still burn in my heart."

As we exit the storehouse, a group of about two dozen workers is outside—a factory work unit on an educational field excursion—patiently waiting for us to finish so that they might have their turn. "I wonder what they're thinking after seeing all that and now having to look at us," whispers Alexandre.

✪

I thought that would be the last of it. But then, there is a *third* storehouse, home of yet another burning atrocity, but by now, I am so emotionally exhausted by the content and overwhelmed with the theatricality of the staging that I have lost track of the narrative. Min points to a piece of graffiti that was scratched into the wall "at the last moment": "Long live the Workers' Party of Korea!" wrote the dying martyr.

Before bidding us adieu, the museum guide makes her conclusive speech. "Please go back to your countries and spread word of the terrible atrocities suffered by our people. The Koreans never wanted a war. We are the most peace-loving people in the entire world." Then, without a pause: "We will never forget what the American imperialists did to us; one day, we will have our revenge."

TWENTY-ONE

AFTER THAT, WE'RE hardly in the mood for revelry, but after much cajoling by Alek and Alexandre, Min announces on the way back to Pyongyang that she was granted permission to take us to the Friendship Club for the Saturday night soirée. A big deal, since tourists typically aren't allowed inside this part of Pyongyang, the diplomatic quarter where most foreign residents are housed. Save for the employees of the embassies and missions stationed there, North Koreans cannot go past the guarded entrance, either. They will have to drop us off at dinnertime and pick us up at 11 p.m. I feel like a teenager again.

Alexandre is excited to get away from our minders. But he also has ulterior motives. He might not be opening Kimchi Baguette anytime soon, but he does have a fantasy of working here someday. Neither Alek nor I can determine what his ultimate goal is. He's clearly obsessed with this place. But then so are we. But whereas Alek and I are mainly just curious to see what life inside the compound looks like, Alexandre is out to network and make contacts. He's already started, even before the trip. In Paris, he managed to get introduced to the head of France's recently opened consular service. This is why Alexandre really bought the phone; he was able to call ahead and secure a personal invitation to tonight's festivities.

Munsu-dong diplomatic quarter is in east Pyongyang, not far from our university. The Friendship Club is situated in a small two-story house. It contains a restaurant and small bar, with a billiards table on the ground floor, while upstairs there is a makeshift disco with a larger bar as well as a karaoke salle. A sort of diluted successor of the Random Access Club, opened by aid workers in the famine years of the 1990s, at a time when there was a veritable lack of leisure options in the city.

The ironically named Random Access Club—access being rather elusive in North Korea—gained notoriety for its Friday and Saturday parties, though perhaps not reaching the level of decadence attained by Kim Jong Il's parties in the early 1980s. In an interview about her years as a kidnapped member of Jong Il's inner circle in Pyongyang, actress Choi Eun Hee revealed that fawning over and toasting the Dear Leader were key components of the evening. Jong Il himself would often sit at a distance and *direct* the evening's proceedings, instructing partygoers when and what to drink, which games to play, with whom each should dance. Activities that would get a normal citizen shot were freely indulged in— Western disco and South Korean pop songs danced to, expensive liquor (including Kim's favorite, Hennessey Cognac) consumed in staggering abundance. Teenage girls from Jong Il's personal joy division were on hand to provide sexual favors for the male guests. If you were one of Jong Il's people, these parties were mandatory to attend. They played a key role in the younger Kim's wrenching of power out of his father's hands. Promotions and demotions could be issued on the spot—as well as, on at least one occasion, an execution. The victim, the wife of an elite, had written an indiscreet tell-all letter to Kim Il Sung, who was in the dark about such fêtes, complaining of the son's decadent ways. Instead of reaching its intended recipient, the letter fell into Jong Il's hands. That night, he announced to all in attendance the instantaneous verdict and death sentence, which was to be carried out immediately. Upon hearing the announcement, the husband of the condemned rose and implored Jong Il to allow him to carry out the execution personally. Jong Il consented, handing him the gun.

By comparison, the Random Access Club gatherings of the subsequent decade were a comparatively mild affair and solely reserved for the expatriate diplomats and aid workers living in Pyongyang as well as the occasional visitor. But the party came to an end in 2012, when a couple of French NGO workers threw a so-called Workers' Party. Guests came dressed in vinylon Mao suits and proceeded to drunkenly slander the Dear Leadership as the evening's festivities wore on. Naturally, the place was bugged and the offensive shenanigans duly reported to the authorities. The responsible NGO workers had their visas revoked and were put on the next plane to Beijing. The Random Access Club was shuttered for good.

We arrive for dinner around 8 p.m. Early, it turns out—the place is deserted. The waitress leads us into the restaurant, addressing us with a flawless American accent. "Welcome to the Friendship Club!" She beams. "We haven't seen you around here before. Where are you from?" When she hears that I'm American, she gives a visible start, followed by an embarrassed smile. "Well…We don't really get very many…Americans around here. Shall I give you a minute to look at the menu?" She scatters off to the kitchen, no doubt to report our presence to her *bowibu* superiors.

We take advantage of the a la carte offerings to indulge in some Western food. After finishing our pizza, hamburger steaks, and fries, we order ice cream for dessert. As we're finishing, Alexandre hears French-speaking voices emerging from the downstairs bar, which is starting to fill up. He excuses himself and vanishes. After settling the bill, Alek and I follow after him.

In the bar, it's the United Nations of Pyongyang. The room is populated with mostly middle-aged career diplomat types and their spouses from across Europe and a few Southeast Asians, plus a smattering of thirty-somethings modeling the khaki, denim, and polo shirts connoting the international aid worker. Loosened ties and casual eveningwear abound in this scene of cocktail hour conviviality. At the center of it all, a beautiful young Korean woman, exquisitely dressed, holds court; she's the "head boss" here, someone pointedly whispers. She darts back and forth behind the bar, greeting all comers, keeping the drinks flowing alongside the conversation. Recognizing the three newbies in her midst, she flows through the crowd and introduces herself to each of us whenever our scattered conversations reach an opportune pause. Throughout the course of the evening, Ms. Lee will ask us each our name, our nationality, our job, where we're staying, and what we're doing here—and in that precise order. I notice she's wearing no Kim badge—probably as a tool for encouraging drunken indiscretions. She introduces me to a tall, handsome young man working for the Swedish Embassy.

"It's his last month here with us in Pyongyang." Ms. Lee bats her eyelashes honeypottishly. "We're going to be so sad to see him go."

He politely shakes my hand. Did I register with the embassy prior to my arrival? Yes, I sent an email a month ago. "Let me know if there's anything I can do for you while you're here." He gives me his card and then skittishly excuses himself.

Like nearly all the Western embassies here, the Swedish mission is small—just two staff members. Since the US has no embassy in the DPRK, Sweden handles the concerns of US citizens in the country—which means it is forced to play middleman whenever an American tourist is arrested and detained.

Everyone we meet is taken aback by our presence—mine, in particular. It is an anomaly enough in itself that non-Chinese foreign students have been granted permission to study here; but an American—that's unheard-of. I am warned, constantly, to *be careful.* I breezily dismiss all words of caution. "I don't plan on stealing any propaganda banners while I'm in town," I tell them. "Or proselytizing." Nobody laughs at my funny joke. "Well, we don't know for sure what *really* happened" is the common response when the case of Otto Warmbier inevitably comes up, as though a consensus had been secretly reached not to trust any versions of the story promulgated in the media.

Upstairs in the disco, '90s dance music plays, interspersed with drunken interpretations of pop classics on the karaoke machine. We're nearing our scheduled pickup time—too early, we realize, as many new guests are only now arriving to merge with the crowd of some two dozen. We try to make the most of what time we have left, gleaning some sense of what expat life is like here. Alek and I make our way to the front door, passing Alexandre, who is bidding adieu to a vaguely hippie-ish Italian forty-something with plaited hair, an engineer from a development-oriented NGO. "Be careful what you say," she tells him, "because you never know when they are listening. Even when they are not listening, they often know things. So it is always best to be honest. They are suspicious of us, of all foreigners. They think we are here because we want to change the system. But the Korean people are happy with the way things are—they don't want it to change." She shrugs her shoulders. "And they do have a right to live as they see fit!"

Earlier, a secretarial staff member from the German Embassy had a far more cynical take on things. "You are studying here?" she said to me, almost accusingly. "Just so you know, for them it's not really about 'cultural exchange'—they're just interested in the money. How much are you paying for this anyway?"

Since we're both Berliners, I asked her about the youth hostel next door to the DPRK Embassy in central Berlin. DPRK diplomatic missions are tasked not only with coming up with their own funding but with generating income to send the regime back home. As such, DPRK embassy staff are believed to have been involved with all sorts of business ventures—of both the legal and illegal varieties. (Diplomatic immunity comes in handy here; overseas ambassadors have been caught smuggling everything from rhinoceros horn to crystal meth.) Since the fall of communist Europe and the reunification of Germany, the sprawling DPRK Embassy in the former East Berlin was needlessly vast for its few staff and family members. In 2008, the larger of its two buildings was leased as a well-known hostel. Backpackers staying there might notice the DPRK Embassy next door, with its display case out front featuring a revolving exhibition of photographs of the Kims giving on-the-spot guidance, but otherwise have no idea where their money is actually going.

"We Germans have been very angry with them about that." She shrugged. "They owe us two million euros in back taxes on that hostel. Which, of course, they will never pay."

⭐

Word quickly spreads in the tiny expat community as to our presence in Pyongyang. When we bump into a Western stranger at a coffee shop or restaurant, we're usually met with something along the lines of: "Oh yes, you're the ones studying Korean at Kim Hyong Jik University. Now are you the Australian, the French, or the American?" Gossip travels fast when there are so few competing distractions. For as exciting as this all is for us the first couple weeks, as we settle in, I begin to realize that for long-term foreign residents, boredom is more or less the unifying force.

The following week, we are invited to a *Stammtisch* organized by the German Embassy in the communal dining area of the building shared by Germany, Sweden, and the UK. The atmosphere is markedly different from the Friendship Club; for one thing, no Koreans are present. The spouses of the embassy employees take turns tending bar, spooning out potato salad, and distributing sausages and slices of brown bread.

Alexandre and I arrive alone at the *Stammtisch*. Our attendance at these events clearly makes Min and Roe somewhat uncomfortable—or perhaps envious, since Munsu-dong is one of the few places we can go where they're not allowed. Alex elects to stay behind to have dinner with them and Comrade Kim. They need to talk business anyway; Tongil Tours has several more tours planned in the coming months.

Because of the lack of Korean faces, the *Stammtisch* attendees feel free to let their guard down and speak a bit more openly—though there's no doubt the place is bugged. Still, the buzz of the crowd would presumably make it difficult to pick up on any one conversation, particularly given the plurality of languages being spoken.

Seven European countries have diplomatic missions in the DPRK, while two more have "cooperation offices." I fall into conversation with one weathered ambassador. "In my experience," he says, "the embassy people working here tend to go through three phases. The first is where you think you finally *get* it and understand how this country really operates. The second, where you get frustrated and realize you don't understand anything. And the last is when you realize you don't understand anything and no longer care because you'll be out of here soon."

I ask if he's personally experienced all three phases. He has, after all, been in Pyongyang for more than a year now.

The ambassador shakes his head. "I'm at stage two. I know I'll eventually get to stage three, but I want it to last as shortly as possible. Because that's where cynicism sets in, and that gets you nowhere—nor does it do any good for the people you're ostensibly here to help."

In the near absence of anything that could be deemed normal diplomatic relations, most of the foreign embassies work very closely with the NGOs stationed here. As these aid organizations tend to be staffed with people from the represented countries, the dividing line is very thin. The feeling of mutual belonging, of quasi-familial community among these outsiders, is apparent.

Moments of frustration are a common theme in conversation. Another newly arrived ambassador joins our conversation. He tells us he had been on a trip the past weekend with two of his Korean staff members. While embassy staff are permitted to travel virtually anywhere they want within Pyongyang city limits, they must apply for permission to travel outside the city and are always accompanied by Koreans. The ambassador began to realize that the answer to every question he asked his Korean colleagues was a lie, so he eventually reached the point where he gave up and chose not to ask them anything. In response, the weathered ambassador ventures, "The most honest thing one of my Korean colleagues ever told me was 'I've been told not to tell you.'"

It is unsurprising that a paranoid regime would be paranoid when it comes to diplomatic missions. One of the implicit tasks of a diplomat, after all, is intelligence gathering. Historians' best source of information regarding the inner workings of Kim Il Sung's early government comes from the dispatches of the diplomats stationed here that were found in the files opened to the public after the fall of the Soviet Union. NGO workers are similarly regarded as potential spies. The Koreans assigned to work with foreigners are naturally tasked to uphold a disinformation regimen.

"I wonder at times whether they lie to each other as well," the first ambassador continues. "I sometimes think it might be even worse here than it was in the GDR, where a father couldn't trust his own son. I suspect it probably is."

"They live in fear," concludes the second ambassador. "All of them."

Again, the Warmbier case comes up. Again, I am told to *be careful*. "You never know," I hear. "They are always looking for a reason. And sometimes, *there is no reason.*"

Opinions are regaled with the tired expressions of those who have been enduring monitoring, conflicting reports, mixed messages, and outright lies for extended durations. Even though they are somewhat sheltered from the harsh realities that Koreans themselves have to confront, have access to the internet (albeit with slow connections that are most likely also monitored by DPRK authorities), and can travel outside the country (as a rule, most embassies and NGOs require their employees to "take a breather" once every three months), the psychological realities of working in such an environment have their consequences. The overall effect is less distrust and paranoia—at least here tonight, they are among friends and colleagues in whom they can confide—and more extreme fatigue, with an underlying sadness and greater or lesser degrees of cynicism.

There are exceptions, of course. People whose power of empathy borders on the transcendent. Those capable of disengaging from those unpleasant aspects of their daily encounters to wrench something of the universally human out of them. One employee of the Polish Embassy studied Korean in Warsaw for several years before she arrived here; she prefers to speak of "cultural differences" between herself and her North Korean colleagues.

Gabriella is an Australian occupational therapist, here with a healthcare NGO. She's been here for less than a month and still retains a cheery air. Her job, however, is not without its difficulties. She works with the physically disabled, from young children to the elderly. I've never seen any disabled people in my travels to the DPRK. I ask her about a rumor that they had been forbidden from residing in Pyongyang since the early 1980s so as not to "tarnish" the city's appearance and status as the showcase capital. She nods her head sadly. "That may have been true up to about five years ago," she says, "but my organization has done a lot of work to change that. People are becoming more educated."

Still, getting around is extremely difficult for those less able, which may account for why they are rarely seen in public. For those unable to walk, there is nothing in the way of electric wheelchairs available. The wheelchairs they do have are rickety things that have been donated. As if that does not make it difficult enough to navigate, none of the buildings have been designed with accessibility in mind. Given the power shortages, elevators cannot always be relied upon.

Despite these hardships, Gabriella tells me, her patients welcome her each day with warmth, kindness, and affection. Their suspicion and distrust of her as a foreigner—which, like all other North Koreans, had been programmed into them from a young age—quickly dissipated; within minutes of their first meeting, the children cuddled in her lap, the elderly addressed her as tenderly as though she were their daughter.

Toward the end of the *Stammtisch,* Alexandre suggests we use our extra time before pickup to go walking through the embassy district. I hesitate. I've been told repeatedly throughout the night that I'm in danger, to watch myself, to be careful. Alexandre, being French, does not have to endure such repeated warnings. Yet he had also been fortunate enough to experience Pyongyang in a comparatively *unsupervised* way, since he was on a student visa last time he was here. The entire trip, he has been itching to get away from the ever-watchful presence of Roe and Min and to walk through the streets freely. Now's our chance—albeit in a rather limited way. The Munsu-dong district is anyway restricted to foreigners, with a Korean guard at the entrance prohibiting all but the authorized from entering. Still, I'm not sure. Something so innocent as going for a walk unsupervised— who knows? Could the Koreans use that as an excuse to arrest me? Claim it as evidence that I'm a spy? If they could accuse a drunken twenty-one-year-old student of working for the CIA, what could they do to a thirty-six-year-old writer?

"It will be fine," Alexandre insists. "Let's just walk to the entrance of the compound. We can wait for them there. They will appreciate it—that way, they don't have to stop and argue with the guard."

I agree, though I am nervous the entire time. Anyway, there isn't a lot to see at night—a row of gates and shrubbery hiding small houses containing the embassies and residencies, the streets eerily bereft of pedestrians and traffic. I'm startled when Alexandre's phone suddenly rings. But it's only Alek—a rare excuse to use those newly purchased Koryolink phones—to tell him they're on their way to pick us up. Alexandre winks at me, tells him we'll wait at the entrance by the guard post.

TWENTY-TWO

I'M NEVER ALONE, and it's starting to drive me crazy. It couldn't have occurred to me, the moment I so eagerly signed up to come on this trip, that the biggest challenge of spending a month in North Korea might in fact be a psychological one. My earlier sojourns had all lasted one week or less—a quick in-and-out back to the polluted chaos of Beijing's familiar streets. Now, it seems I underestimated the duress of spending an uninterrupted month in the strangeness of this otherworld. As a writer, I am accustomed to spending a great deal of time alone; that's normal for me. It's what makes me feel comfortable. I'm not anti-social—I enjoy being around people, people I like, at least—but it has to be balanced by an equal or greater amount of solitude, or else I find myself approaching a discomfiting edge. Being around people constantly, it's exhausting. People you hardly know. People you only have a limited means of knowing. You are never able to let your guard down and relax under such circumstances— you are constantly having to perform. Especially here, where your self-censoring device must be turned on at all times. This might come naturally to the Koreans born and raised in this environment, who have been conditioned from childhood to operate in this way. But for everyone else, such restraint requires a great deal of mental energy.

Then, at those rare moments when you *are* alone, it feels creepy. As though someone is either watching you, unseen, or else listening. Or both. *They hear everything... Even when you don't think they're listening, they often are.*

On the way back to the hotel, staring out the window at the empty, well-lit streets of the nocturnal city center, I experience wells of a strange emotion I haven't felt for a long time: fear. In my half-drunken exhaustion, a menagerie of voices swells up in my head, but where I feel it the most is my chest.

Everybody is reporting on everyone else… They're all watching… Always telling… They know everything… Great danger, great danger…

It suddenly strikes me how cut off we are here. We haven't had news from the outside world in the past two weeks. We had our chance tonight and last week— we could have asked the expats, who all have internet access. Any news from outside? But strangely, it didn't even occur to any of us to ask. We've forgotten. How easy it would be for the outside world, then, to forget all about us, were we to disappear.

I am, in fact, *completely alone* here—while paradoxically *never* being alone. The insanity of the situation… What have I gotten myself into? Here I am, sitting in a van with a group of strangers, all of whom would be completely and utterly helpless to come to my aid were I to get into trouble. Sure, Min is great, the "cool" North Korean. But in the event that someone, someone high above her, decided to make an example out of me, would she really be able to do anything about it? To do so, really, would be to put *herself* at risk. That's how the system operates. You report on others, turn others in—but certainly don't come to anyone's defense once they've been accused. To do that would be to admit complicity, your participation in their crime. If it's your own spouse, save yourself— volunteer to pull the trigger.

And Alek and Alexandre? I have great affection for them both. But as I look at them, it suddenly occurs to me that they're kids. It's not even an age thing— even if they weren't ten, twelve years my junior, what help would they be in dealing with the arbitrary arrest and detainment of a fellow student?

Then there's the Atrocity Museum, to which I continue to return in my mind. As gory and brutal as the contents of the museum are, they are actually the least disturbing thing about the entire experience. Clearly the model for the Sinchon museum are the holocaust museums and memorial sites tourists can visit in Europe. But those places are suffused with a historical context that is utterly absent in Sinchon. A history that we all know, that has been verified by countless sources. When you visit, say, the House of the Wannsee Conference in Berlin, where the mass murder of Europe's Jews was coolly plotted by the Nazi elite, the layout of the place is rooted in a chronological, detailed outline that emphasizes not merely *what* took place but *how* and *why* the events depicted and documented came to occur. In Sinchon, there are no hows, no whys. What you have, besides the set of gruesome displays, is a rhetoric that boils the conflict down to an imaginary battle between *good* and *evil*. The pure, innocent-hearted Korean civilians and the heartless American bastard imperialists. Never once are the Americans clarified as *soldiers,* either. When they are referred to, it is as "American imperialists"—or else, to make them less than human, wolves. Animals. The entire context in which these crimes allegedly took place is erased. It was a war. A *civil* war.

To say that these crimes were perpetrated by "Americans"—not American soldiers or even, perhaps, the US government, but simply *Americans*—is to imply that not only were all Americans complicit in these actions but all Americans are *essentially like that*: animals, as it is repeated throughout, up until the very end. Finally, by putting the blame on the American bastards, the North Koreans are able to evade the painful and traumatic truth: that the horrendous crimes committed against them—and that they committed against others—were Korean on Korean: the *civilness* of the civil war has been eradicated.

The lack of self-reflection and criticality in the North Korean education system means that Koreans often don't even realize it when they blatantly contradict themselves in speech. As anyone who has tried to make their way through one of Kim Jong Il's books or speeches—or read an editorial in the *Rodong Sinmun*—will tell you, the rhetoric of the propaganda is such a mishmash of impassioned confusions, of chest-beating bellicosities, that very little in the way of coherent sense can be extracted from it. This is damaging because, for foreign visitors at least, it obscures any shred of truth regarding what might have actually taken place in Sinchon. What we're presented with is a fake historical museum that appeals only to the emotions. This, indeed, is one of the key tactics that the system uses to infantilize its populace, teaching them to *feel* rather than *think,* where the only guiding principle is this primitive notion of *good* and *evil.* The same primitive notions that certain Western politicians like to promote when propagandizing against North Korea ("the axis of evil"). Reason and logic are completely absent in such environs. Irrational fear, paranoia float in to fill the gap.

TWENTY-THREE

SO WHAT REALLY happened in Sinchon?

In his novel *The Guest,* which is based on a series of interviews conducted with a North Korean pastor who had been living in Sinchon at the time that the massacres took place, Hwang Sok Yong attributes two foreign guests, imposed on Korea during the process of colonization and division, as the ultimate ideological causes of the unrest and violence: Christianity and Marxism.

Christianity had been introduced to Sinchon quite early on. During the Japanese occupation of the country, there were also a large number of pro-independence freedom fighters active in the region. Economically, Sinchon was situated in one of the wealthiest regions above the thirty-eighth parallel. After Korea was liberated from Japan, many of the young people living there opposed the communists' suppression of religion and policy of land distribution. They were left with two choices: either defect to South Korea or stay and form covert anti-communist underground operations, sporadically putting up resistance against the forces of the Korean People's Army.

According to South Korean historian Han Sung Hoon, when the North's military units retreated from Sinchon in October 1950, local communist guerilla units formed to take their place, battling the South Korean and US-led UN forces that had moved into the area. In short, Sinchon and its surroundings had been a hotbed of both rightist and leftist aggression in the moments leading up to the massacre of late 1950. When US and South Korean forces moved in, it gave the rightist guerrillas the upper hand in the battle. Although the Korean People's Army was forced to retreat from the Sinchon region during this period, neither the US nor South Korea was able to gain complete control over it either, owing to the confused morass of multiple guerrilla factions and the spate of retaliatory killings that would occur whenever one of these groups managed a brief triumph over the others. Han writes: "This kind of revenge killing reveals the nature of the *civil* war in Korea, which cannot be understood as a mere temporary flash of emotional vendetta. From the end of Japanese colonial rule and national liberation to the formation of the Democratic People's Republic of Korea, the war was the explosive result of continued economic and religious conflict between the left and the right."

In the years following the massacre, with the Korean War raging on, the Belgium-based International Association of Democratic Lawyers—alarmed by rumors of a civilian massacre in Sinchon—dispatched teams of human rights specialists to the region to investigate in 1951 and 1952. On each visit, they interviewed numerous witnesses. In the resulting report, the group stated that they found overwhelming evidence that US soldiers *had* carried out mass and individual killings of civilians, including women and children. (This is the same report in which it would come to light that the US had deployed chemical weapons and germ warfare against the enemy, something that the US continues to deny.) For his part, Hwang, in the process of researching his novel, interviewed a number of witnesses from Sinchon who claimed the massacres that took place had actually been perpetuated by Koreans against Koreans and that the violence was committed on both sides of the political divide. Kwak Pok Hyon, a South Korean who was himself part of an anti-communist guerrilla unit during the war, has claimed that the massacre was carried out by Korean right-wing security units. Kwak even admitted that he himself had taken part in the massacre of civilians but that the number of civilians killed was greatly exaggerated by the North Koreans.

According to Kwak, one of the acts of mass murder took place not long after the US crossed the thirty-eighth parallel and Christian right-wing guerrilla forces took over the security of the area surrounding Sinchon. After hiding out at a military base in nearby Mount Kuwol, communist fighters began coming back to Sinchon because they were starving. They were rounded up by the Christian rightists, who then led dozens of communists into a mud hut in an apple orchard and set it ablaze. Anyone who attempted to escape the mass incineration was hacked to death with pitchforks.

Other sources claim that the massacres were carried out by a secret police unit dispatched by South Korea's dictator Syngman Rhee shortly after the US troops took control of the area. This would imply that, while the US troops themselves did not carry out the massacre, they certainly would have witnessed or at least known about it and did nothing to stop it.

The Sinchon massacre, concludes Han, "cannot be understood simply as killings between the left and the right. It must be understood three-dimensionally, as the explosive result of the contradictions emanating from the colonial period after liberation, combined with the division and establishment of two separate states in the North and South, and eventual war, which exacerbated internal problems of class, hierarchy, and religion."

✪

Why did the North Koreans wait until 1958 to build the museum in Sinchon?

The answers to this are rooted in that politically crucial period in the country's history. In 1956, Khrushchev gave his notorious "Secret Speech," whose contents would soon become not so secret, spreading throughout the communist world. In the speech, he denounced the crimes and personality cult of his predecessor, Kim Il Sung's role model Josef Stalin. Behind the scenes in the DPRK, factions engaged in a fierce ideological battle, with many in Kim's government expressing sympathy with the currents being espoused in the Soviet Union. Currents that essentially amounted to a repudiation of Stalin-esque personality cults—such as the one that Kim Il Sung and his circle of supporters were very much keen on emulating.

Steps had to be taken to curtail these currents. To isolate the country from Soviet influence and assert that there would only be one way—"*our way*"—forward. The Songbun system was created. Juche, the doctrine of ultra-nationalistic self-reliance, was asserted, eventually overtaking Marxism-Leninism as the official state ideology. Purges eliminated all competing factions, putting an end to all political pluralism in the DPRK by early 1959.

Kim's turn toward ultra-nationalism was motivated by more than just a domestic power struggle. There were also military concerns. Kim had called for *all* foreign troops to withdraw from the Korean peninsula. In 1958, the Chinese People's Volunteers, which had troops in the North to support the country in the event of another war's eruption, followed suit. The Korean People's Army became the sole military force in the North, a situation that endures to this day. Not only did the US in the South *not* follow suit, in 1957–1958, Americans installed nuclear weapons in South Korea, essentially breaking the Armistice Agreement. This greatly alarmed the North Koreans, who protested the move, all to no avail.

The fear and paranoia within the regime and populace provoked by the US's installation of nuclear weapons on the peninsula exacerbated anti-Americanism into official state doctrine. The North Koreans had, of course, been anti-American ever since the Korean War, but the virulence with which it continues to this day had its origins in the late 1950s. And the first major, state-sponsored iteration of this anti-American sentiment was the construction of the Sinchon Museum of American War Atrocities. This is the museum's real historical significance.

In the DPRK, history cannot just be history in the way it is in most developed countries—a dormant thing, lying in the past, a passive actor in the construction of present and future. To North Koreans, it is as though these atrocities took place yesterday. They also serve as warnings that the very same thing could very well happen again, tomorrow even—or in an hour from now. Hypervigilance, then, is demanded of all citizens. It is one of the things that *makes* you a North Korean: your past, current, and potential future victimization at the hands of hostile forces. A nation whose traumatic past cannot be merely buried but continues to inform the psychopathology of daily life. Fear *must be* deeply and endlessly ingrained in the populace for the enabling belief to continue, and it is the role of the regime and its propaganda to perpetuate that fear.

Just like the top-down political structure, fear also operates vertically in the DPRK. This is the ultimate source of all the paranoia you begin to detect on street level—and experience personally, when you stick around for long enough, as I have come to realize. It is something deeper than the *mere* Orwellian nightmare of the police state, of being under constant surveillance, of your fellow citizens spying and reporting on you. That might be bad—but surely it can't be worse than the nefarious forces of the outside world, which want to see you destroyed in the most gruesome way possible.

To North Koreans, though, there is a remedy for that constant threat. There is one more building in the museum in Sinchon that foreigners are not allowed to enter: an "oath-taking" spot, where groups are meant to congregate after their tour of the museum, curse the American imperialists for committing these crimes against them, and vow to take their revenge. An expression of solidarity. Unity through hatred, but unity nonetheless.

PART SIX

VICTORY DAY

TWENTY-FOUR

IT'S A HOLIDAY, so no school. Victory Day is celebrated each year on July 27, the day the armistice that ended the Korean War was signed. The day the DPRK "won" the war.

The national imperative to commemorate this date surfaces even in consumer culture. The brand of cigarettes smoked by Kim Jong Un is 7.27. They come in luxurious cream-colored packaging, gold letters bearing the brand name embossed above a gray engraving of a soldier wielding the victory flag. Priced at seven dollars, they are the most expensive cigarettes for sale in the country, outpricing even imported foreign brands.

The day starts with a visit to the zoo, which Alexandre and I requested because we've never been. And Alek hasn't been since the renovation. Like virtually every amusement avenue in Pyongyang, it was recently refurbished at great expense. In fact, the opening was just last weekend, according to the new edition of *The Pyongyang Times*.

Hwa drives us through a thick swarm around the huge tiger mouth forming the main entrance. It's only 9 a.m., but already there's quite a crowd. We step out into this panoply of Pyongyangites representing all walks of life—families and soldiers and students and elites with young children, all decked out in their Victory Day finest, pressed shirts and colorful galoshes following the morning's light showers.

During the Kim Jong Il years, the Pyongyang Zoo enjoyed a rather dismal reputation among foreign residents. Tales abounded of half-starved beasts howling in miniscule cages. Rumor had it that they were nourished with the flesh of executed political prisoners. Conditions have improved enormously since then, though that's not saying much; it's still a zoo. In a country whose circus still makes use of dancing bears, an animal rights discourse is decidedly absent. The concept alone would sound comical to most North Koreans. Man is the master of the universe—not bear.

Inside, children shriek with delight as they throw chips and crackers into the cages. Signs indicate not only breed but through which Kim the animal was gifted—whether directly or indirectly, via some other dubious luminary of Second and Third World politics. An elephant from Ho Chi Minh, presented to Great Leader Kim Il Sung in Juche 48 (1959). A Cuban crocodile presented to the Dear Leader Kim Jong Il by the Cuban Embassy in Juche 69 (1980). A lion from Robert Mugabe...

There is a separate house for dogs and cats. Household pets are uncommon in Pyongyang, so according to local logic, such creatures should naturally be showcased in the zoo. A trio of gray mutts stand at abrupt attention at the end of a steel cage, separating us by a waist-size concrete partition. "Go ahead, the one in the middle hasn't had one yet," a young mother instructs her toddler, who gleefully tosses in a cracker and then watches the dogs fight over the morsel before popping one into her own mouth. When another cracker lands on the concrete partition, just on the other side of the fence, Hwa approaches and nudges it with the end of his umbrella till it lands within dog reach.

There's a long, unmoving line waiting to get inside the penguin house. Apparently, as foreigners, we're allowed to jump it, as we're immediately ushered in. Inside, we join a group of college-aged elites for whom a private viewing has been arranged. They stand around casually chatting and snapping photos and videos of the penguins, who swim back and forth in the aquarium against a painted desert island backdrop.

Another popular attraction is the talking parrots. Min elbows her way through the crowd of children to record the creatures, which have been trained to croak out 안녕! ("Hi!") when you toss them a cracker. Elsewhere, a mobile photo studio offers laminated photos of your tots seated on a live pony. Sample photos show entire families weighing down the poor beast's back.

In a windowed enclosure, two vultures groom each other's elongated necks. "They're fellating each other!" Min exclaims. I grimace, suspecting a misused verb, but decide to leave it. Perhaps they *are* fellating each other. What do I know about vultures?

"Oh look—he has scratches!" Min squeals in childish delight. "It looks like he has a skin condition."

"Maybe it's disease," I suggest.

"No." Min shakes her head and points at the other vulture. "It's definitely this big guy."

Out in the parking lot, several "grasshoppers"—the poorest women of grand-motherly age who dodge the authorities from place to place illegally selling all sorts of goods out of their knapsacks—squat, briskly exchanging candy and wrapped ice creams for won and hard currency. We hover near the Kim Il Sung monument as we wait for Min to return from a bathroom break. Standing around our van, I notice some security types—young and tall with attractive, well-fed features, in pristine navy blue suits and trendy South Korean haircuts, gaze shielded behind Ray-Bans. Suddenly, like an owl nabbing its prey, one of these guys swoops in on an old lady vendor and drags her off violently. I try to follow their path discreetly, but they disappear behind a row of buses in the rear of the parking lot. Wherever she's been taken, it's not going to end well for her.

★

Speeding through Pyongyang, a feeling of lightness overtakes me. It's cloudy this afternoon, but the trees are still in bloom, the eerie caterwauling of a folk song blares through the radio speakers, and the darkness within has temporarily melted away; I guess I've been struck with the Victory Day spirit. Outside, the streets are filled with young people. Everyone looks so beautiful, the boys in suits, girls decked out in multicolored flowing *joseon-ot*. It's a national holiday, and they're on their way to a mass dance. We're going to join them. But first, we'll stop in for a quick coffee at the Changgwangsan Hotel, across from the conical Pyongyang Ice Rink.

I hum along to the chorus of the Moranbong Band's "Let's Go to Mount Paekdu!" These catchy tunes, they're everywhere—the car radio, sure, but also in every restaurant and shop you go into. The music singes itself into your brain. After a few days, you start to hear it even when it's not playing. The will of the peo-ple, the single-minded unity, to be discovered in these sweet melodies, the never-ending soundtrack of North Korea. Decode the harmonies to discover the truth.

Perhaps it is far too easy, an overassumption, to say that *everyone* here is living a lie. It is more like no one is lying—it's just that nobody is quite telling the truth, either.

Pulling into the roundabout hotel entrance, we see a North Korean girl in university attire standing next to a doe-faced guy with blond hair and blue eyes. They turn toward our approaching van. He gives us an intense stare. "Who the hell is that?"

"*Putain.*" Alexandre curses and emits an ominous sigh. "I know that guy. And he's not supposed to be here."

The Changgwangsan's entrance is crowded with young people going in and out to use the lobby bathrooms. The mass dance is to be held at 3 p.m. across the street in front of the Pyongyang Indoor Stadium. I've never been inside, but according to a local guidebook, it was completed in Juche 62 (1973) and is the largest indoor stadium in the country. It is here where Dennis Rodman played basketball in front of Kim Jong Un.

"Actually," says Alexandre under his breath, "I know both of them. The girl, too."

He climbs out of the van, Alex and me close behind. The Korean girl in the Kim Il Sung University uniform is speaking in Parisian-accented French to the young man. She's one of the Koreans who came to Alexandre's university as part of the exchange. When she sees Alexandre approaching, her face lights up. "Alexandre! Mon frère!"

Alexandre bows and embraces her. Myong Hwa looks after all the French students studying at Kim Il Sung University; at the moment, there is a grand total of one, and he is standing before us. Patrice and Alexandre greet each other stiffly. Last time Alexandre was in Pyongyang, he and Myong Hwa forged a special bond. She even bent the rules and helped clandestinely arrange for him to have dinner one night with a businessman he had met at a North Korean restaurant in Dubai.

Malheureusement, now she really has to go. She was just bidding adieu to Patrice when we drove up.

"Shall we have a beer?" Patrice asks after waving her off.

"I don't drink," says Alexandre. "Not when I'm here, I mean. But I'll have a tea or something."

"Bon. On y va."

The rest of us trail behind them into the Changgwangsan lobby, where we're greeted with a large oil painting of Kim Il Sung and Kim Jong Il grinning on top of Mount Paekdu. We make a sharp right and turn into the ground-floor restaurant. Though much of the hotel has fallen into modest disrepair and is now mainly used by budget-conscious Chinese businessmen, the restaurant is still a favorite among well-heeled residents of the central district.

"I've been doing nothing *but* drinking," Patrice spits out in rapid-fire French, pleased to be speaking to a compatriot for the first time in four months. "It's so fucking boring here, there's nothing to do but drink drink drink. It takes me four beers just to get into bed at night—otherwise I can't sleep! And you know something funny?" He leans in. A strange expression—glassy-eyed paranoia. "I never drank before I came here."

Patrice shoots us a quick smile, his eyes darting back and forth. His teeth have a weird gray gauze to them, almost as though they are sheathed in some transparent substance. An artificial glaze. Alek and I will later debate whether it's due to all the drinking or else some kind of newly acquired mineral deficiency. For now, Alek has already retreated to another table with Min and Roe.

"Your friend here, he understands French?" I do but decide to play dumb. Patrice turns and addresses me—in Korean, of all languages—even though I'm as blond as he is and Alexandre has already mentioned I'm American. Abruptly, he rises and makes his way to the bar to order another beer.

"Will you come back?" Alexandre calls after him, confused and exasperated.

"Oui oui."

"Travis," Alexandre says, now turning to me, "I'm very sorry for this. But could you please go over there and sit with Alek? I promise I will tell you everything later."

★

Anyway, the festivities are about to begin, so Alek and I venture across the street to the square fronting the Pyongyang Indoor Stadium. Mass dances, featuring hundreds of young people, typically university students, are held in cities throughout the country on virtually every national holiday. For men, the required uniform is black slacks, smart black dress shoes, a white collared shirt—can be long- or short-sleeved—and red necktie. For women, *joseon-ot,* color optional; today, a flourishing of pink and lavender. Expressions on the students' faces range from blank to awkward to just plain bored, revealing the inevitable lack of enthusiasm for these typically drafted activities, whether they be military parades, mass dances, or manual labor—participation is mandatory when your number is called, lest you pay to get out of it or otherwise find someone to take your place.

At the preordained time, the dancers congregate in orderly lines in the parking lot. When the announcement is made via the huge speakers erected on either side of the entrance to the building, the students move forward. With uniformed marshals guiding them, they are led into circular formations. The music begins, and they commence a stiff shuffle. Each song features a specific choreographed combination. Nothing very challenging: ballroom-lite. A couple of steps toward your partner, swing your arms back and forth, twirl around once arm in arm, detach, three steps back, raise arms to the heavens, clap, repeat. Next: a variation on the foxtrot, with as little bodily contact as possible. One defector I met in South Korea who had herself once been drafted to participate in a mass dance told me that there wasn't any preparation; there are some who just appear to *know* the steps, others follow. Keep one eye on the girl in front of you, another eye to your right to copy what the guy beside you is doing. As the circles rotate at given moments, your dance partner will change throughout the afternoon's repertoire. The circles are imperfectly gender-balanced; where they are, boys dance with boys, the girls with girls. It's all fairly mechanical, and most of the couples strive to avoid making eye contact. And it all takes place beneath the watchful eyes of the Kims, who smile down upon the crowd from their enormous official portraits posted above the stadium's main entrance.

Guards block off the square from the street. Beyond the barricade, a few local onlookers stand and watch. But mostly, the scene seems to be set up for foreign tourists, who are free to mill about, film and take photos, even join in, which a few do, to the amusement and embarrassment of most of the participants, who are forced to integrate their clumsy improvised steps into the circles.

After a few tunes that sound hopelessly dated to the whimsical 1940s, the energy lifts as the opening bars to "Dash Towards the Future" resound. A sudden enthusiasm infects the dancers, as they launch into their routine: three steps forward march, three steps backward march, three to the right with arms raised in flight, clap, spin to the left with hands on hips, then do it all over again.

Forty-five minutes into it, the mass dance comes to an abrupt, fanfare-less end. The dancers leave their orderly circles to form orderly lines. A command is shouted into the microphone, and off they march into the parking lot. Some get into waiting buses. Most, however, merge into the pedestrian traffic, off to home or perhaps a next assignment.

In the parking lot, Patrice and Alexandre wait next to our van. This is Patrice's last day in Pyongyang, it turns out, so this brief hello was also a good-bye.

"It was nice to meet you," says Patrice, turning to me and Alek, finally drunk enough to speak English. "Have a great time here. The Korean people are the best." He flashes an insincere smile. "Really."

★

Later that night, Alexandre tells me all about Patrice on my balcony. The two of them, it turns out, were planning on coming here together at one point. They had both applied to Kim Il Sung University through their North Korean contact in Paris—the same one who had arranged Alexandre's earlier trip. Apparently, Patrice had been accepted, while Alexandre hadn't.

Patrice was himself an elite, albeit of the French variety. The nephew of a former prime minister, son of a Hong Kong–based billionaire. When they met in Paris to discuss their shared ambition of studying in Pyongyang, Patrice had been very blunt about his real intentions. When one has money and connections, sanctions are but a minor inconvenience that can readily be sidelined when not overlooked entirely. In Pyongyang, there were business opportunities galore. Didn't Alexandre agree?

Well, no, not really. His interests in North Korea were purely academic; he really did want to learn the language, study the culture, find out as much about this country as he could; for his sociology degree, he had written his undergraduate thesis on the DPRK. But Alexandre also realized that the North Koreans would bend over backward at the mere whiff of a potential investment from someone of Patrice's ilk. Alexandre didn't have that kind of capital behind him. His only way in, then, would be to try to become as friendly as possible with Patrice in the hope that he could at least attach himself temporarily.

What kind of business, Alexandre didn't know. Patrice's family had their hands in all kinds of ventures throughout East Asia: hotels, wine, cosmetics. Probably ventures of a less licit nature as well. Alexandre could only speculate.

When Patrice suddenly stopped replying to his emails, Alexandre knew he'd been dropped. "He probably figured, 'Who cares? I'm going, he's not.' He was definitely surprised to see me there today." Alexandre sniffs. "Of course, he didn't *need* me for anything. I would just be in his way. So he must have told the Koreans that it'd be best if he came alone."

What's more, with Patrice's profile, it would be essential that *no one* knew he was in North Korea.

"My uncle doesn't even know I'm here right now," Patrice told Alexandre that afternoon as he drained his third beer.

Bullshit, thought Alexandre. "Everyone knows his uncle is in Hong Kong doing business all over Asia. There's no way Patrice just came here as an independent agent, to learn a language he had no interest in. He could have gone to South Korea easily if he wanted to study."

"These Koreans are all so stupid," Patrice had ranted under his breath between sips. "It's unbelievable how brainwashed these people are. Unable to fathom the simplest concepts in business! You have to explain *everything* to them—not that I'm here to do business, of course... But, you know, while I'm here, I can try to be of some use. A gesture of *politesse*... But you have to understand, Alex, there are some things I just cannot tell you. I know things. Actually, I know *everything*. I was even at the last Workers' Party Congress. They invited me there. And I saw *him*. The Marshal. The Man. Up close. Do you know what that means? They trust me, these idiots. They need me. Imagine. I am one of the only foreigners in the world to have *shaken hands* with ..."

His voice trailed off, out of fear of saying Number Three's name aloud in a crowded restaurant.

"I know everything," Patrice said, leaning in. "I even know things about you, Alex. Things they have told me."

"What do you know?" Alexandre asked. "Who did you speak to?"

"I cannot say. I have many contacts here. I know *many* secrets."

Patrice's eyes darted around the restaurant paranoiacally as his voice dropped even lower.

"They know *everything* we do. Even when we masturbate. You have to be careful what you say here, who you say it to. You might make some minor complaint, off the cuff, only to have it repeated to you days later by a complete stranger. They talk to each other, you know. They have networks. They are all crazy. And they know *everything*."

"Are you okay, Patrice? You seem a bit ... nervous."

"No! I'm fine. Why?"

"You keep looking over your shoulder."

"Nonono. I'm not nervous! I'm completely fine. Why do you ask such things? Waitress! Another beer. And one for my friend."

"I don't want a beer. I'm not drinking."

"Then I'll drink it for you."

TWENTY-FIVE

IF KIM JONG Il tried to make the most of his artistic pretensions in formulating a Juche-oriented literature and cinema, today the most seductive instrument of the state propaganda machinery is music. You hear it in every shop, every restaurant, every taxi you climb into. The sound is quaint, old-fashioned, with its soaring melodies and lyrics of ideological affirmation, but it sinks in quickly. After a few days, you're humming along, every tune recognizable. In those rare moments of silence, I often find myself missing it.

Around Alek, I've started jokingly referring to this genre as *Norkore,* the North's very own version of K-pop. And it is the only acceptable, state-sanctioned style. What it is, really, is a stylistic hodgepodge of virtually every known mode of the anthemic: Disney and Broadway musical ballads, gospel uplift, Chinese synth pop, Russian disco, patriotic folk—and with maximalized sentiment etched into the overall with operatic, usually soprano, vocals. Norkore's borrowing from all of these genres does nothing to diminish its *Volkish* appeal to mass sentiment; if anything, its defiant hijackings serve as righteous affirmation of survival, of *victory,* in a world where, let's face it, everyone hates them. It is so catchy, so sticky sweet, that there's something almost sinister about it.

The hottest Norkore act is the all-female Moranbong Band. It's really the DPRK's house band, each of its members handpicked by Kim Jong Un for not just her musical talent but also her attractive features. The twenty-member band performs in matching nursing uniforms with—gasp—short skirts and high heels, a look that must have shocked the audience when it held its first performance on July 6, 2012. It was, after all, only a few years before that Kim Jong Il had decreed that the ban on women wearing trousers was to be lifted; skirts ending above the knee were something new and salacious indeed.

Moranbong's brand of pop wouldn't be out of place aside many of the entries at the Eurovision Song Contest. Lyrics extoll the greatness of the country, the military, but also the Marshal. His father, Jong Il, also had his own house act, the Pochonbo Band. One's lifelong musical taste is often forged early in life, and Kim Jong Il's was reminiscent of the oompah-pah songs of the Soviet era that formed the background soundtrack of his childhood and adolescence. By 2012, Pochonbo's Russian disco-inspired tunes sounded embarrassingly old-fashioned. The masses were bored. Kim Jong Un had to grapple with any number of inherited unpleasantries—among them, the undeniable fact that Western and South Korean pop music had begun to flood in through the underground markets. There was a desperate need to upgrade the country's state sound, to discard all the accordions and Soviet-esque stompery to appeal to the youngest generation, of which Kim was a part. After all, he needed them on his side. Fittingly enough, the Moranbong Band's first public performance was for an audience of university students in Pyongyang.

We know from Dennis Rodman that the Marshal's two favorite songs are the themes from *Rocky* and *Dallas*—tunes that undoubtedly implanted themselves in the young Jong Un's brain during his own adolescence, growing up in Switzerland—which were played over and over again by an orchestra on the night of their banquet together upon the basketball player's first visit to Pyongyang. In addition to this stylistic influence, the Moranbong Band has layered electronic beats, dance breaks, and soulful vocal acrobatics that channel Whitney and Mariah. Concerts are replete with synchronized dance moves, laser light shows, and digital video backdrops showing footage of missiles blasting off into the sky, ecstatic marching soldiers, and the biggest rock star of all, the Marshal himself, swarmed with hysterical citizen-fans.

The oversimplified sloganeering and sentimentalism that so often fall flat in cinema and literature and the propaganda banners that fill the landscape prove memorable and persuasive when encased in the gold of pop overdrive. "Dash Towards the Future," that song that elicited shouts of "Hooray!" at the mass dance, is the anthem of youth, with its calls to reunify the country by staying up all night studying. A celebration of a new country in a new era—the great era of the Workers' Party—a time when the fatherland should be celebrated and extolled for all its wonderful achievements and inventions that have been made famous all over the world. A time that includes, above all, you, the youth of today. Victory Day, every day.

Then there's the driving rhythms of "Let's Go to Mount Paekdu!" The beat is infectious enough that one could easily lose oneself in it on the dance floor—if such a dance floor actually existed anywhere in the country. But you can goose-step to it! Soldiers sing it aloud as they march in regimen.

At its climax, the melody is transposed to a higher octave, soaring the spirit even higher. Over the chorus, the soulful improvised wails of a soprano hit those Mariah Carey highs, her heart swelling uncontrollably with love of this supreme signifier of the motherland, the sacred mountain of the Korean people. Mount Paekdu, where Tangun, the mythical founder of Korea, emerged. Mount Paekdu, where Kim Il Sung held fort while bravely fighting off the Japanese. Mount Paekdu, where Kim Jong Il is said to have been born to continue his father's fight. It is the place "where miracles and fortune are called upon this land," as the lyrics go.

Don't make the mistake of thinking it's all just frivolous fun for these bonging Moran babes. There is a serious, sentimental side to the Norkore sonaesthetic they espouse, one that suits more contemplative inquiries into the heart of what it means to be Korean. The Norkore canon wouldn't be complete without this ongoing series of slow, moving ballads that one can hardly goose-step to but that nevertheless serve as sentimental wellsprings for delving into the spirit of the day. With titles like "Confession," "Burning Wish," and "Voice of My Heart," a non-Korean speaker might be fooled into thinking these are mere conventional love songs. While they may not sound so unlike the songs you first slow-danced to in your junior high school gym, these love songs differ in that they are nearly all addressed to one particular human subject.

In "World of Compassion," soloist Ryu Jin Ah meditates on just what it could be that draws so many people—the entire world, really—to Comrade Kim Jong Un. Could it be his warmth? His affectionate style? "How can it be I feel him so close?" she sings. "How can it be I feel the heat / of his heart burning with love?" Just like the crowds that follow him everywhere, smiling and weeping tears of joy, "blindly I was also drawn to him / by his mind flaming with compassion."

After a lilting string solo, all seven vocalists rise in a chorus:

> *His compassion worth more than tons of gold*
> *Envied by the whole world*
> *Even at the end of the sky*
> *A world of endless compassion.*

His love for us, the Korean people, who "all share the same bloodline in our veins," Ryu passionately intones, kneeling forward to push the racial affirmation out of her lungs. These songs, like nearly all solos, tend to be sung with so much passion, it sometimes sounds as though the singer is about to pass out for want of oxygen.

There's the lilting ballad "Burning Wish," in which the Marshal is addressed directly. Marshal, soloist Kim Yu Kyong intones in her endearing soprano, we know you are about to embark upon a long journey late at night—as you must do every night, in your selfless devotion to the country—but just to let you know, we are all thinking of you. The drums, mic'd up for maximum reverb, kick in, as the chorus rises to its apotheosis: Marshal, we only have one burning wish: that you are in good health. Our happiness, our fate all depend on you, dear Marshal.

Flaming heart. Burning wish. Lyrically, it's all so hot, and sonically, the fire it most evokes is St. Elmo's. Dwelling on it for long is likely to give you a burning sensation in one part of the anatomy that is never mentioned in any of these songs. The DPRK's brand of socialism has a painfully limited vocabulary, but what it lacks in words, it makes up for in pure melodious sentiment.

Of course it is overblown—as is all state propaganda. Yet music is the Dionysian form where outpourings of over-the-top unbridled passions of all sorts don't seem out of place; propaganda passes best in this format. The Moranbong Band also does its own version of old DPRK classics, showing how the flashy sounds of the moment build on this illustrious canon. The slow, sentimental numbers clearly have their roots in songs like 1961's "We Have Nothing to Envy in This World," one of the first songs children are taught in school, while the upbeat pop tracks belong to a lineage that includes "Whistle" from the late 1980s, with its instrumental medley slyly hijacked from ABBA's "Gimme! Gimme! Gimme! (A Man after Midnight)" (and which was subsequently used for Madonna's 2005 single "Hung Up"—hey, a global pop canon!).

I admit that "Norkore" sounds like a rather heavy-handed riff on "hardcore," a slightly absurd commentary on both the intensity of the state-sanctioned sound's content and the implicit violence contained therein. But the "Kore," besides being short for "Korean," can also be thought of as the *core* of overbaked emotion, of sentimentality, that drenches each of these songs. Like Japanoise and other regional subgenres of extreme sonic expression, Norkore is not likely to gain the mass international following of K-pop—though in design, it's certainly catchy enough to appeal to the masses.

TWENTY-SIX

ENTERTAINMENT FOR THE masses—*by* the masses.

Mass expression has always been a canonical form of entertainment in the DPRK. Up until 2013, the annual event that attracted the most visitors to the country was the Arirang Festival, also known as the Mass Games. "Arirang" is a folk story that is used as an allegory of Korea's division, in which a young couple is torn apart by the wiles of an evil landlord. The story went on to become a popular song—which was also popular in South Korea at one point—but has become something of an unofficial national anthem in the North.

Featuring more than one hundred thousand performers—among them acrobats, athletes, singers, dancers, brass bands, banner- and flag-wielding marshals, oh my—the Arirang Festival enacted the revolutionary history of the country in ninety minutes on über-monumental scale, the likes of which can't be seen anywhere else. Or, to be precise, would be impossible to reproduce elsewhere. (As I heard one overexcited tourist exclaim: "This could never happen in a capitalist country. We're just not *organized* enough.") I attended one of the final iterations of Arirang in 2012 on my second trip to the DPRK. Word at the time was that a whole new spectacle was being planned for the future, but it has yet to materialize. The Mass Games, it seems, are a relic of the Kim Jong Il era.

The Arirang Festival had originally been "invented" by Kim Jong Il in 1972 as part of his father's birthday succession—though that's yet another dubious claim, as mass gymnastics demonstrations had also been a mainstay throughout the Soviet realm and, before that, were a showpiece of a number of nationalist movements in Europe in the nineteenth century. Originality aside, Kim and his cinematic staff spectacularized the event, transforming it into yet another achievement of succession art, along with many of the monuments making up contemporary Pyongyang.

The scene outside the Rungrado Stadium that night was reminiscent of the organizational nature of most activity in the DPRK; when people aren't following instructions, they're often standing around or squatting, waiting to be told what to do. Families stood in clusters around a fountain, watching it spit water under the illumination of a revolving rainbow of colored lights. Several regiments of soldiers stood in line, waiting for their orders to march into the stadium and take their seats in the Korean-only section of the stadium. Besides soldiers, the most ubiquitous group was the red-scarved members of the Children's Union, who were more amenable to smiling and waving at the foreign tourists sequestered at the rear of the parking lot as our guides counted heads and issued tickets. Finally, the spectacle of the costumed performers themselves marching orderly toward the rear of the stadium.

The enormity of what we were about to witness became evident the moment we entered the stadium to take our seats, with thousands of flag-bearing marshals lined up on the stadium floor. Behind them stood another several thousand young girls in gymnast attire. Twenty thousand schoolchildren flipped colored cards in perfect synchronicity to form the world's largest LED screen. A start cue was issued somehow, somewhere; the children shouted out "Hey!"; the marshals on the ground stepped forward and then swooped back, as thousands of young women in *joseon-ot* came surging forth. Lights dimmed and a festive symphony swelled—as did the adrenaline of the crowd.

The narrative begins in 1905, a relatively idyllic time in the nation's history, only to be soured five years later when the country comes under occupation by Japan. Rather than dwelling on the ruthless nature of the Japanese imperialists— there is plenty of that in DPRK cinema and literature—there is an emphasis on the inherent goodness and purity of the Korean people here. A female vocalist sings "Arirang"; painted mountain scenes unfold across the live LED screen. A traditional fan dance is performed by rows of thousands of women on the stadium floor below. Suddenly, a red sunrise appears, signaling the birth of Kim Il Sung. The audience breaks into applause. The history of the nation begins.

Two pistols, inherited by the country's Eternal President upon Kim Hyong Jik's death in 1926, according to the official history, flash their way across the screen as dancers in military garb march below in clockwork synchronicity. The guns, it is said, were used by the family patriarch in the anti-Japanese revolutionary struggle. Kim Jong Il would inherit the same two pistols from his father, as, presumably, would Kim Jong Un, legitimizing—through symbolism—the filial succession.

And then, there are the kids. The ones we cannot see, of course, who form the background screen on the opposite side of the stadium. But then a circus instrumental plays, and thousands come running across the field, landing in perfect lines and embarking upon a routine of synchronized cuteness, much to the delight of the squealing audience. "Children are the kings of our nation," Kim Il Sung was fond of saying. But look at them out there, smiling and, well, just *perfect*. How do they do it? The answer is simple: In the DPRK, they aren't raised by their parents. They're raised by the state.

Most of the tourists who watched the Arirang Festival could little understand the symbolism. But that's fine as well. What's unmissable, in such extravaganzas, is the dynamic symbiosis that emerges in the energy field formed between the performers and the audience: the real intended audience, of course, is the Korean people—who simultaneously serve as the performers. In the course of the ritual, any division between us and them, participant and audience member, is dissolved in the experiential spectacle of mass being.

★

Nobody knows for sure why the Mass Games came to an end. Some speculate that the new regime recognized how deeply unpopular they were among the participants, particularly the parents of the schoolchildren drafted to form that LED screen. The yearlong preparations for the performances were famously grueling and tortuous, with children pulled out of school for months at a time to learn how to flip those pages perfectly. Some say that the kids weren't even allowed to use the bathroom for hours during rehearsals, flipping pages over and over, learning to subordinate their thoughts, actions, and bladder to the collective will.

TWENTY-SEVEN

THE ESTABLISHMENT OF schoolchildren's palaces throughout the country
is a testament to not only North Koreans' love of children and devotion to their
care but to their willingness to foster talent for propagandistic purposes from an
early age. It is here, in afterschool extracurricular lessons, where the country's
most talented tots may nurture their natural abilities from early on in life.

After the mass dance, we ride across town to the Schoolchildren's Palace of
Manyongdae, the district where Kim Il Sung was born. This is the most prestigious of these training grounds. Among other distinguished alumni, most
members of the Moranbong Band trained at Manyongdae. A visit to the Schoolchildren's Palace is one of those classic well-choreographed DPRK tourism experiences. Since it was renovated in 2015 under Kim Jong Un's instructions, one
of the star attractions now is the architecture and remodeled interior, which at
times threatens to outshine the children. The scale of the building is truly palatial, a massive glass-and-concrete semicircle that is meant to evoke the embrace
of the Supreme Leaders Kim Il Sung and Kim Jong Il, whose official state portraits occupy the front and center of that circle, just above the main entrance
doors. Above them, a glass-encased flying saucer–esque structure must offer
great views of surrounding Kwangbok Street. Before the entrance, we pass by
one of Mansudae Art Studio's kitschier copper creations, two winged horses,
the Chollima beast, with a wagonful of overjoyed children pulling the reins: the
nation's kings have arrived.

Once we get inside, the eye-grabbing fun begins. After passing by the bright,
illuminated urn-shaped wall relief where a handwritten blessing by Kim Il Sung
has been etched in gold lettering, we glide through the corridors, which, from
floor to ceiling, have been doused in color according to the themes of the various

sports and art forms pursued here. At certain points, the ceiling opens up to reveal all eight floors, whence multihued chandeliers descend.

A Young Pioneer–scarved girl leads us through a series of ornate halls. The Hall of Science showcases a huge floor relief of the Korean peninsula, behind which stands the replica of a satellite missile branded with the DPRK flag. The Hall of Arts features a massive wall painting of a musical staff rendered in rainbow lines extending in a bright blue sky, beneath which sits a purple stage that upholds a grand piano. The hallways are dotted with framed color photographs documenting visits by Kims Il Sung, Jong Il, and Jong Un, surrounded by admiring youngsters.

Next, we're taken through a series of classrooms where we get to witness the prodigies in action. In a rehearsal room with gleaming hardwood floors, a prima donna conducts a class of young female dancers in black dress and pink bonnets. One class is devoted to the gayageum, perhaps the most typical Korean instrument, a series of thick ropelike strings erected by pegs across a wooden board, requiring a muscular expenditure of force, pressed fingers on one hand, a firm pluck with the other. In another, a junior accordion orchestra delivers an instrumental rendition of "We Have Nothing to Envy in This World." Other classes are devoted to the visual arts. Children as young as five practice calligraphic strokes on paper, dipping their horsehair brushes into inky wells beneath the approving smiles of the leaders' portraits; the more advanced students, seated on the other side of the classroom, are already rendering full propaganda banners in elegant running script. Another room has children as young as five working on elaborate floral needlepoint textiles.

The visit culminates in a performance. In the auditorium, we are seated in front of a row of teenagers in matching uniform, the girls in tasteful blue-and-white *joseon-ot,* the boys in white short-sleeve dress shirts and navy slacks. "Zainichi Koreans," Alek whispers.

★

"Zainichi" is a Japanese word meant to designate temporary residents of that country. But Zainichi Koreans are actually permanent residents of Japan; their families having been there for generations. Most trace their family background to the colonial period, when Koreans immigrated to Japan for work or study opportunities and then remained after Korea's liberation and subsequent division. A formidable ethnic minority, often discriminated against. And like many ethnic minorities the world over, they formed their own community within the larger society, in part, at least, as a result of this stigmatization.

In postwar Japan, two Zainichi Korean organizations emerged to protect and promote the interests of the minority. Mindan was loyal to South Korea. But far more popular, at least in the beginning, was the pro-Pyongyang Chongryon association. Chongryon was one of the main forces behind the voluntary repatriations of ethnic Koreans from Japan to the DPRK begun in 1959. Thanks to deeply ingrained racism, xenophobia, and political paranoia, it didn't take much prodding to get support for this exodus from the Japanese government, which was eager to get rid of as many Koreans as possible. Until the spring of 1960, North Korea managed to settle the new arrivals successfully, at a rate of around one thousand per week. These earliest arrivees seem to have been the luckiest, with many of them rewarded with apartments in Pyongyang, in what was considered a propaganda coup for the DPRK government. Early letters sent back to relatives in Japan often contained positive words about their new living conditions.

But then, as time wore on and more and more settlers arrived to their new-old homeland, those letters began to dry up. When letters did make it back to Japan, they were often disturbing in content, consisting largely of words of flattery for Kim Il Sung and platitudes about the glories of life under socialism, ending with requests at the end for the family to send basic necessities that even the poorest of the poor had easy access to in Japan, which seemed to contradict all those preceding statements about their bounteous new life. Cryptic references to hard work and implications of resettlement in remote, far-flung rural locations were intended as warnings to family members remaining in Japan that they might wish to reconsider their intention to make the same journey; others would conceal more bluntly discouraging warnings in miniscule script behind the postage stamp.

From some of these repatriates who managed to subsequently escape North Korea during the famine of the 1990s, we now have a better idea of what happened to many of them. What at first was a propaganda coup eventually became a burden, a strain on the DPRK's limited resources, as the settlers arrived in ever-increasing numbers. Most of them could see immediately the wide gap between what they had been promised and the reality of life in their new homeland. Waiting for them at the harbor of Chongjin on the east coast, where they would ultimately land, a cheerless mass of locals would be organized to greet them with chants, song, and bouquets. The Zainichi Koreans on those boats would later describe how a wave of disappointment descended upon them the minute they saw the shabby clothing and sunburnt faces, the gray, ugly buildings forming the cityscape, and, once they were off the boat, the empty shelves in the shops.

At first, some of the Zainichi Korean families managed to thrive in the North. Those with family members still in Japan could arrange to receive regular shipments of money and goods that they could barter, sell, or enjoy for themselves, much to the envy of ordinary Koreans, who would often turn against them for these reasons. And many of them fell victim to more official forms of discrimination because, having lived their earlier lives in enemy territory, they were considered politically suspect. It is not known how many eventually ended up in the gulag, but at least one defector, Kang Chol Hwan, himself a Zainichi Korean who was interned with his family at the Yodok concentration camp, maintains that a great number of them suffered similar political persecution.

After South Korea normalized relations with Japan in 1965, the repatriation program tapered off, though it would continue on a smaller scale until 1984. These days, there are no new settlers, but the Chongryon association is still going strong, maintaining a network of schools in Japan where Zainichi Koreans grow up learning of the great exploits of Kim Il Sung and Kim Jong Il. Each summer, teenage Zainichi Koreans are sent by their families to Pyongyang, where they enjoy a program of tourism and cultural and educational activities.

The lights dim. A small girl, about six years old, smile plastered across her face, makes her way to the microphone. She welcomes the audience, which seems to be composed mostly of parents in addition to the foreign tour groups, in the quivering style of overbearing excitement famously employed by DPRK nightly newscaster Ri Chun Hee, a style that is probably rooted in the melodramatic Japanese Shinpa theater that was popular during the colonial period, something that most Koreans today are likely unaware of. She gracefully floats offstage, the red curtains part, music swells from the orchestra pit, and the spectacle is launched, missile-like, at full force.

The performance is structured as a variety show, featuring one magisterial act after another. Many are rooted in ancient Korean art forms, with a good dose of

DPRK-style propaganda added to give it all a "contemporary" flavor. A group of girls perform the *buchaechum,* an elaborate traditional fan dance. A chubby five-year-old boy belts out a solo in a piercing alto that could wake Ethel Merman from her death slumber. Another boy executes an impressive routine of clown acrobatics. A solo dancer places a porcelain urn upon her head and spins wildly across the stage, never once losing her balance or breaking the wide smile plastered across her face. A chorus of eight teenage girls sing a melody accompanied by a boy accordion player. Another group of accordionists battle each other at top speed; the accordion is a favored instrument, and some musicians outside the country claim that the DPRK manufactures the finest specimen.

In the penultimate performance, before a widescreen shot of the tri-phallic Party Monument, a full adolescent orchestra comprising both Western and traditional Korean instruments, conducted by a thirteen-year-old boy in a Young Pioneer scarf, plays the backing soundtrack as a young girl makes her way toward the lip of the stage, reciting a poem about the glories of the motherland. She is then joined by two lookalikes, adorned in the same outfit, and the trio launch into a harmonized paean to the wonders of the Workers' Party. A preadolescent girl swathed in *joseon-ot* performs a dizzying solo on a set of eight Korean leather barrel drums. She is joined by an entire stage of petite drummer boys and girls, each strapped to a single drum of varying size and shape, who join in on the fast, complex rhythm; together, they operate as a single machine, bowing to wild applause when the final beat is hit.

Everything executed with pitch-perfect precision. Every move graceful, every note hit, no matter how high. The curtains rise and fall at the precise moment. Even when motion does not take center stage, when it is a chorus of children singing a song of praise for their leader, all exhale and sway in effortless synchronicity, as though attached to the same battery. There is something chilling about it—though such reflections only come later, after the final bows have been taken.

Making our way to the van, we pass by the Zainichi kids having a group photo taken in front of the palace. Sitting behind us in the darkened auditorium and adorned in this typical clothing, they could nearly pass as ordinary North

Korean teenagers. Seeing them in broad daylight now is a disruption to the senses. "Look how tall they are," I whisper to Alek. And it's true—they tower over the North Korean adults surrounding them. Their hair is naturally shiny and of the deepest black, their complexion clear, their skin white in stark contrast to the sunburnt faces of most North Korean men, pockmarks denoting childhood malnutrition noticeably absent. In a word, they look *healthy*. Seeing them standing there, cheerfully hugging one another with smiles unforced, it becomes shockingly apparent that they come from a very different world. I'm jolted when I realize how normalized the stunted appearance of North Koreans has become by now. Three weeks in, and it's starting to feel a little like home.

TWENTY-EIGHT

To know and not to know, to be conscious of complete truthfulness while telling carefully constructed lies, to hold simultaneously two opinions which cancelled out, knowing them to be contradictory and believing in both of them, to use logic against logic, to repudiate morality while laying claim to it, to believe that democracy was impossible and that the Party was the guardian of democracy, to forget whatever it was necessary to forget, then to draw it back into memory again at the moment when it was needed, and then promptly to forget it again: and above all, to apply the same process to the process itself. That was the ultimate subtlety: consciously to induce unconsciousness, and then, once again, to become unconscious of the act of hypnosis you had just performed. Even to understand the word "doublethink" involved the use of doublethink.

—George Orwell, *1984*

OUR FINAL STOP on this busy Victory Day tour is on the outskirts of Pyongyang, in a rural area. It's newly opened, and none of us—including Min and Roe—have been here before. We know nothing about it, other than its status as a "revolutionary site," which designates any place where one of the leaders carried out activities of national importance. These sites play a pivotal role in fomenting state mythography. One such revolutionary site is Kim Il Sung's native home in Manyongdae, near the Schoolchildren's Palace. Another is Kim Jong Il's fake birthplace on Mount Paekdu.

Our van makes its way down a long, narrow drive surrounded by immaculately manicured lawns and ornate landscape architecture, every rock polished, each flowerbed formation enunciated in perfect geometrical flourish. "What the fuck is this? The wonderful land of Oz?" I whisper to Alek. He shakes his head. Alexandre has no idea, either.

We get out of the van. Soldiers everywhere, most of them manual labor units at menial tasks, putting the final perfecting touch on the accumulated sheen. The echoed commands of a battle drill can be heard in the distance. A unit marches past singing the chorus of "Let's Go to Mount Paekdu!"

"Is there a military base nearby?" I ask innocently.

"That's not…a question I would feel comfortable asking," Min warns with an awkward smile. "Don't know and don't want to know!"

Okay then.

A young female soldier and older male officer approach our vehicle. She'll be our guide, and he's there to monitor all that is said and done until we vacate the premises. It's one of those places. Sensitive.

"Comrade Min," the guide exclaims with surprise.

"Comrade Li Gyong Sim," Min responds, emitting a bolt of laughter.

Turns out they were in the same class at the University of Foreign Studies, though they hardly knew each other. Still, something about this chance meeting has them both stifling giggles.

"So I guess you don't need me to interpret," Min says to her former classmate. "You can do the tour in English yourself. Your English is probably even better than mine!"

Comrade Li shakes her head firmly in the negative, a brief sideways glance acknowledging the presence of the senior officer next to her. She launches into her introductory spiel, leaving Min no choice but to translate for us.

We are welcomed to the Gonjiri Revolutionary Site, where Kim Il Sung spent late 1950 to 1953 commanding the Korean War. Or so they would like us to believe. I raise my camera to take a photo of the artificial hillside grass cave entrance. Min raises her arm in front of my lens just as fast. "You can leave your camera in the van, Travis." She smiles. No photos here.

Inside the cave, an open-floor museum has been created. We are led through a series of installations, the highlight of which is Kim Il Sung's office, where, we are told, he held more than two hundred meetings. Fake stars glimmer from the night-blue ceiling above. The office is a theatrical stage set with desks and chairs that look like restored high-end antiques, gleaming with a fresh paint job.

"Is this the original office?" I ask. "Or a re-creation?"

"It's the original office." Comrade Li and the senior officer study my face, as though trying to gauge whether I'm buying it.

"Oh wow." I give them a wide-eyed nod.

The guide points to a bullet hole in the wall, evidence from the day "the enemy attempted to assassinate our General." Well, it looks as real as anything else here.

The path takes us through a series of military tunnels out the back, where we are shown a small classroom. "This is where the Dear Leader Kim Jong Il took his lessons while his father worked in his office." Out of the corner of my eye, I spy Roe trailing behind us, typically silent but attempting to stifle his laughter.

"This was the bedroom of the Dear Leader Kim Jong Il from June 25, 1952, to August 16, 1952." A simple affair, with a tiny child-sized bed covered in a pink-and-white-striped sheet, garish red carpeting, and a small table with a tablecloth of a clashing shade of red. Like the office, this sacred ground is roped off to prevent visitors from sullying it with footprints.

As we circle our way back toward the parking lot, we meet an arriving tour group, this one composed wholly of soldiers. They seem more interested in us than the introductory spiel their guide is presenting.

We pause between four chairs arranged in a circle in front of the cave's entrance. "This is where Kim Il Sung met with the first three hero soldiers of the Fatherland Liberation War." I study the chairs, puzzled by a sense of déjà vu. That's when it hits me. I have the same chair at home in Berlin. Who knew IKEA exported its designs to Korea in the 1950s?

★

The day ends with another sporadic appearance by Comrade Kim, eager to check on the status of his latest pet project. "I want to show you my favorite bar in Pyongyang," he tells us in the van.

The joint he takes us to is brand-new, hidden down an alleyway behind the Tower of the Juche Idea on the eastern banks of the Taedong River. On the ground floor is a shop vending the usual miscellany and a pharmacy selling a range of imported medicine, from Tylenol to antibiotics, behind a glass display case. Upstairs, the bar is rendered in exquisite oak paneling and varnished wood tables. Everything glistens and, save for the Moranbong girls on TV, you could easily be in an upmarket sports bar in Chicago or Boston. The tables are filled with *donju* and Chinese businesspeople. They stare at us with bemusement, unaccustomed to seeing Western foreigners here.

Comrade Kim orders beers and kimchi pancakes for the table. "So," he says, "I heard you went to Gonjiri today. Now you know the *true history* behind the Korean War!"

As he smiles at me, he gives me a sly wink.

Kim, as we have learned, is the son of a prominent officer. It suddenly dawns on me: of course he must know the truth. They all must know. All the prominent families here, they are the descendants of the people who fought in the war. People who were actually there, who must have passed down the stories from generation to generation. Pyongyang was bombed to near total annihilation; the entire city was destroyed. Kim Il Sung and his closest advisers, the entire Politburo, had to be evacuated to the border with China, where they remained until the war came to an end and they could safely return to Pyongyang. Gonjiri, like Kim Jong Il's birthplace on Mount Paekdu, is a total stage set.

★

"Let's talk," says Alexandre as we make our way down the hall to our rooms. These nightly chats are a means for both of us to retain our sanity as the days wear on.

Alexandre starts venting right away, in the whisper we've taken to adapting as a measure of safety whenever we're alone. "Do they really think anyone believes this shit? They are all mentally ill. They *have* to be."

From my balcony, we look out onto the lights of the city before their nightly extinguishment. I've been having my own mental travails of late, though that's not something I'm eager to share. They've manifested themselves, in the past days, in difficulty getting to sleep at night. Thankfully, I prepared for this inevitability in advance by bringing a stash of sleeping pills.

"Fucking crazy," he continues, "this whole system. A system of ass-kissing is what it is. It started with Kim Il Sung, his sick fetish for Stalin. And the next one, who exacerbated it all to get in his father's good graces. And this one now— he has no choice but to continue it and doesn't have the brains to do it any other way."

"But what about what Simon told us?" I ask.

"Simon who?"

"Businessman Simon. The Chinese guy. He implied that...*Number Three* wanted to change the system. It's the old men surrounding him, his advisers, the old guard, who won't let that happen."

"I don't buy that."

"Then...what's going on in his head? Is it that he grew up so sheltered in his Swiss chalet that he doesn't know what's real and what's not?"

"It's partly that he doesn't know," Alexandre speculates, "and partly that he doesn't care. They're afraid of him, so they have to hide certain things from him. But the reality they do show can be just as deceiving. The songs they sing for him. The constant reminders of who he is—which is who his father and grandfather were.

"But here's my theory. It's the tears that get him the most. Tears are a powerful thing. The people sobbing with joy wherever he goes. I think he must see them and think to himself, 'Hey, those are *real tears*. Not something you can fake. Sure, I do some bad things. But when the people see me, they cry because they love me. They *really love me.*'"

"And those bad things"—I contribute to this exercise in armchair psychology—"he can rationalize those. Things he *has* to do. That he's been *forced* into doing. Because of his position in life. Who he is, what he was born into."

"The ones I feel the most sorry for are the people on the ground who have to deal with the foreigners," says Alexandre. "Not guides like Min and Roe. They have some distance from it all. I'm talking about the minders who get tasked with accompanying the NGO workers, the foreign embassy officials. They're the ones who really have to *live* the contradiction. The ones who see the truth and know what's really going on and then have to lie on the spot. Going out into the countryside to find out what happened to all the food or medicine, seeing what really happened, and then having to invent a lie to tell the foreigners. Having to deny that what is there in front of them is real. At the end of the day, imagine how fucked up their heads must be. It reminds me of something my teacher said the other day in class. We were learning some new vocabulary, something to do with food and drink. The teacher was giving an example of a sentence: 'When I have a headache, I drink alcohol.' I thought, wait, that doesn't make sense—he must mean something like when he drinks too much, he gets a headache. Then I realized, no, I had understood the sentence correctly. He drinks when he gets a headache. Your head must ache at night, with all this bullshit, all these lies you can't even begin to unravel. This fake victory, this triumph of socialism that is really a triumph of oppression. Your head aches from it all, and you want nothing more than to have a drink, to annihilate all the wreckage in your mind."

Alexandre studies the dim glare of the city blanketed before us.

"What were the North Koreans you met in Dubai like?" I ask. "Did they still believe in the system? In any of it?"

"Some do, some don't," Alexandre replies. "They've seen the outside world. And they're torn. They suffer from . . . let's call it an *inner conflict.*"

"Double consciousness," I offer. "Chinese intellectuals talk about this."

"What it comes down to is dedication and belief. Those are two different things. There are some who genuinely *believe* in the system. Then there are those who are *dedicated* to it without necessarily *believing* in it. I met both types in Dubai. As foreigners, of course, we will never, ever meet someone who is not benefiting from the system in some way or other. That's what makes it hard to gauge what it is they actually believe. That's where the dedication comes in: you might think it's all bullshit, a lie. But you don't want it to end if you know how it works and it's rewarding you."

"So I guess you weren't serious about Kimchi Baguette."

"No! Of course not," Alexandre spits. "These joint ventures, ha! This is how it works: they take your expertise, they use it, you teach them until they've mastered it. Then they see they have no further use for you, and you—and your investment—are shuttled out of the picture. It's happened to a lot of businessmen who have tried to do joint ventures here. 'Oh, sorry, because of the political situation, we can't get you a visa. And your funds? They are frozen in the bank here. We can't get them out. Sorry, and have a nice day.'

"A childlike criminality pervades this entire system. The people's sense of right and wrong is completely perverted. This government that defaults on its foreign loans and then brags about it in the state media to its own people. What a great business model! That's why the economy is in the dumps, has been for so long. They can't get any credit from anyone, anywhere. The only way they can do business is the criminal way. To do business here as a foreigner is to set yourself up to get robbed!"

"But don't you think the *donju* are the ones who are going to change the system? People like Min and Kim—these are enlightened people. They know how it works in the outside world."

"I don't think anyone can change the system," Alexandre says. "It's too late for that. And you want to know why? It's because the people who designed the system are dead."

The last syllable, though whispered, cuts a resonant swath through the night air, sending a chill up my neck. A factory on the Potong River suddenly emits a strange fiery light into the night sky. The thought that all this has been solidified into an inalterable permanency—that nothing, no imaginable shift in the narrative, can ever arise, no hope on the horizon—in my exhausted state, it is too much to take. Alexandre sees from the expression on my face that he has gone too far, wishes me good night, and retreats to his room.

Belief and dedication. One can be expressed through words, the other only through action. There is, of course, an entire spectrum that lies between. I want to believe there are more directions in this moral compass than what has been sketched out, beyond the dumb naïveté of blind obedience and the pure selfishness of cynically upholding it for personal gain. I close my blinds to the creepy solitude of my empty hotel room. As muddy as the facts are, as impenetrable as something that's supposed to be crystal clear as truth is in this confused place, there is still something that we cannot access, a togetherness spawned by these mad and perilous conditions, a unity that we will never fully have access to. Those ties that bind, that cannot be expressed in language—for it is far too dangerous—but make themselves apparent in other ways. A sly grin. A wink. It is, after all, a kind of victory. Not in any war, whether real or imagined. But victory in the sense of endurance. Of survival.

PART SEVEN

HOUSES OF FRIENDSHIP

TWENTY-NINE

IT STARTS TO make sense after a while. The vowel combos no longer appear or sound like such odd juxtapositions but come across as familiar as the face of a friend you see every day. Together with the consonants, they merge into words that sound not so distant from English after all. Even the syntax of the sentences, which seems exactly backward to an Anglicized ear, becomes less of an obstacle as it solidifies into a logic. I'm on the precipice of understanding.

Three weeks in, Pyongyang has grown used to our appearance on its streets, and we feel ourselves growing less immune to the mindfuckery of everyday life in which everyone around us is enmeshed. A small conspiracy emerges among our teachers at Kim Hyong Jik University, and their whisperings have reached Min, who is only too eager to stir the pot. One day after class on our way to lunch, she announces: "Travis is winning." What on earth are you talking about? we ask her. She relays that our professors have designed an impromptu ranking system and determined that I have made the most progress. "And Alexandre," she reports glumly, "is the worst."

"But that's not really fair," I protest. "We're at three different levels. I started out at the lowest, as a total beginner, so of course I'm going to make the fastest progress—because my course is the easiest."

Min shakes her head. "Ms. Pak said that it takes her Chinese students one month to learn what you mastered in the first week."

"But why compare me to them? And why compare the three of us to each other? Alek is pretty much fluent, so any progress he makes is going to be negligible—at a certain point, there's just not much more you can learn. And Alexandre is right in the middle—which is the most challenging part when learning *any* new language. You of all people should know that, Min. I'm sure learning Spanish wasn't such a walk in the park."

Min and the others listen to my argument in silence, but I get the feeling that they're dismissing it as false modesty. And, since it's all rather embarrassing, especially for Alexandre, everyone silently agrees to let the subject go.

If only Min would let it. Over the course of the following days, she continues to bring it up whenever we're in the van traveling somewhere—moments, I've come to realize, of unofficially designated privacy, when we can all talk relatively freely without worrying who might be listening in. Even though she usually brings it up teasingly, it's clearly an act of passive aggression.

Finally, one afternoon when Min is seated next to Alexandre in the middle row of seats, with Alek and me behind them in the van, she turns to him with a more serious expression.

"I spoke to your teacher today," she says. "He's very frustrated. He says you're not learning. What's wrong, Alexandre? Why are you not studying at night?"

"I *am* studying," he explodes. "How can you say that? I'm studying most nights together *with you*!"

It's true. I've been opting for alone time in my room. Alek and Alexandre, on the other hand, have taken to spending a couple hours each night reviewing their lessons with Min and Roe in the lobby after dinner.

"But it's obviously not working," Min says. "You're not retaining what we learned. Your teacher keeps complaining about you."

"Look, I told you over and over again. *I need the dictionary app.* There are many new words, new grammar, and there is no English explanation in the texts they are giving us. I can't *go online* to get it. The teacher does not speak any English or French. This makes it very difficult to learn."

"But Roe and I have been helping you at night, explaining everything, and you still don't understand."

"How many Korean words do you know?" Roe suddenly interjects.

"I don't know," says Alexandre, taken aback. "Do you know how many English words you know?"

"Yes," he replies satisfactorily. "Four thousand three hundred seventy-three words."

A silence as we all take this in. As though memorizing a list of words is the key to learning a language. But maybe this kind of quantitative assessment is the norm here. Roe is, after all, a graduate of the University of Foreign Studies.

"You can't possibly explain everything he's giving me each day," Alexandre goes on, "and I can't possibly learn everything the minute you explain it. It takes time. I am not Travis, I am not Alek. It's not fair of you to compare us like that. I have to learn at my own pace, and you have to accept it."

Min remains silent for the rest of the ride. When I look over, I notice there is a tear running down her cheek.

✪

Alexandre's take on the situation is that this kind of passive aggression is an internalized symptom of totalitarian mass psychology, and that Min probably doesn't even realize she's doing it. That everyone here is traumatized by the bullying they are victims of from a young age, and so they in turn take every opportunity to terrorize those who are perceived to be in any way beneath them on the social scale. Such a top-down structure of terror, Alexandre reasons, is key to ensuring that no groups are formed. Because groups always pose a threat. They have to be broken up.

I have my doubts. Then I notice our teachers getting in on the act.

My bladder's always full at break time, so I make my way to the men's room at the end of the hall. There's no plumbing, just a waist-high tiled sink filled with water and a small bucket on the side. After pissing, I go to the sink, fill the bucket with water, pour it in the urinal. If you shit in one of the two squat toilet stalls, several trips from the sink to the toilet are required to clean up after yourself.

I'm coming out of the bathroom one morning when I catch the gist of an exchange between Alek and Ms. Pak. Alek makes the customary bow expected of university students when passing a professor in the hall. "How are you doing today, Comrade?" Ms. Pak stops to ask. "You look a bit under the weather."

Alek gives a weak smile. "I'm okay. I just haven't heard from my girlfriend since I've been here. I've sent her several texts, but she hasn't responded."

"Well," replies Ms. Pak coolly, "we have a saying in Korean you might find useful to learn: 'Out of sight, out of mind.'"

She smiles and sashays toward the teachers' office, shutting the door gently behind her.

As our course nears its end, Ms. Pak has developed an affection toward me that at times feels maternal, at others flirtatious. Not only am I the first American student she's ever had—the first American she's ever encountered in the flesh, actually—I am also her oldest student. At thirty-six, I'm only two years younger than she is.

There's a mischievous jokester in her that endears her to me. She flutters her eyelids when we get on to family vocabulary and I tell her, in response to her query about my domestic arrangements, that I'm not married; then she laughs out loud at her own daring. Like Min, she has a certain no-nonsense toughness at her core, though she is less likely to take her position of authority very seriously. As the days progress, she grows increasingly eager to use the themes of the lesson as prompts for conversation about our personal lives. These conversations take place in a whisper but also seem quite relaxed—the door is left open for the entirety of the lesson, but footsteps are almost never heard in the hallway. She asks about my apartment in Berlin. I draw a map of the floor outline for her. We determine that we more or less share the same square footage. She nods her head at this, intensely interested.

She asks whether I keep a diary. I tell her yes, that I write more or less every day. How about you? "Yes," she says, "but only for special occasions. Or if I am feeling sad." She makes a mock sad face to illustrate and then bursts out laughing. Though the way she laughs implies that that might be a bit more often than she'd care to admit.

Besides the photography incident with the leaders' portraits early on, there is only one other time when I sense external forces meddling with our lessons. One day, as Ms. Pak is sitting at the desk next to mine watching as I complete a writing assignment, she looks up at me with doe eyes, a sweet look of nurturing sincerity she gives whenever she's genuinely impressed with my progress. "Comrade Travis," she whispers with a sly smile, "I think when you go back to your country, perhaps you will get a job in Washington. You have learned much about Korea. Perhaps you could be of use to your country."

I understand immediately what she is implying and also intuit that she hasn't thought up the question herself but has likely been put up to it. I shake my head firmly, launching into my elementary Korean.

"No work in politics. No work for government. Me—writer. Intellectual, like you. Brush on the Workers' Party Monument. Novelist."

She appears visibly relieved. Excited, even.

"Novelist! Yes—novelist!" She claps her hands, as though she's finally got me all figured out, and obviously quite relieved. On earlier trips, I was always afraid of revealing my actual vocation. Western journalists are forbidden from entering the DPRK on a tourist visa, and although I have never considered myself a *journalist,* I realize that the fine distinction between *writer* and *journalist* is obscure to many people—perhaps especially those in positions of power. When applying to visit China, another communist country, I once had a visa rejected for putting "writer" in the job description field; by the time I visited Cuba for the first time in 2015, I knew better than to admit this on my visa application. From a US perspective, it is too easy to bemoan this as further evidence of the lack of freedom of the press; but from the perspective of these countries, they are, in fact, engaged in an international propaganda battle against the media of the Western, US-led First World, a battle that they have long been losing.

Whether we wish to admit this to ourselves or not, the fact remains that nearly all our reporting on North Korea is ideological. Diligent observers of the media might have noticed that, despite our "freedom of the press," there seems to be an unwritten rule that nothing positive can be reported about North Korea. This unofficial yet consensually agreed-upon policy seems to encourage or allow for a willful neglect of the rigorous fact-checking that any other subject warrants. Of course, the reasoning goes, it is impossible to carry out normal fact-checking procedures with anything Pyongyang-related, since *normal* journalism does not exist there and the regime is so belligerent and intentionally lies to its own people. Then there's the language barrier. Few Western media outlets employ fluent Korean speakers. The remedy to both these problems, more often than not, is to rely on translated South Korean news dispatches with regard to the North. Yet this problematically overlooks South Korea's own ideological bias against the North. South Korea has been engaged in a propaganda war against North Korea since the day the country was split in two. South Korean media is responsible for originating some of the more outlandish rumors about the North, rumors picked up by wire services and reported worldwide as fact that have turned out to be false, such as the story that all university-aged North Korean men were required to get Kim Jong Un haircuts. As one South Korean journalist admitted, at his paper, the editorial policy goes that it is better to publish a lie or unconfirmed rumor about North Korea than nothing at all.

Even when South Korean media cannot be relied upon to confirm our prejudices, elevating groundless speculation to the plateau of fact is the preferred tactic. Before the 2017 governmental ban on US tourists visiting North Korea, the US media drummed up its support by endlessly repeating the State Department's assertion that the money paid for these tours *might be* going toward the country's nuclear weapons program. Readers of such stories were, of course, easily led to ignore the conditional tense of that verb. In fact, would the State Department be so troubled as to sit down and talk with Simon from Koryo Tours, Alek from Tongil Tours, or any of the other Western travel agencies that bring tourists into North Korea, it could find out almost exactly where those tourism dollars are going. The cost breakdown for these all-inclusive tours is provided by their North Korean counterparts, men like Comrade Kim at the Korean State Travel Company: the Air Koryo flights into and out of the country or the train from China; the hotel, which varies depending on the quality of accommodation and amenities (the Sosan Hotel, where we're staying, is in the lower-budget range of options); the cost of the mandatory two guides and driver; the cost of food for the duration of the trip; and so on—not forgetting, of course, the commission that the Western tour companies, which are completely unaffiliated with the DPRK government, take as salary for their own guides who often accompany the groups and as profit. Since North Korea remains an abstraction for so many of us, it is easy for us to base any number of assumptions on what little we are told, to imagine that every dollar spent goes directly into Kim Jong Un's personal coffers, rather than the reality that tourism in the DPRK is an *industry* composed of any number of competing profit-driven business enterprises.

Perhaps this argument is still unconvincing for some. "Sure, North Korea operates its own for-profit businesses just like anywhere else," one might say, "but because of the vertical nature of the country's economy, there is always the remote possibility that any dollar spent there *could,* in fact, *eventually* go toward the development of nuclear weapons." In truth, owing to the secretive nature of the North Korean regime, nobody can know for sure where the small profit earned from tourism each year will go. North Korea does not publish statistics on the budget for its military defense, and because we refuse to have any diplomatic engagement with the North, it is impossible for us to gather that kind of information on the ground.

We do know, however, that the profit earned by tourism is a relatively small figure, since the few tour agencies that take Western tourists to North Korea have openly divulged *their* numbers: around five thousand tourists annually, as of 2017. By comparison, France receives more than eighty-five million tourists each year.

✪

There are other details of my personal life that I will not, cannot disclose to Ms. Pak. I cannot tell her that I do not, in fact, live alone in Berlin. There is no discourse on otherness here. An ethnically—and sexually—homogenous nation. The first question I am asked, each time I meet someone new, is where my wife is. In an extremely conservative, traditional family–centric land cut off from the rest of the world, it is very difficult to fathom that one might elect, by either choice or born necessity, to live a different way. That a woman might—gasp—make the decision not to marry or have children. Or not to marry yet have children anyway. Sex, already, is a taboo subject in this prudish society that will not even show two lovers kissing in its cinema. Sex education is completely absent from the educational curriculum; homosexuality, as a concept, does not exist in the DPRK. Even though there is no law against it. Even though, with one of the world's largest standing armies, the act presumably goes on behind closed doors in the segregated barracks, there is no word for it, no identity concept to embrace. Most North Koreans you ask have no idea what homosexuality is; presumably non-heterosexual North Koreans live a life of extreme confusion, unable even to articulate these feelings aloud.

So I've gone back into the closet. I am, after all, here to learn, not to teach. If they were to find out, it would at best result in awkwardness, confusion, and endless questioning; as an American, I'm already enough of a walking freak show. I don't fear overt physical violence; I fear the unbearability of humiliation, of having to explain myself constantly everywhere I go—which, of course, is a form of violence unto itself. Silence on certain matters, I knew well in advance, is what I was signing up for. And I am, after all, here to learn—not teach.

Endurance; survival.

THIRTY

AT THE END of our third week, we take an overnight trip to Mount Myo-hyang, "Mysterious Fragrant Mountain." Home to the International Friendship Exhibition. This enormous treasure trove is where the leaders display all the gifts they've received over the years from foreign guests. Such exhibitions were main-stays of communist countries during the Cold War, but North Korea now boasts the largest surviving one. Actually, not just one—a few days earlier, we had vis-ited another, less famous house of friendship in Pyongyang, one whose existence I was previously unaware of.

It was a blisteringly hot summer day, and to get there, we had to drive down a long stretch of road in the nether regions of west Pyongyang's Manyongdae dis-trict. Though it is still technically Pyongyang, the area is rural and undeveloped. The entrance to the friendship house was guarded by a Kalashnikov-wielding soldier. Entering the building, one must undergo a detailed security check. Belongings and mobile phones (no photos allowed) are stored in lockers. Your body is scanned with handheld metal detectors. You walk through a machine that blows dust off your shoes as you enter the main exhibition hall. There you are led by a young female guide cloaked in the inevitable *joseon-ot*. The four-floored building, she tells us, was inaugurated on August 1, 2012. We're led into the first room, which is dominated by two large white marble sculptures, around forty feet tall, of Kim Il Sung and Kim Jong Il set against a garish illuminated pink background, and told to bow. Formalities out of the way, the tour can begin.

In this vast theater of kitsch curiosities, Alexandre and I understood implic-itly to refrain from making eye contact throughout the duration, lest we crack each other up. A white-framed, two-sided circular painting depicts, on one side,

Kim Jong Il adorned in armor, seated on the back of a tiger in front of the volcanic lake at Mount Paekdu; on the back, he is adorned in army fatigues on Hosan Mountain in South Korea, tiger resting behind him. This was gifted to the museum from "an anti-Japanese Korean fighter abroad" in 1992.

Then there are those objects that were subject to everyday use, such as a turtle shell penholder plated in gold used by Kim Il Sung up until his death.

The friendship house also holds a number of acquisitions of flattery to the latest incarnation of the Mount Paekdu bloodline. One "Korean living in China," according to the placard, has presented a monumental work of kitsch sculpture, a jade mass weighing more than three tons, of an orange-and-gray tiger. The pedestaled inscription: "Because we have the Marshal Kim Jong Un, the future is bright." Another present that makes more sense to regular Pyongyang watchers, familiar with the Marshal's love of the game, is a 2010 Spalding Pro NBA basketball signed by LeBron James; I somehow doubt James was aware of whom he was signing the ball for and would probably be surprised to learn where it has ended up.

There is an entire floor dedicated to gifts from overseas Koreans, such as a volume of *Kim Jong Il: Lodestar of the Twenty-First Century* by one Kwang Myong Sa—likely a pseudonym, as beyond this title I have never been able to uncover any further information about the author.

For his birthday on February 16, 2000, Kim Jong Il was presented with what the guide described as a "treasure coffin"—something must have gotten lost in the translation—though, on further reflection, this could be an apt description of the entire Pyongyang friendship house. The one she pointed out to us, however, was actually a hand-sized green jade box that, when opened, had been filled with 216 hundred-dollar bills, the serial number on each note ending in -216. I asked if the money was still inside the treasure coffin. The guide gave me one of those looks as she shook her head no.

Besides these ornate and obviously valuable gifts, there was also an entire range of mass-produced CDs, buttons, fridge magnets, and bumper stickers contained within the glass display cases. Anything that comes across as *foreign* must appear exotic and important to local eyes. An honorary doctorate for Kim Jong Il from "Oxford University, Los Angeles, California." Finally, Alexandre and Alek and I found ourselves standing at a glass display case pondering a mug from the ABBA-themed Broadway musical *Mamma Mia!* Min and the guide approached us.

Min turned to me wide-eyed. "Travis," she said, "what is *Mamma Mia?*"

Suddenly, a thud. We all turned to see our guide landed in a pile of yellow *joseon-ot* fabric on the ground. Min rushed over, picked her up off the floor, escorted the poor young woman to a nearby bench.

Alexandre came up behind me. "Do you see that?" he whispered in my ear. "She fainted."

"Yes, I noticed."

At the end of the hallway is a rooftop terrace, providing views of the surrounding countryside. We stepped out into the heat of day. They had opened up a refreshment stand for us, the sole visitors, on the balcony. I bought a can of iced coffee for myself and a bottle of water for the guide, who gave me an embarrassed smile when I handed it to her.

That put an end to our tour. It would be impossible to see all four floors in a single day anyway. And it was too hot to linger for long on the rooftop terrace. There wasn't much to see, save for the surrounding greenery and the long driveway leading up to the friendship house. Alek promised me that the International Friendship House on Mount Myohyang was much more impressive.

When we got back in the van, Min told us that the guide was five months pregnant. And indeed, she had neglected to eat breakfast that morning.

★

By the time we reach Mount Myohyang after the four-hour drive from Pyongyang, my back aches. The highway was constructed in the 1980s just before the economy collapsed and hasn't been upgraded since. We arrive late at night. The dark road approaching the hotel is largely bereft of traffic and people, save for a few soldiers walking here and there. Our van lights illuminate a woman dressed to the nines, albeit in a very formal North Korean sort of way, in a dress covering her knees. "Night flower" is the elegant name assigned to women on the game here.

We're led into the hotel restaurant, where we're the sole guests, save for a table of soldiers drinking in tattered undershirts; our Korean guides and driver are taken off to a separate dining room. We're greeted with a dinner that is largely inedible. The chicken is all gristle leaking off a set of disassembled bones, the soup gruelish, the vegetables nonexistent. I down most of the beer they bring to our table and then excuse myself for the night.

I wake up feeling horrible. Back at the restaurant, the breakfast looks as unappealing as last night's dinner. Outside, the searing heat disorients me further. Thankfully, Hwa's already got the air-conditioning in the van cranked up.

We make our way down a winding road running along the Myohyang River until we arrive at two traditional palatial houses—Socialist body, Korean head—that denote the entrance to the International Friendship Exhibition. We pull into the broad, empty expanse of the parking lot. The gift exhibition houses burrow their way deep into the surrounding mountainsides. Two young soldiers bearing silver-plated machine guns march between the buildings. When they see us climbing out of the van, one cracks a joke under his breath and the other breaks protocol, bursting into laughter. As we approach the house devoted to Kim Il Sung's gifts, their laughter subsides and they step aside to open the four-ton bronze doors with white-gloved hands.

Sweltering outside, but inside this mountain palace, the temperature has been kept glacial by what must be the world's most robust air-conditioning system, energy shortages be damned. Our *joseon-ot*-ized guide instructs us to remove our baseball caps, place our phones and cameras in a storage locker, and sheath our sneakers with cloth sacks she provides. Led through a metal detector and another dust-removing fan into the holy entrance room, we bow before Kim Il Sung, represented here in front of Mount Paekdu. If it would take at least two days to see the Pyongyang friendship house, I wonder how long it would take to make our way through all seventy-one thousand glass-encased gift items in the one hundred rooms of this palace.

Standing in front of a stuffed crocodile holding a tray of drinks, I realize I am shivering with cold. Too bad all those glasses are empty. Ennui is combining with the delirium of these daily surrealities to send warning signals shooting up my spine.

The staggering quantity, but also the oddness of all the gifts, must seem impressive to the average North Korean factory worker brought here to see the evidence of the esteem their leaders enjoy around the globe. What they will not be told, of course, is that the exchanging of gifts is diplomatic protocol the world over, that most of these items were not donated directly by foreign admirers of the Kims to the Kims but received by any number of party functionaries participating in this mundane act of exchange in meetings with their foreign counterparts. The display of the gifts, then, is meant to show not only the reverence and respect that the three Kims enjoy worldwide but the generosity of the Kims in "sharing" all these gifts with their people. Socialism *our way*.

On the balcony of Kim Jong Il's house of gifts, we defrost ourselves outside while snapping photos of the mountain valley below. As the friendship exhibitions rank among the country's most sacred sites, Min pressures us into signing the guest book. To do so is not a simple affair of scribbling your name next to a peace sign; rather, visitors are expected to fill an entire page with their ebullient feelings about the place and their love and respect for the leaders. Then your guide has to translate what you've written verbatim into Korean. Alexandre and I feign flightiness, distraction, taking photos of the scenery around us and wandering around the gift shop annexed to the balcony. Bowing in front of statues is one thing; inscribing your name permanently into the propaganda machinery with written praise, no matter how sincerely felt, is quite another. That leaves Alek to do the task on behalf of all of us. I feel sorry for him. Then again, Tongil Tours is his gig, not ours.

Making our way back to the van, I feel faint. I tell Min, choosing my words carefully, that I do not want to have lunch at the hotel. Noting my pallor, she nods but looks troubled. Everything has been prearranged; making last-minute changes is never easy, and we must pay out of pocket. At this point, I could care less—I need to eat something at least vaguely nutritious.

On the way back, we stop at a giant, pyramidal hotel. Apparently there's a fondness for this shape when it comes to luxury accommodation. The Hyangsan Hotel, Roe tells us seriously, is a "six-star" property. The bow-tied concierge greets us in the empty lobby. Roe asks whether we might have lunch in one of the hotel's numerous restaurants. What follows is a lengthy conversation, a wordy explanation that amounts to *only hotel guests are permitted to eat here.* The truth is a bit more obvious to the naked eye: there are no guests, so there is no food.

Luckily, outside, some enterprising soul has set up a barbecue stall right next to the hotel. They're more than happy to grill some meat for a couple US dollars. We sit at an empty table across from a lone group of teenage soldiers. It's not the best meal I've had, but it's useless to complain.

By the time we get back to Pyongyang, it's dinnertime and my throat is swollen, my back and ass ache from being jostled by all the potholes in the backseat. I recognize that all-over feeling of wobbliness that signals the onslaught of flu. In the lobby of the Sosan, I tell Min to apologize to Ms. Pak, but I will have to miss class tomorrow morning. I need some time to myself.

★

It's not just my body that is sick. The symptoms I have are too random, too flagging; they don't add up to a complete picture. I'm constipated from the food and also from being cramped up in the tiny, uncomfortable van for so long, my back and neck are in knots from the bumpy ride, my stomach queasy and empty yet my appetite nonexistent, my head pounding. But ultimately, I think it is my soul that is most sick.

I'm fatigued. Worn out. I haven't been alone for days, weeks, it seems. Every day a roller coaster of thought and emotion—I am bored at one moment, absorbed by intrigue the next. I find myself charmed to tears with the sweetness and earnestness of the people I encounter; the next second something will occur that reminds me how horrific it all is, the systematic oppression, the fear it breeds, the intellectual enslavement that leaves the people bereft of any idea of how *wrong* it all is, any language for questioning. My hope for the future of humanity rises and falls with each passing minute, wild and uncontrollable. Paranoia comes and goes. Lying in bed at night, trying to sleep, I wonder whether they *have,* in fact, bugged our rooms. Can they hear Alexandre's and my whispered conversations on the balcony at night? Where could the bugs be—in the phone? In the antique nightstand radio that doesn't really work? What about the smoke alarm? I look up at the ceiling. Okay, surely there must be an audio bug somewhere—but what about video? Could they be *watching* as well? What about my laptop, my notebook that I leave so carelessly in my desk—are they coming in during the day while I'm at class and *reading* what I wrote the night before?

Of course I'm being paranoid, I tell myself. Then I realize there's no real way of knowing. Just forget it?! . . . Sleep doesn't come easy. When my alarm goes off, my appetite still hasn't returned. I wait until I'm sure the others have left the hotel and then take the elevator down. Not to the breakfast room. I'm going to get a massage, I've decided.

On the second floor, there's a recreational services lounge, where you can arrange to swim in the indoor pool, take a sauna, get your hair cut, see the doctor. The attendant presents me with a laminated price list. Full-body medical massage, $20. I point to it and nod my head in the affirmative. She leads me into the massage room, instructs me to strip down to my underwear and lay on the massage table. Then scurries off.

I wait there for what could be five minutes or twenty—time passes so slowly here, I've lost my ability to gauge it. Finally, I hear the door swing open. An old man enters, smiles and nods, gestures at me to flip over on my stomach. He must be the house doctor. Massage is an integral component of Eastern medicine, and Sosan Hotel is, after all, in the middle of the sports district. These days, while there might not be many foreign sports teams staying here, the doctor is most likely called upon to attend to the local athletes practicing tae kwon do, swimming, basketball, and gymnastics at the surrounding stadiums. They probably had to fetch him from one of them.

Without communicating a single word, the doctor's fingers immediately gravitate to all of the problem areas. There's a lot wrong with my body. He figures it out right away. Every single sore point in my neck and my back, his fingers arrive at by instinct, applying a strong pressure that brings with it a modicum of pain followed by an explosion of relief. There is, as corny as it sounds, a healing power to touch. I haven't had any physical contact with another human being since I arrived, and the result is that I have become detached from any notion of sensuality whatsoever. My body has lost all self-awareness in its total surrender to manic cerebrality, and sickness is the inevitable result.

When the doctor flips me over on my back and commences a deep-tissue acupressure attack on my torso, his fingers make their way to my gut. Gradually, he goes deeper and deeper, his fingers digging beneath rolls of fat, until he is massaging my liver. I belch, and the old man giggles. I've had many massages, but this is the first time my internal organs have been targeted. Again, I didn't have to tell the doctor that there was anything wrong with my stomach—he wordlessly sensed it. Whatever he did, however he managed to intuit all that was wrong, with that single belch, it is as though all sickness is ejected from my body. When he finishes, he bows slightly before me and quickly leaves the room before I even have a chance to say thank you. I stand, realizing instantly that everything that was broken an hour ago has now been fixed. Body and soul realigned. I'm cured.

✪

That afternoon, we make a spur-of-the-moment decision to break the rules. We ditch our guides and take a walk.

Health regained, I join the others for lunch after they finish classes. I even feel refreshed enough to return to maintaining my caffeine addiction. Our plan is to visit the Foreign Languages Bookshop off Kim Il Sung Square, but first, I insist on a stop at the Viennese coffeehouse for a shot of espresso.

In a way, it's Min who abandons us. She gets out of the van and starts instantly walking ahead toward the coffee shop, texting away on her phone. Alexandre and Alek and I linger behind, calling out that we're going down to the river to take some photos of the Juche Tower across the way. She waves her approval and then continues toward the coffee shop, immersed in whatever new business deal she's conducting via SMS.

"Guys," says Alexandre after we snap some pictures, "let's take a walk."

Alek and I look at each other but don't say a word.

"Just along the riverbank. Just down there. Come on. She's not looking. Let's just do it. Why not? Nothing's going to happen to us."

It doesn't take much prodding. We've been cooped up for three weeks, unable to operate under any shred of agency on our own. Besides, we're not going far. Just a little ways down the river. We're staying out in the open, so it's not like we're breaking any rules, engaging in suspicious activity.

So we walk. Assuming as casual an air as we can manage. We head in the direction of "Dubai," the fancy new apartment buildings, past the playground, continuing under the overpass, until we get to the Okryu Restaurant, where people have already begun queuing up for its famous cold noodles. By now, we are being stared at by pedestrians. They notice we're unaccompanied. We ignore their stares and continue walking as though we're perfectly entitled to this small freedom. Outside of the staring, nobody dares say a word to us. For all they know, we could be family members of Russian Embassy employees, aid workers. We take a left on the street across from the restaurant and calmly walk back toward Kim Il Sung Square.

"Last time I was here," says Alexandre as we pass by a shiny new complex of shops, "I saw a fistfight. Right here, two young guys beating each other, right in the middle of the street. I think it was a money thing."

Alek pauses to take a photo of the apartment tower across the street. Alexandre and I chew him out. "Dude, what the fuck are you doing? We can't look like *tourists*."

The entire situation, of course, is absurd. The amount of nervous energy being generated among the three of us, for what? All we're doing is *walking down the street.* In the back of my mind, I reason, Min is so spacey, she probably doesn't even realize we're gone.

Well, I'm wrong. As we approach the Foreign Languages Bookshop, Alexandre whispers, "Shit, there she is. Act normal, guys, like nothing happened."

We act "normal." Whatever that is. But it's not convincing.

Min is furious. She bangs her umbrella on the pavement, oblivious to the throng of pedestrians passing by.

"What are you *doing?*" she cries. "You guys had me so scared! I am *responsible for you while you are in my country.* What if something happened to you? What if you were hit by a car?"

She is crying, furious. I try to diffuse the situation by acknowledging the publicness of our surroundings. "Look," I say under my breath, "can we just go in the bookshop and deal with it there?"

Inside, Min doesn't say a word to us. She makes her way to the couch and sits down with a huff, her face bright red. We spend an awkward five minutes browsing the titles of books by and about the three Kims, but no one's in a buying mood.

We pass the next hour in a strained silence. "Hey, don't worry about it," Alexandre whispers. "She'll get over it. In a few years from now, just think, we're all going to laugh about this."

★

Later, we drive to a local laundry shop, where Roe covertly drops off a bag of our dirty clothes. It's not allowed, but it'll be much cheaper than what they charge at the hotel, and since none of us have packed blue jeans or clothing with American flag insignia, Roe can pretend it's his own.

In the lot of the apartment complex where we're parked, a blanket of millet has been laid out to dry under the sun, watched over by two old ladies. Min spies a vendor and hops out of the van. She returns with three wrapped ice creams—a peace offering.

"I'm sorry for yelling earlier," she says. "But don't ever do that again if you come back to Korea. Especially not to another guide. An *ordinary* guide, I mean."

The day before our final lesson, Ms. Pak breaks off from her lecture to stare at me with glassy eyes. "Comrade Travis," she says, "we do not have enough time to finish this chapter. Tomorrow will be our last day."

We stare across the room at each other. A lump forms in my throat. It's not like we can keep in touch through Skype or Facebook.

"When you come back to Pyongyang, we will see each other again," she says, hopefully. "When you find a wife, bring her here." She clutches my arm. "I want to meet her. We will eat together. We will laugh."

I smile. She smiles. We both know it will never happen. There's no way a foreign visitor can simply ask to go meet a private citizen without first going through a labyrinth of bureaucratic protocol, without there being a damn good reason that would prevent one or both parties from falling under suspicion. But one thing I've noticed people living in police states are remarkably skilled at: their ability to dream.

THIRTY-ONE

THAT AFTERNOON, IT'S Alexandre's turn to be sick. He made it through class in the morning but wants some alone time at the hotel for the afternoon. Roe also needs some time off to heal his stomach—yesterday, I presented the guides with some chocolates I had bought at duty-free in Beijing, and I'm pretty sure Roe ate the entire box alone in his room last night before Min could get to them.

So besides Hwa, it's just Alek and Min and me.

The Pyongyang Film Studios! I've been wanting to visit for years, but it hadn't been on the itinerary of any of my previous trips. One of Kim Jong Il's favorite haunts. His father only visited the film studios twenty-three times in his life. Jong Il is recorded to have visited three thousand two hundred thirty-one times. Virtually every day that a film was in production, Jong Il would show up on the set. These statistics are etched into a plaque near the main entrance.

Kim Jong Un doesn't seem to share his father's passion for the cinematic arts. Our guide, a ruffled middle-aged gentleman in a Mao suit, informs us sadly that the Marshal has yet to visit the film studio—"though he will be welcome here anytime," he is quick to add, as though any of us would have the means of passing on the message. In a square across from the mandatory bronze statues, a multi-figure wall mural painting of Kim Il Sung surrounded by costumed actors, looking to the Great Leader for guidance. The building it's attached to is the Museum of the Ministry of Art and Culture, which, somewhat predictably, is a temple dedicated to Kim Jong Il's tenure as head of said ministry.

Given the torrid heat, our guide politely requests we tour the outdoor studios from the comfort of our air-conditioned van. The grounds of the studio are near empty. I ask if there are any films in production at the moment. Two, he replies, and both with female protagonists: one about the Girl Mother, and another about a traffic controller. Perhaps a remake of that immortal classic *A Traffic Controller on the Crossroads*?

The outdoor sets give some insight into the limited themes that make up DPRK cinema. There's the traditional Korean houses, for those period pieces depicting the idyllic period prior to the invasion of the Japanese; here, a photo stand has been set up, where cosplay enthusiasts can choose from among the studio's costumes and props and have their photos taken for a small fee. A street meant to evoke the sleaziness of capitalist Seoul—or at least what the city resembled in the 1960s; a Little Tokyo of the same era. Both replete with visual signifiers of exploitation, hand-painted billboards advertising prostitutes. For flicks with Euro settings, an English cottage. Unlike Hollywood, all the buildings have been constructed with interiors to match the exteriors, so if the outside is a pharmacy or bar, you find the same when you go inside. This was a brilliant innovation of Kim Jong Il, the guide informs us, a definite improvement over the wasteful Hollywood soundstage model!

Suddenly, Min squeals and asks Hwa to pull over.

"Is it really . . . *them*?" she asks the guide, pointing at three graying men walking out of what must be one of the crew's huts.

It is indeed. Three of Min's favorite movie stars. We climb out of the van to take photos with these icons of Norlywood, stars of such box office hits as *Our Fragrance, Order No. 027*, and *The Nation and Destiny, Part 61*. But Min wants in on the action, too—she hands Alek her phone, and he snaps photos of her posing with the celebrities.

★

On the ride back from the film studio, driving past a remote stretch of the Potong River, we spot a newish suburban apartment block in the distance. "You see that?" shouts Min. "That white building? That's where I live!"

"Ah, really? Let's stop by for lunch!" I joke, knowing full well that no *inminban-jang* could ever be bribed enough to allow an American bastard onto the premises.

"Sure, why not?" Min goes along with it. "Though not today. Next time you're in Pyongyang."

"Haha, okay."

"But that means you have to come back." Min dangles her pinky figure in front of me. "You promise?"

My pinky locks with hers. "Promise."

THIRTY-TWO

IT'S THE LAST day of class, and our teachers have organized a graduation ceremony in the department office. A private ceremony—just our teachers, the department administrators, our guides, and Comrade Kim—but still a big day. Alek makes sure that the whole thing is documented, Min tasked with filming the proceedings so that he can upload clips on Tongil Tours' social media back home. Alexandre outshines us all, showing up in a suit and tie.

Today, we're rewarded with a tour of the campus—which is actually restricted to the university's single-room museum on the ground floor: as banal as it sounds.

Earlier in the week, Min had taken us to a photo studio around the corner from the Changgwangsan Hotel, where we had our portraits taken, each of our faces grafted onto a matching suit, thanks to the miracle of Photoshop. Now, our certificates are presented. My photo has been pasted on to the paper, a typewritten notice alerting all who read it that Comrade Travis Jeppesen has completed a Korean language course at Kim Hyong Jik University, seal embossed with the insignia of the Ministry of Education.

Outside, we pose for photographs with our teachers in front of the university. Alexandre, in the excitement of the moment, asks our timid administrator for the department's phone number so that he might personally arrange to come back and study on his own. She laughs uncomfortably.

"Alexandre, it's not possible to do it that way," Comrade Kim interjects. "You can contact *me* if you want to come back and study."

"Why can't I contact them directly?" Alexandre asks defiantly.

We say our good-byes. I bow in front of Ms. Pak. I shake hands with the other teachers and administrator and then climb into the van. As we pull out of the parking lot, I look behind at Ms. Pak and wave one last time. She sees me and smiles, gives a quick wave, and then briskly turns away as our van merges into midday traffic.

PART EIGHT

FOLDING SCREEN

THIRTY-THREE

THE MORNING FOG. Through it, a single ray breaks, signaling the start of another day. I open the door to my balcony, trying to absorb it all. Through my own fog: the fog of my brain. I've just gotten out of bed but am having a tough time. My mental state is shattered; I'm exhausted, a condition likely abetted by the sleeping pills I've been needing to shut my eyes most nights.

It will all be over soon. School is finished. Today, we leave for our final weekend excursion.

I throw some clothes and supplies in my backpack. Min has arranged permission with the hotel for us to leave the stuff we don't need in our rooms. It's not likely there will be much demand for them while we're away. Other than the occasional Chinese tour group or businessman, we're the only guests.

Down in the lobby, a surprise. Comrade Kim is waiting for us alongside Min and Roe. "Come on, we must go shopping! Supplies for the journey..."

In the car, Kim congratulates us on finishing our courses. "You are the first Westerners to have completed the Korean language program here. You have made history!"

Beaming, he is clearly as proud of himself as he is of us. And he should be. He has cracked open the door to one of the capital's most prestigious universities to the outside world. It might not seem like much, but in the North Korean context—where progress tends to take place at the pace of glacial melt, where every step forward seems to require a backtrack of fifty miles—he has managed to pull off something quite remarkable.

In the middle of Chongchun Street, a jaywalking young girl steps absentmindedly in front of our van. Rather than slow down, Hwa accelerates forward and lays on the horn, narrowly missing the girl, who looks back at us with a dazed expression. No one takes notice. We've grown used to local road customs by now.

At Kwangbok Street Department Store, Min and Kim take charge. They fill a shopping cart with an outrageous quantity of snacks, beer, water, soju—way more than we could possibly consume in the three days we have left. Kim pays for everything. I'm running low on won—running low on currency, period— but realize this will be my final chance to pick up some Kims to bring back as a souvenir, so I trade in some euros at the wooden currency exchange booth on the ground floor. I get a mixture of old and new 5,000 won notes, the largest denomination printed—worth less than a dollar according to the unofficial exchange rate, the one everyone abides by. (Confusingly enough, pricing in all shops follows the official exchange rate published by the government, which nobody actually uses, so all shopkeepers have a calculator next to the cash register for the complex arithmetic required to determine the actual price, based on whether you are paying in Korean won or one of the more preferable currencies: US dollars, euros, or Chinese renminbi.) The old ones have the Great Leader's face on them; the new ones feature his birthplace. The rumor is they're getting ready to introduce a 10,000-won note, hence the need to preserve the founding father's face. But so far, it's just speculation.

As we're loading the goods into the van, Kim asks me if I'm looking forward to the trip. "Have you been to Mount Kumgang before?" I tell him no, though I've been to Wonsan, where we're heading first.

"What will you do this weekend?" I ask him.

"Now? I am headed back to the office."

"Really? Why don't you come with us? It will be more fun."

He nods his head, much to the surprise of Min and Roe. That didn't take much convincing. He's curious about the Mount Kumgang resort, built by the South Koreans and then abandoned shortly after when relations soured. And, frankly, any excuse to avoid those Saturday study sessions is always welcome.

★

On our way out of town, I witness the police engaged in the act of administering justice. Three officers circle a young guy in his late twenties, shouting. He's handsomely dressed, clutching a leather file case, all signifiers of the respectable middle class. One of the officers grabs him by the collar of the wine-colored shirt that has become so fashionable in Pyongyang of late and hurls him to the ground. He lands near the foot of another officer, who uses it to boot him in the chest. The guy stands up and grabs his carrying case, as though about to make a run for it; the second officer kicks it out of his hand and punches him in the face, sending the guy flying back to the ground, where he is descended upon by a flurry of punches and kicks. Although it's all taking place in bright daylight on a busy street corner, the pedestrian traffic moves coolly past—no one stops to intervene or even watch. Just pretend like nothing's happening.

Min, who's missed it all, notices the alarmed expression on my face as I twist my neck around, trying to catch the outcome. But we're driving too fast, and soon it all becomes a blur.

"What? What is it? Is something wrong?" she asks.

"No—it's just... They were... The police. They were beating up that guy..."

Min responds with a blank empty smile and then resumes staring out the window, as though she hadn't understood a word of what I'd just said.

The long drive to Wonsan takes us through mountainous terrain over yet more potholes. Outside the window, fertile fields embedded in the mountains, sun-baked people with backs bent laboring beneath the harsh late-summer glare. Others walk slowly down the side of the deserted highway or squat roadside, waiting for God knows what to happen. Our boredom is nothing next to theirs.

Spotting Alek's headphones, Min asks if she can listen to his music. He plays her Sleater Kinney, God Is an Astronaut, Rise Against, and a drum-and-bass DJ, Logistics. It reminds her of the music she used to listen to in Cuba, she says. "Do you have any Green Day? Any Matchbox 20?" Later, when no one is looking, she will hand Alek an empty USB stick and ask him to copy some music for her. "It's kind of against the rules," she says, "so don't mention it to the other guys."

Alexandre entertains us with his bitingly accurate impersonations of various non-native English-speaking people's attempts to speak English. He ranges through Hindu, Italian, even parodying French by slathering on an exaggeration of his own accent. The Koreans love it. The entire car is rolling with laughter. "Now do an American!"

Alexandre turns to me. "Okay, Travis—now it's your turn."

"Oh, I couldn't—"

"Come on! I made fun of the French. Now what does a typical American tourist sound like?"

I clear my throat, preparing my best George W. Bush redneck drawl; as a southerner myself, it doesn't require much effort to coax it out. "Boy, what the sam hell you doin goin to daggawn cotton-pickin *North Korea*? They're a bunch of goddamn *communists* over there, they wanna take away our *freedom*!"

The Koreans howl. In the passenger seat, Kim claps his hands, unable to control his laughter. It all goes to show what Henry James well knew: a rare creature, the American innocent, beloved as the buffalo, wherever he may roam.

★

After snaking our way across several hours' worth of bucolic mountain scenery and through a number of pitch-black tunnels, including one that extends for nearly two and a half miles, we arrive in Wonsan, a coastal city and the country's third largest. Wonsan has existed since the Koguryo Dynasty, though it received its current name during the Koryo. Its name is said to mean "folding screen," and this comes from the zigzag shape that is seen to emerge as the hills make their way toward the natural harbor. The mountains surrounding the city are filled with gold, and mining it—whether officially or covertly—is how most of the privileged few have managed to make their fortune around here. The view from the port is the best scape of the city, with its high-rise apartment buildings jutting like jagged buckteeth toward the water. Like Pyongyang, it was completely destroyed during the Korean War, so everything around us has been built in the ensuing years.

The Folding Screen City is also Roe's hometown, though he doesn't have much to say about it. He appears as bored and listless here as he does in Pyongyang.

We head straight for the beach. On the road leading to the shore, a traffic cop appears, waving his stop sign at us. "Ignore this asshole," Comrade Kim mutters to Hwa. We zoom past.

THIRTY-FOUR

DURING THE TIME I spent in Seoul, I met several North Korean defectors. One of them, who became a close friend of mine, is Un Ju, who grew up in Wonsan. I wonder if Roe knew her, her family—though I know better than to ask. Save for some short spells in Pyongyang, she lived here her entire life until the age of eighteen, when she began her long, perilous journey to the South, following in the footsteps of her mother, who had left a few months earlier. Shortly after that, her little brother would make the same journey. Her father, whom she hasn't seen since, still lives here somewhere.

Un Ju and I met through a mutual friend and somehow clicked right away. It was unusual to meet a North Korean from Wonsan in the South—and unusual for her to meet an American who had been to her hometown. By lucky coincidence, Un Ju happens to be incredibly thoughtful and articulate. In the many hours I spent with her, I sat back and listened as she dissected the fabric of her autobiography with an objectivity and distance that I found astounding given the pain she has endured.

Most of the defectors I met in the South came from the provinces bordering China. Although the border is heavily guarded on the North Korean side, it is actually quite porous, especially when compared with the impenetrable boundary of the DMZ, with its miles of minefields on either side. Geographical strata delineate the Sino-Korean border, namely, the rivers Yalu and Tamen and the impassable Mount Paekdu. There are places where the rivers become so narrow, one can merely hop across to the other side. And since the famine of the 1990s, bribing the border guards with a pack of smokes or hard currency has enabled anyone with the means at their disposal to cross back and forth relatively easily.

Many merchants do exactly that, bringing back goods from China to sell in the markets at home.

The border is a long way from Wonsan. But through the services of a broker, a journey there and across can readily be arranged for the right price.

★

In the eighteen years she spent in her home country, Un Ju experienced all the highs and lows. She came from a well-educated family with decent Songbun, her father a scientist, her grandfather a university professor. They lived in a house on the outskirts of Wonsan that her father had built with his own hands. At a young age, Un Ju's talent for singing and dancing was discovered and nurtured by her parents. She auditioned and was rewarded with a spot at the local school-children's palace. Performing became her life, and after years of training, she made it into an elite troupe of young female singers. She would spend weeks away from home in Pyongyang, staying at the Potonggang Hotel. At night, she and her fellow performers in the troupe would be whisked away in a van with blackened windows so that they couldn't see where they were being driven, to sing and dance for Kim Jong Il and his entourage at lavish parties on one of his hidden estates.

But the Arduous March put an end to the relatively idyllic years of Un Ju's childhood. Wonsan, like most of the country, was hard-hit by the financial catastrophes that saw the collapse of the public food distribution system and widespread famine. The corpses of people who had starved to death littered the grounds surrounding the train station, the streets of the city, and the mountains surrounding her home where people would go desperately foraging for food. Thieves regularly broke into her family's house to steal anything that could be eaten or sold. Her mother began making illicit trips to China to smuggle in food and goods, which Un Ju and her brother, who was only six at the time, would sell in the black markets that popped up throughout the backstreets of Wonsan.

Un Ju estimates that about 50 percent of her classmates died. One day, her teacher didn't show up for class; the students were able to intuit for themselves her fate. Most starved to death or else suffered starvation-related illnesses that they were unable to cure. Others perished in industrial accidents, in the rubble of collapsing buildings. As factories ground to a halt and the workers ceased showing up, people would rummage through decrepit buildings looking for anything that could be sold, from machinery and support structures to screws and copper wire.

The mountainous terrain surrounding Wonsan is rich in natural resources that the government, through ineptitude, corruption, and a systematic privileging of political loyalty over economic pragmatism, has never managed to sustainably exploit. Un Ju's parents had been wise enough over the years to invest their savings in gold, which, owing to the government's ignorance and incompetence, could be bought for cheap, way less than its actual value. This savvy investment is one of the mechanisms that likely spared Un Ju the fate of her friends and classmates. To earn extra money, Un Ju would travel to a small village, Haejung, outside of Pyongyang, where children as young as four and five worked under perilous conditions in a gold mine. It was common for children and adult laborers alike to die as a result of poorly coordinated dynamite explosions or by slipping and falling into the depths of the mines, where they were forced to crawl around without any protective gear whatsoever. Still, Un Ju preferred working there. You could earn a lot more money in the mines than you could selling food in the markets, where you had to be on the constant lookout for thieves.

Un Ju grew immune to the stench of death that welled up from every street corner. The corpses were a daily unpleasantry to which one soon grew accustomed. But then one day her father, though not a religious man, began to partake in a bizarre, quasi-shamanistic practice. Whenever he came across a dead person, he would pick up the corpse, sling it over his shoulder, and bring it into their house, despite the protests of Un Ju's mother. There he would dress the deceased. For the ones who had clearly starved to death, he would place rice in their mouths. The family always slept together on the floor, in traditional Korean style, warmed by the underfloor *ondol* heating system. The corpses would spend the night in the same room with them. In the depths of winter, when the temperature dropped to well below freezing, the dead person would be allotted the warmest spot on the floor, at her father's insistence. When morning came, the family would lug the stranger's lifeless body into the mountains for burial, a task that could take many hours of tough labor on those days when the ground was frozen solid.

As strange as it sounds, Un Ju insists, this wasn't a mere eccentricity of her father. Many others did the same thing, caring for the dead, performing impromptu funerary rites for complete strangers. Despite all the desperation, the insane acts and often brutal depths people plummeted to in order to survive, there was also a less apparent struggle at stake, a struggle to retain some common thread of human dignity as the years of the Arduous March wore on.

Still, those memories left their mark. To this day, Un Ju's dreams are haunted by the ghosts of those dead ones. At night, she has a chronic sleepwalking problem. Once, shortly after her arrival in Seoul, the police found her walking down the street in a somnambulant state in the middle of the night. They managed to wake her and drive her home.

The dead. She almost never knew their names, the people, but she can vividly recall the faces of everyone her father took in. She has forgotten the face of her father but not them. The nightmares will not let her forget.

May you live in interesting times goes the apocryphal Chinese curse. All the members of her family survived the Arduous March, but given what lay ahead, this could be described as a mixed blessing.

THIRTY-FIVE

IN WONSAN, THE beach is segregated: one side for Koreans, the other for foreigners. Divided by a wooden pier, extending into the water, with floating diving rafts on either side. As on all my other visits, we're the only visitors on the foreigners' side. The Korean side, however, is packed.

Alexandre and I swim out to the floating diving boards. Alek, who never learned how to swim, remains on the shore together with the Koreans, who have begun to gorge themselves on the snacks they bought earlier.

"I have something I want to show you," Alexandre, treading water, tells me with a mischievous glint in his eye. "But you have to do what I tell you."

We climb onto the float. The wooden planks are rotting, the diving boards rusted. It seems unsafe. Plus I'm afraid of heights.

Alexandre insists we climb up to the highest. No way, I tell him. But finally, slowly, I manage to make it, my knees quivering beneath me.

"Over there," he indicates with a lilt of his chin. "Can you see it?" He doesn't want to point in case they're watching us from the shore.

"See what? I see Songdowon." I feel like I'm going to barf. I have to get down.

Songdowon Children's Camp. A summer camp that parents from friendly socialist countries could send their kids to in the summertime. It's still in operation, though I can't imagine there are many parents these days who would consider sending their children to summer camp in North Korea.

"No—look closer," Alexandre says, "behind the camp. Do you see it? Those buildings. In the hills. On the other side."

I strain. I can just make out some rooftops without my glasses.

"It's *his* house," Alexandre insists. "Number Three. That's where he took Rodman. You can find it on Google Earth."

Indeed, it's well known that the Marshal has a house in Wonsan—though I had no inkling it was visible from the top diving board. In Seoul, I met a Canadian guy who had accompanied Rodman on that trip, serving as an interpreter. He also mentioned Wonsan. Said they had even gone jet skiing with the Marshal—an image I have a great deal of trouble conjuring.

"This raft, it's special to me for other reasons," Alexandre continues, surveying the seascape. "On my first visit to this country, in 2012, I swam out here by myself. There were a bunch of rich kids from Pyongyang hanging out here, elites. One of them actually spoke French—he had studied in Paris. So we had a conversation that none of the others could understand. He asked me what I thought of his country. So I said the standard polite things one says in those situations. And he said yes and then added more of the standard polite things. Then there was this loaded pause. And I don't know what motivated me to say it— maybe it's because we were out here, floating in the East Sea, away from all that political bombast on the shore—but I did. I told him, 'I don't actually believe any of those things.' And he just smiled back at me and said, 'Neither do I.'"

We decide to swim across to the raft on the Korean side. Which is allowed, apparently—it's okay to share the water but not to intermingle on the shore, according to some obscure logic—likely a directive barked out without a second thought from one of the visiting leaders.

The dozen young men hanging out on the raft eye us nervously as we swim up. By now, Roe has caught up with us, breaststroking just behind. He climbs the ladder up to the raft. I ask him if he's going to dive off, gesturing to the board high above us. "Me?" He laughs. "No. I'm like you. Don't like heights."

"Come on, Travis!" Alexandre is already halfway up the ladder. "You can get an even better view from here," he says through his teeth.

Everyone oohs and ahhs as the foreigner ascends to the highest board and gracefully dives off following a brief study of the horizon. When he was younger, Alexandre trained to become a professional diver. He's put on a few pounds since then but still retains the posture and some impressive moves.

I'm not going to make it to the top. The diving boards here are even more dilapidated than the ones on the foreigners' side—after all, they see a lot more use. Large gaps between each of the wooden boards reveal the underlying barge and slivers of sea, fueling the acrophobe's paranoia.

On the second-highest diving platform, I step shakily toward the edge. A thumping sound from behind startles me; I freeze. A teenager with one leg hops past, one board at a time. He gives me the once-over before skipping his way to the very edge. The stump at the end of his right leg resembles a bundled foreskin. He hollers down to his friends on the raft below; they shout back their affirmation. One final hop, and he is descending toward the rippling green of the East Sea.

Back on the shore, Min and Hwa and Kim are frolicking like children in the sand. Alek sits on a beach towel watching impassively as Hwa dives back and forth in the water, returning to the shore each time with a handful of clams—a skill he learned in the army, as troops are often required to forage for their own food. And this beach is a gold mine—a clam mine—since nobody except for foreigners can use it, and the foreigners rarely come. The more he finds, the more excited he gets. We will bring the pile back to the hotel with us, give it to the chef to prepare for dinner tonight.

Meanwhile, Min and Kim busy themselves drawing huge hearts in the unleavened sand with their toes, snapping photos on their phones. Kim writes the name of his daughter in the middle of one. Min writes the name of a boy she likes, takes a photo, and then quickly erases it as Alexandre approaches, wrapped in a towel.

THIRTY-SIX

WHEN SHE WAS sixteen, for reasons she still can't fathom, one of Un Ju's closest friends ratted on her. The *bowibu* did a search, found a couple of South Korean K-pop CDs. She was sent to prison.

She was beaten by the guards on a nightly basis. For no reason—all unprovoked. The beatings were savage and severe; she permanently lost her sense of smell. Still, she managed to avoid the fate of one of her cellmates, who was taken away by the guards each night and raped. This girl, Un Ju told me, became like a zombie. During the day, she would stare straight ahead, unmoving or else rocking herself, unblinking, never uttering a word.

Un Ju quit bathing, smeared dirt in her hair, did anything she could to make herself appear as ugly as possible so that the guards wouldn't want to touch her.

Finally, after two months, her parents managed to come up with enough money to bribe the authorities to release her.

✪

Unlike most of the refugees who defect to the South, Un Ju's reasons for leaving the DPRK were political rather than economic. Toward the end of his life, her grandfather, the university professor, became enlightened or else afflicted with loose tongue syndrome, depending on how one sees it. He began blabbing. Speaking his mind a bit too freely, to both his students and colleagues. Funny ideas—dangerous ideas. Things you're not supposed to think, let alone say aloud. That this mess they were living in was not *real* socialism. That Comrade

Kim Jong Il obviously didn't care about his own people. A *real* leader would never allow his people to starve, putting all the money into the military instead. That America was partly to blame, for sure—but another cause of the problem was right here, in Choson. That together, the people could do something, to change it—rise up—bring back *real socialism* to the homeland.

The final straw came when her grandfather was invited to Pyongyang to give a lecture and began speaking in this way. Shortly after his return to Wonsan, he came over to Un Ju's house one day to visit the family. As he approached their front door, a black car drove up to the house. Two men got out, grabbed her grandfather, and drove off.

They called the local police station. They called the security bureau. The party cell. Every office they could think of, day in and day out, trying to find out what had happened to her grandfather. Nobody would give them any information.

Eight months later, they received a phone call. "We have your father," the police said to Un Ju's mother. "You can come collect his body."

✪

Her grandfather's corpse was battered and bruised, nearly unrecognizable. Un Ju couldn't even begin to imagine the long, drawn-out pain and suffering he must have endured. Over the course of those eight months, they had managed to break every bone in his body.

To this day, she is tortured by mixed feelings about her grandfather. "He's my hero," she'll say when referring to him, her voice swollen with love and admiration for his bravery. Then, a few minutes later: "How could he have been so stupid? Why did he *say* those things? What the hell was he *thinking*?" After they buried him, there was no sense for Un Ju to remain in Wonsan, in North Korea. Her grandfather had damaged the family's Songbun so badly that her days in the performing troupe were finished. She would never be permitted to sing or dance on a stage again. Her art was her life, and at the age of eighteen, her life was now over.

THIRTY-SEVEN

AS THE SUN sets, we check in to the Tongmyong Hotel, one of the DPRK's bizarre architectural masterpieces. A structure that uncannily looks both hopelessly dated and like the prototype of some future building. Or else a model from an undergraduate architecture class that, in any other country, would have never been green-lighted. A diamond-shaped structure sitting just on the lip of the shore, from which a rickety bridge crossing commences the Jangdok Jetty. The hotel's exterior was recently lavished in a marine blue—on my first visit to the country in 2012, it was sea green. Beside the entrance to the hotel's main nine-story bulk, a two-story Streamline Moderne extension juts out to the right, almost like an afterthought, culminating by the edge of the pier with an elegant wraparound staircase that takes you up to a balcony that circles around the building toward precious sea views.

Enter the dim lobby—outside the capital, electricity is rationed sparingly, even in tourist-designated buildings. Squint to make out the details of the fantastic kitsch undersea sculpture that greets you: surrounded by potted plants, enormous plastic lobsters and sea urchins compete with an arrangement of shells against a rocky blue background. The circular open floor plan allows you to look up at the top-floor ceiling, from which dangles a massive chandelier with long tentacular hairs of fake diamonds.

From my room, I'm treated to the daily show of the sun descending into the mountains over the East Sea. Somehow I arrive at the perfect moment. I sit in one of the low chairs, positioned right in front of the window just for this performance of nature, and absorb every moment until the mountain has completely swallowed the gold orb and sky's phlox gives way to nocturne.

Along the jetty, locals climb over rocks, searching for mollusks and other tasty treasures of the sea. The jetty culminates in a lighthouse-crowned islet, from which some of the best views of Wonsan can be enjoyed. I recall walk-ing out there on an earlier trip, stepping over two slumbering drunks who were passed out on the lighthouse steps. I tried to enter, but the doors were locked. I followed the climb down to an unofficial fish market for enterprising local residents, where a woman with a bucket and a couple of knives had set up an improvised restaurant. For the equivalent of a few pennies, I enjoyed a sashimi breakfast composed of the morning's catch.

The hallways are perpetually shrouded in darkness, making it difficult to get around, especially at night. On my way up to the restaurant, I make a detour to the eighth floor to see if I happen to run into Mark or Simon. They had told me in Pyongyang that they rented the entire floor as their DPRK business headquarters. Indeed, I see a bunch of Chinese businessmen hanging around in the hallway, smok-ing outside their rooms, but not our drinking buddies from the Sosan. I consider asking if Simon or Mark is around, but my instincts caution me against that idea.

Upstairs, we are ushered into a private room Comrade Kim has reserved for our group. On the TV screen, instead of the standard Moranbong Band concert or nightly news broadcast, they're showing a DVD of the animated film *Kung Fu Panda*. The moment they walk into the room, the Koreans' eyes attach them-selves to the monitor. They're enraptured by every detail—the sophistication of the animation, the inventiveness of the characters' supernatural acrobatic abili-ties, the thrill and humor of the story line, the catchiness of the music. The same fascination, come to think of it, as a foreigner watching the Mass Games.

The waitresses lay out a magnificent spread. *Naengmyon* and roast chicken and scrambled eggs and kimchi and bulgogi and green bean pancakes and potato salad and rice, plus some Western dishes like spaghetti and french fries, together with all varieties of crab and the shellfish caught by Hwa as well as the fresh catches from the East Sea down below, pollack and herring and mackerel and cod, all dressed in herbs and spices.

And then there's the profound quantity of booze purchased earlier at the Kwangbok Department Store, now sprinkled in tiny soju cups across the table. We pour for each other, following the Korean custom of never serving yourself. The meal wears on, and jovial chatter is intermittently dispersed among the sunken fascinated glares at the film and the commentary it provokes among the Koreans. Min proudly displays her familiarity by reciting lines seconds before the characters on-screen. As postmeal cigarettes are lit, I submit to a beery haze as I chatter on amiably, relaxed enough after nearly a month in these people's constant company to let my guard down to a reasonable level, just above carelessness.

Without rising, Kim casually commences an after-dinner speech.

"Many of the foreigners who visit our country do not understand it," he begins. "I think the reason why is clear enough. It is because we are a socialist country. Very different from how the other countries do things. We all know this. But you, gentlemen..." He turns to the three of us. "You are different, too. You are not ordinary tourists. And I think we, all of us at KSTC, recognize this. The main reason I am interested in this tour is because it is for intellectuals. I also don't speak with *ordinary* people."

It is not the first desultory reference Comrade Kim has made to *ordinary* people. I'm starting to understand what it means here. That young man on the beach in Nampo who wanted to practice his English who told us he was just an *ordinary* worker. Min warning us never to do what we did to an *ordinary* tour guide. It is a covert reference to a class system that is said not to exist. Being elite or a *donju*—or an intellectual—makes you *extra*ordinary, it seems.

"You have a good understanding of our country," Kim continues, "how we do things here. This, Alek, is what makes Tongil Tours different from other tour companies. And I want you to know that KSTC will *always* be here to welcome you to our country. To facilitate the interests, the curiosity, of intellectuals like you."

We toast one last time and utter our words of thanks and appreciation to Comrade Kim. The end credits of *Kung Fu Panda* roll in the background.

"Of course," says Comrade Kim, adding a final word, "one of the most important things is security. Especially for Americans."

He turns to me.

"Alek and I have been careful to arrange that. And I was sure to speak to my contact in the Ministry of Foreign Affairs," he whispers. "When you travel with us, Travis, you will never have to worry."

He winks. I smile, unsure how to respond.

Making our way to the elevator, Roe grabs my hand, a wide, earnest look in his eye. "Comrade," he begins, "please promise me something."

"Yes?"

"Promise me you will always think good things about our co—" I feel my eyes starting to roll back in my head in expectation of yet another expression of nationalist zeal I've so often heard from North Korean men in states of drunken exuberance—"mpany."

Wait—did he just say our *company*? Not our *country*? Well, okay then. Startled, I step back and smile, returning his grip affectionately.

"Don't worry," I tell him. "KSTC will always have a place in my heart."

THIRTY-EIGHT

UN JU'S MOTHER was the first to leave. She was the one familiar with the route. A few months later, she sent a broker for her daughter. They landed in Shenyang in 2006; shortly after, they were able to earn enough to send for Un Ju's brother, selling the traditional Korean-style clothing they made. Shenyang has a large Korean community, including a sizeable population of defectors from the North. For them, it is a dangerous place, like all of China, because the police periodically do crackdowns. If caught, they would be sent back to North Korea, where slow, painful but certain death in a concentration camp likely awaited them. They worked and they saved until they had enough to pay a broker to take them the rest of the route, through Laos and Thailand, and then on to South Korea.

Un Ju's battles didn't end in the South. The plan had always been for her father to eventually join them, once they had enough to pay a broker. It is much more difficult, and thus expensive, for men to defect than women. Whereas women have the option of staying home as housewives, men are required to work, and work for the state. Since they're more highly monitored, that makes it much more difficult for a man to slip away for enough time to make it across the border to China.

Brokers are among the richest and best-connected people, and live a gangster-like existence. Since their work is considered highly criminal, and since they need access to a constant flow of cash in order to bribe all the officials it takes to turn a blind eye and allow them to conduct their activities, they show no compunction about blackmailing former clients when times are tough. Those former clients usually have families they have left behind, and those families are in a vulnerable position; if it is discovered by the authorities that someone from their clan defected to South Korea, they can be punished. (Recently, Pyongyang has sought to dispel this notion, using the case of high-profile defector Thae Yong Ho, a former diplomatic official at the DPRK Embassy in London. Months after Thae's defection, CNN's Will Ripley, in an amazing piece of reportage, was astoundingly granted permission to interview Thae's brother and sister in one of their homes in Pyongyang. They looked healthy. The sister claimed that nobody in their family had been punished. The brother, however, hinted at the inevitable stains on the family's Songbun. "If I don't wash this sin away by myself," he said, "my sons and future generations will have to work harder, to pay for this.")

As Un Ju and her mother and brother adjusted to life in the South while struggling to save enough money to buy their father's way out, the broker back in the North began threatening to report their defection to the authorities and land the father in a concentration camp if they didn't send hush money. They endured the psychological torture of this blackmail until eventually reaching the painful decision to cut all ties with the broker, giving up the dream of being reunited with the family patriarch.

THIRTY-NINE

IN THE MORNING, I awake to what can only be described as a *crinkling* sound. Is there a malfunction in the air conditioner? Perhaps even a fire somewhere? I lift myself out of bed, groggy, to investigate. It seems to be coming from the direction of the window, so I pull the blinds open. Seven stories below, directly beneath my room, a "volunteer" work unit of some three dozen, all diligently at work in squat, crushing rocks with hammers. Punishing my lazy bourgeois ass for daring to sleep till seven on a Sunday. And I thought Sunday was the designated day off for everyone. Not in Wonsan, at least.

I have a shower, go upstairs for breakfast. I feel strangely unaffected by last night's drinking. Everyone else is already seated at the breakfast table. This time, we're dining communally, in a room overlooking the harbor. Min is in a particularly dapper, chatty mood. As the waitress pours my coffee, she asks about my university studies. She knows I've just finished my PhD at the Royal College of Art in London, but what about my undergraduate years in New York? I tell her I studied literature and philosophy. She asks if I abide by an "official philosophy." I ask her what she means by that. "Well, you know, here in Korea we have the Juche Idea," she replies. "Is there an official philosophy in America or Germany?"

I tell her no, that in the West, philosophy operates differently. That there's no one central idea that is meant to sum up the meaning of all life and reality. Instead, philosophy serves as an open-ended quest for truth, one that necessarily has no finite conclusive point.

She appears unsatisfied with my answer.

"Well, there is one parable that I've always liked, that holds great philosophical sway for me," I say. "You've heard of Socrates, who is regarded as the father of Western philosophy?"

Min nods. Rings a bell, at least.

"He was asked who the wisest man in Athens was. He said in response, 'I don't know. I know a lot of wise people, but I don't know who the wisest of them could be. Give me one week to figure it out.' So he went around Athens, interviewing all of the wise men and women he found, asking them to tell him all that they knew. And at the end of one week, he returned to the man who had asked him that question. He told him, 'I've figured it out. I'm the wisest man in all of Athens.' The man was aghast. How had he reached this conclusion? 'Because,' said Socrates, 'I'm the only one who knows that I know nothing.'"

Ha, Min laughs and then looks perplexed. "But what does it mean?" she asks.

"Well," I try, "it illustrates how philosophy is meant to function—at least in the Western tradition."

"But how can you be smart and know nothing?"

"He doesn't say he *knows* nothing. He says *he knows he knows* nothing. Philosophy is knowledge about knowledge, thinking about thinking. So what the story means, I think, is that certainty—about anything—is an illusion. Even if we are told something is a fact, we can never really be sure that it's true. Because, Socrates would say, there is no such thing as certainty. There is always the possibility that what we believe to be true, that *what we have been told* is true, is merely an illusion—or *propaganda*. In a sense, there is no such thing as truth—there are only greater and lesser arguments."

Min ponders this as Roe translates the parable for Hwa, who had been looking on at our exchange with intense curiosity. At the end of the story, he gives a similar laugh and then assumes a ponderous gaze. Roe and Hwa discuss it, puzzled, and then Min relays my interpretation of it. Hwa pauses to consider it and then digs back into his bean paste soup.

Alexandre glares at me from across the table, a slight grin on his face. *What?* I mouth. I was cautiously indirect, though I realize how dangerous the implications of everything I've just said are. But I can't be bothered to fret over it. Maybe it's reckless, but I don't care. I even feel relieved somehow. Far from being a gesture of defiance, it was more an act of self-assurance. More for me than for them. A way to demonstrate, however meagerly, that I still have a foothold in a reality much larger than the web I am currently caught in.

I finish my breakfast in a state of total calm and relaxation, like how a Catholic must feel after a morning spent at the confessional—relieved of all taxing psychological burdens, forgiven and blessed to continue onward.

I go back to my room to pack up and prepare for checkout. The crinkling sound continues. I look out the window. They're still at it, those citizens of Wonsan, pounding away, turning rocks into rubble. They'll be there all morning. *Breaking up big rocks on the chain gang / Breaking rocks and serving my time.*

FORTY

A FEW MONTHS after Un Ju's arrival in Seoul, a major news station asked to interview her about her experiences as a defector. A pretty standard request: North Korean defectors suffer systematic discrimination in the South and often experience difficulty finding gainful employment; one of the few ways they have to earn money is by selling their stories to journalists. Un Ju agreed to the interview, with the stipulation that her face be blurred so as to protect her identity—and her father back home in Wonsan.

When the piece aired, Un Ju was enraged to see that they did nothing to conceal her face. She contacted a lawyer and was preparing to pursue legal action against the station for breaking its agreement.

"But you're a performer," the representative from the station argued in response. "Don't you want to be famous? Now everyone knows who you are. This is going to help your career!"

"No," she said. "I'm a *stage* performer. I have no desire to be famous on-screen—and certainly not at the expense of my father."

When it became clear that she had no intention of reneging on the lawsuit, the station's representatives upped their game. They told her that if she was going to behave this way, she would never make it in South Korea. That she would earn a reputation for being difficult, for being a brat, and that no one would ever give her a job, that she would wind up a failure. She considered this. She was a new arrival in the South, after all; perhaps they were right. She still only had a limited means of understanding how the society functioned. Dissuaded, she agreed to drop the case against them.

It was too late, anyway. Soon after the piece aired, the police in Wonsan came for her father. He was thrown in prison. Luckily, by this time, she and her mother had earned enough money to send to North Korea—enough, at least, to buy her father out of prison via another broker.

In order to save himself—for the DPRK now had clear, televised evidence that the family had defected—her father had to divorce her mother in absentia, publicly denouncing his former family. Soon after, he remarried. The last time Un Ju spoke to her father was four years ago. With a broker, he had traveled to a border region where mobile phones can pick up signals from China. Defectors often speak to family members they have left behind in this way, but they only have one or two minutes—if they speak for longer, the security apparatus might pick up the signal and be able to locate them. "The call was nothing," Un Ju told me. They couldn't have much of a conversation in that tiny sliver of time. "My father just kept repeating 'I'm sorry' over and over again."

Since arriving in South Korea, Un Ju's done a little bit of everything, work-wise, to survive, minus some of the more unpleasant jobs her female compatriots have unluckily fallen into since leaving the North. Un Ju herself had been used, virtually raped, any number of times since leaving—mainly in China, when she was still green to the ways of the outside world and would believe anything any man told her, only to see him vanish as soon as he got what he wanted. She knew that any kind of sex work—be it online chatting or real-world prostitution—wasn't for her.

Nor has she ever opted to become a professional victim. Which is what, she says, participating in the celebrity defector culture effectively amounts to. She's seen so many go this route, and she can't really blame them. Though it is a rule that every student learns on day one of any introductory journalism ethics course—any information you pay for is bad information—South Korean and foreign journalists alike are quick to forget it when it comes to interviewing North Korean refugees. Since the years of the Arduous March, which launched an exodus of economic migrants on that perilous journey through China and Southeast Asia to South Korea, the defector's tale of woe and suffering has become a cottage industry in publishing and the media. Defectors quickly come to learn of the harsh reality of life in the South—a reality that nothing in the North prepared them for. It's well known that South Korea is considered one of the most competitive societies, but what does this really mean on a day-by-day level?

To understand the prominent role that nepotism plays in South Korea, one need look no further than the Chaebol system. "Chaebol," which means loosely "wealth clique" in Korean, refers to the powerful family-run conglomerates with close ties to the government, companies like Hyundai and Samsung. Undoubtedly, these Chaebol are responsible for the rapid acceleration of South Korea's economy since the 1950s.

Ironically, the Chaebol system has many striking parallels to the elites occupying the top of the Songbun system in the North. In both countries, a certain number of powerful families form the unofficial upper crust, securing all wealth, power, and opportunity for themselves and their minions. In the DPRK, these families historically aligned themselves to the Kim dynasty, while in the ROK, these families, most of whom opportunistically served the Japanese during their occupation of the peninsula, similarly married themselves as closely as possible to the seat of political power; it was under South Korean dictator Park Chung Hee that the industrial empire of the Chaebol system was established thanks to the granting of government loans.

The Chaebol system operates a trickle-down effect. As a result, South Korean society is tribal, clannish. Those in positions of power are more likely to give jobs and other opportunities, when not to family members, to those they went to school with, those they grew up in the same neighborhood alongside. Outsiders have no hope of penetrating such a system.

Very few South Koreans wish to have anything to do with North Korean defectors; among those few, one finds the typical range of opportunists—Christian pastors, right-wing politicians, exploitative employers, and journalists—eager to use the extremely vulnerable outliers toward the accomplishment of their own dubious ends. Socially and economically, the majority of the South's some thirty thousand North Korean defectors are left to suffer the humiliating consequences of their systematic exclusion from the mainstream of ROK life. That in their home country they were conditioned to view themselves as little more than human instruments of propaganda makes them all the more ripe for exploitation upon arrival in this new land of freedom.

Finding every door of gainful employment shut to them, Un Ju explains, some refugees unsurprisingly have found that there is at least one, potentially highly lucrative, way to make ends meet: by telling their stories. North Korean defectors have become best-selling authors and television celebrities and are highly sought after on the lecture circuit. Un Ju—like many defectors who happen to have that winning combination of being bright, physically attractive, and articulate—has dabbled in this world. But ultimately, she sees it as a dishonest spectacle. Defectors are incentivized to exaggerate and fabricate. And it is an endless cycle: the more one talks to the media, the more famous one becomes, the more one is expected to give them. Add to that the psychological ailments that many defectors suffer from—not only from whatever they might have experienced growing up in the DPRK but from the traumas they've experienced in China and Southeast Asia on the escape route, not to mention their subsequent ostracization and exploitation in the South—and you have a situation ripe for unreliable testimony.

Because the media, in the end, only want one thing. "When you say that line on the air, we need you to cry," the talk show producer instructed her friend when she went on a popular television show where North Koreans talk about the horrible lives they endured in the North while boasting of the great freedoms they enjoy in the South. "Can you cry for us? Real tears. Because otherwise, no one will believe you."

For the biggest stars of the circuit, a peculiar problem eventually arises: once you have given the media everything, what more can you give?

Invention, as well as "borrowing" details from others' life narratives, becomes a necessity. That borrowing, it turns out, isn't all that hard to finagle; the defector community in the South is quite close-knit, and everyone knows each other. Un Ju remembers the email she got from one young woman she knew who went on to become a major star on the defector circuit. The email was sent out to "practically everyone," Un Ju says, asking for traumatic details from their lives in North Korea and subsequent defection for a book she was writing. She had gotten a deal but was clearly having difficulty piecing together the kind of victim narrative that her publisher and journalist coauthor were after. Un Ju ignored the email; others didn't. Their stories became hers in the course of writing the book, forming a gruesome "autobiography" of life in the brutal police state and the perilous yet ultimately redemptive passage to "freedom."

Her fellow defectors didn't complain publicly that their stories had been stolen; people who are disempowered seldom do—and even when they do speak up, they are usually ignored. Minor controversies over inconsistencies in her story have erupted since the book's publication, but they have been largely chalked up to psychological trauma, the burdens of childhood memory, and the celebrity defector's difficulties with communicating in English. To Un Ju's annoyance, nobody has called into question the larger, systemic problem in which these issues are rooted. The book continues to sell in large quantities all over the world, her TED talk—featuring, of course, *real tears*—is a favorite share on social media, and her appearances on the lecture circuit are rumored to command fees of five- and six-digit figures. Says Un Ju, "When I look at her, I just see a person who is really confused. I genuinely believe she no longer knows what's true and what's not. She no longer belongs to herself. She's become a tool—from one system of propaganda to another."

★

What bothers Un Ju more than the apparent corruption of the celebrity defector industry—she is wise enough, after all, to realize that corruption is rampant everywhere one looks, even here, in the so-called free world—is an even more nebulous form of dishonesty that, to her, is profound in its power to corrupt. It is that people forget who they are when they come to the South. And they forget without ever reconciling with the past. When Un Ju finally made it to the South Korean Embassy in Thailand, she was thrown into a waiting cell with about four hundred other women. At that time, there was a particularly high number of defectors coming through, and for whatever bureaucratic reason, the embassy told them that only five could fly to Seoul at a time. She would have to wait her turn with the others.

"They turned into *animals*," Un Ju said. "It was like we were trapped in this cage. It brought out the worst in everyone—we were no longer human beings."

Since the women were not, in fact, being held prisoner but merely awaiting their transport to freedom, they were pretty much left to their own devices in the overcrowded communal space—which they couldn't leave, since it would mean leaving South Korean territory and losing their place in line. A gang-like atmosphere of terror prevailed, with the toughest women setting the rules and brutalizing all those who didn't obey. "One teenage girl was five months pregnant," Un Ju relayed. "She secretly went to the embassy officials and asked whether she might skip the line because of her condition. When the other women found out about it, they surrounded her, a gang of them, and beat her until she miscarried."

Each of the brutalizers commanded her own territory, the area on the floor surrounding her mattress. If you even accidentally stepped on to that "territory" when walking past, you were liable to receive a beating.

Un Ju was selected at random to become one of their regular victims. In retrospect, she can't blame them. They themselves, she recognizes, had been brutalized. There were the regimentation and authoritarianism of daily life in the North, sure, and any number of traumas experienced there that they were running away from; what's more, many of these women had been trafficked or else escaped from similar situations of captivity in the course of their route through China. It was to be expected that, for lack of empowerment, they would then exercise their own brutality over anyone they perceived to be weaker than them.

The terror became so great that Un Ju one day decided to escape from the holding center. It would mean she would never make it to the South, never get to see her mother again—who by then had already made it to the ROK. But anything would be better than the hell of being trapped in a cage with these animals. She was scaling the wall of the embassy when a security guard saw her and pulled her back down.

Finally, one day after the women tried to attack her again, she grabbed a nail file she had hidden under her pillow and charged at them, growling like a rabid dog. "Look at her!" the women said, stepping back. "The bitch has lost her mind!"

Un Ju played the part accordingly. Imitating a madwoman, it meant she was isolated and friendless for the rest of the time she spent in there. But at least she was left alone.

Such accounts, Un Ju points out, are noticeably absent from all those bestselling defectors' tales. And there are good reasons for this. By those who were with her at the holding center at the embassy in Bangkok, at least one of those celebrity defectors—so beloved by the media for her sweet, gentle demeanor—has been remembered as one of the worst bullies.

FORTY-ONE

I'M ALWAYS TAKEN to the same restaurant in Wonsan, on the same street as the hotel stretching along the port. I remember well my first visit here in 2012 because it was also the night of Kim Jong Un's first public address. The one in which he famously stated that the people should never have to tighten their belts again, subtly distancing himself from his father's tarnished legacy of the Arduous March and implying a renewed focus on economic development. We walked into the main dining room, and there he was on the large screen, all the restaurant employees and customers standing around in complete silence. My guides stopped in their path and joined them. Kim Jong Il rarely spoke in public—this was something new indeed. The deification cult of Kim Jong Un had hardly gotten under way, and most North Koreans simply didn't know anything about him, let alone what his voice sounded like. On my first night in the country, when I had asked one of my guides what she knew about the new leader, she stalled. "I heard he is very kind—very nice..." Then she asked carefully whether the Western media had reported anything about him. "Only that he was raised in Switzerland," I said. She nodded her head, though that was clearly news to her. And now, there he was, live on television, for the entire nation to see—and hear. Speaking aloud. Telling them that it would all be okay. A new era had arrived.

★

After lunch, we stroll down the gingko-lined boulevard, past a typical shop selling everything from socks to household appliances, from televisions to antibiotics, to the provincial art gallery. Upon entering, you're met with an array of mostly underwhelming stock images on canvas, a mixture of classical East Asian ink motifs but also Norkorealist oil paintings and Chosonhwa scenes of abundance and happiness in the Korean People's Paradise. It has all become a bit stale and cliché by now. As I make my way further through the gallery's corridors, however, I come upon something I have never seen before. I call the gallerist over. Who made these?

"Oh, the one of the waterfall, that's Kuryong Falls. Have you been there? It's very famous, in Mount Kumgang... The artist is Lee Ryong Hee. From Wonsan. He represents the newest style in Korean oil painting."

The work in question is on a tiny canvas, the paint applied in such thick impasto in places that it borders on abstraction. The sludge forms two mountains delineated by extreme color contrast; on the left, a clump of rich dark greens occasionally coalesces into a dire blackness, while the mountain overtaking the right side of the canvas consists of competing tones of white and beige applied in hurried though delicate swaths—strokes that alternate between thick and thin—in some spots so thin, in fact, that the canvas material becomes apparent. The sliver of flowing water between the two mountains you have to strain to see—it is all but annihilated in the emotional swell of the paint. Follow it to the bottom, and it's not the colors but the sculptural formation of the paint, a snaky swirl, that pronounces the ultimate landing of the falling water. But the pool, such as it is, isn't actually there; for it is the same flesh tone of the rocky landscape hovering over it. And to the left, following the dark mountain's descent toward the landing stream, a clash of violets arises amid the increasingly grassy green: the birth of springtime, of florescence, is witnessed here, at the bottom of it all.

Taking note of my enthusiasm, the gallerist disappears into the storage room and reemerges with a massive canvas. "This," he exclaims, "is Lee Ryong Hee's masterpiece—and it's not for sale." And it really *is* a Wonsan painting. A portrait of an old fisherman, seated on the rocks of the Jangdok jetty, not far from where I enjoyed that sushi breakfast once upon a time. He is an old man, his jacket rendered in mustard yellows. But it is the details of the wrinkles on his sun-battered face, the weathered, reserved glare of seriousness, of sadness, as he stares at the other end of the fishing rod, that gives the painting its rich melancholic atmosphere. Fishing is an activity typically enjoyed by older men upon retirement in North Korea, a time when there is little left to do in passing one's final hours. But Lee's painting would never make it into the Korean Art Gallery in Pyongyang. There is no joy in his subject's face, no visible display of contentment with life's rewards. No hackneyed signifiers of happiness under the Supreme Leader's guidance. It is far too true to life, too lacking in idealism—too dangerous in its myriad potentialities of interpretation—to ever fit well into the Norkorealist canon.

I'm surprised to find a painter so deeply involved with the raw materiality of his art. As innocent as the painting may appear at first glance, such stylistic bluntness is as subversive as any I've encountered so far, in all my travels in the DPRK. It hearkens back to that moment so long ago, during the Japanese occupation of the country, when, north of the DMZ at least, Korea's art historical evolution was effectively halted. I recall those Mun Hak Su landscapes in the gallery on Kim Il Sung Square and wonder if Lee has seen them as well, if he is conscious that he seems to be picking up where Mun left off. When Korea was occupied by Japan, ambitious Korean artists would go to Tokyo to study. Japan was the first place in East Asia to import Western styles of oil painting as early as the 1860s. French impressionism and academicism—a combination of romantic and neoclassical styles—became the overriding influences. When the Second World War came to an end and Japan was forced to give up Korea as a colony, these styles were among the most popular in both the northern and southern halves of the peninsula. Whereas art in South Korea would continue to grow and evolve on par with an increasingly globalized diversity of styles that eventually fell under the aegis of "contemporary art," something else happened in North Korea—art's evolution came to a halt with this style or else evolved according to its own new state-sanctioned dictates, depending on one's point of view.

But Lee has taken painting further, into an even more individualistic mode of expression. The gallerist smiles at my excitement, leads me into the back room where he begins to lay out stacks of unstretched canvas across a small wooden table. More canvases by Lee but also similar works by two other Wonsan painters, Choi Ho In and Pak Ung Gwon. All of the canvases are quite small, like Lee's. Still, I'm amazed to find, here in Wonsan, what amounts to a new school of expressionist landscape painting. None of these paintings can be found in Pyongyang; the artists are unheard-of there. It makes you realize the extent to which not only is North Korea as a country cut off from the rest of the world, but most of the cities and regions *within* the country are similarly cut off from one another.

In one of Choi's paintings, a farmer is shown mending a fence. Unlike the standard propagandistic works in this genre, depicting agricultural effort as the collective endeavor it is officially meant to be, this farmer is solitary, alone—a clear reflection of the new era, where people have taken to growing their own food for both personal consumption and profit, a practice that began in desperation and defiance but that the government gradually had to legalize. As in Lee's painting, it is the colors that make everything come alive, that transform what could otherwise be a rather grim scene (and probably is in actuality) into a captured moment of deep reflection and beauty. This is cerebral painting, melancholic in its finessed affect, miles away in distance and sensibility from the obvious kitsch of the capital. It signals a subtle pragmatism—everything may be broken here, but we will just repair it, as we always do, since nothing new, no replacements, will be on their way. We must make do with what we have, with what we've inherited.

Finally, there's Pak Ung Gwon, who, the gallerist tells me, is the oldest of the three artists, already in his eighties. Unlike the other two, Pak gives more care to the human form in his painting of a narrow lane dividing a hillside village. Four small figures are seen making their way up and down the street—children on their way home from school, made obvious more by their colorful backpacks than their diminutive stature. More than the houses and network of telephone poles, the Cézannean strokes forming the mountains in the background, your eyes are drawn to the sunburnt face of the small girl coming toward us. Amid the beige white of the houses making up the side of the street, the eyes might nearly overlook the form of a distraught beggar woman—or grasshopper vendor—crouched against one of the houses, a shockingly revealing painting for any DPRK artist, which is likely why it is partly erased.

These paintings tellingly depict the lateness of the day, the hour—a quiet rebellion. For me, it is an invigorating moment of discovery. No one else has seen these works—the gallery is empty, after all; presumably not even locals care to visit. Probably no one else will see them for a very long time, if ever. It dawns on me just how truly *isolated* these artists, these people, are—but also I feel momentarily rescued from the well of cynicism I have lately fallen into by the realization that it is still possible to discover something wholly new in this world. Here, far from the prying eyes of officialdom, you have artists resisting state-sanctioned idealization in favor of a synesthetic, highly individualized perception of blunt reality. A small sign of resistance, perhaps, but one that cannot be underestimated: there *is* such a thing as expression here.

I climb back into the van with Hwa, who's pulled up next to the gallery. Suddenly, the traffic cop from yesterday, the one we'd snubbed, appears. He demands Hwa roll down his window. Asks to see his license. Hwa produces it. The cop grabs it out of his hand and continues walking toward the square up ahead.

The rest of our entourage takes their seats in the van. Hwa tells Comrade Kim what just happened. The traffic cop is standing at the intersection up ahead, just at the entrance to the main square. Kim tells Hwa to drive up, park in the middle of the square, leave the engine running. Kim slams the door behind him and runs back toward the cop.

A lengthy argument ensues. The cop has no reason to disguise his repugnance. *These arrogant assholes from Pyongyang think they can come to* my *town and piss all over it. You want your driver's license back? Well, guess what. Your driver disobeyed a traffic cop, Comrade. Oh, I'm sorry, you've got foreigners in the car? Are you losing face here? Well, tough fucking shit. This is Wonsan, asshole, not some backwater stinkhole. The Supreme Leadership has a house here. Tourists don't make you and your driver exempt from following the traffic laws of Choson.*

As the argument wears on, the price in the officer's mind increases. First Roe gets out, thinking he can pull some local sway. A true son of Wonsan, after all—maybe they know the same people. Min follows shortly thereafter. Hwa remains frozen in the driver's seat, scared shitless. What can he do? He was just following the big boss's orders when he accelerated past the cop. Now, it is up to the boss to get him out of this disaster.

He has a perfect driving record so far. He's never had an accident, never a single traffic violation. North Korea operates on a three strikes system. You hit three, and your license is taken away—your driving career is over when that happens. Of course nowadays, you can bribe your way out of it. He is hoping that's what Kim will do—worst-case scenario is that he emerges from all this with a strike on his license. He'll get shit for it back at the office in Pyongyang, regardless of whose fault it is. But it's out of his hands at this point.

Alek and Alexandre and I wait in the car with Hwa. The argument drags on for more than forty minutes. I study the huge ship docked at the port at the end of the square. The *Man Gyong Bong 92*. This is the passenger ship that used to go between Japan and North Korea. The *92* refers to its year of construction, a gift for Kim Il Sung's eightieth birthday, built with funds raised by the Chongryon association in Japan. For a while, the ship would transport cargo as well as Zain-ichi Korean visitors between the shores of the two countries, until 2006, when Japan finally banned North Korea from entering its waters. After that, the vessel was briefly used as a tourist cruise ship between the Rason special economic zone in the far north of the country and Mount Kumgang. Since 2015, it's been docked here, dormant. For Zainichi Korean repatriates living in Wonsan, it must serve as a painful daily reminder of their separation from the loved ones they left behind in Japan and the increasing unlikelihood of ever being perma-nently reunited.

It is not Comrade Kim's first run-in with the authorities. But most North Kore-ans have had an encounter with the fuzz at one time or another—that's just one of the inevitabilities of life in a police state. Local cops are little more than thugs in uniform, most of them looking for bribes of cash and cigarettes and nothing further. They are by far easier to deal with than the *bowibu,* the Ministry of State Security officers charged with investigating offenses of a political nature and who operate the country's notorious prison camp system—once *they* become involved, it's either far too late or else the amount of the bribe will increase a thousandfold, beyond most citizens' ability to ever pay. With these lower-level cops, unless of course it is a very serious crime such as murder, an agreement can usually be reached. The trick is making sure it doesn't escalate to the point of blows, as they won't hesitate to deliver a severe beating on the spot in front of everyone who happens to be passing by. Which, if you're unlucky enough to get caught up with one having a bad day, you might get anyway.

The presence of our foreign eyes, as well as Comrade Kim's announced cre-dentials as the son of a prominent Pyongyang officer, spares him from such a punishment. It's getting the price down to an amount he is willing to pay, while securing the least repercussions for his driver, that forms the basis of the conflict.

Whereas the cop sees in Comrade Kim a bratty sense of Pyongyang entitle-ment, Kim merely suffers from the very same deep-seated hatred of authority that is inborn in all inhabitants of a police state. It is this bottled-up hatred that frequently erupts in manifestations of physical violence. Kim is too proud and sophisticated to engage in such skirmishes—and anyway, he was never much of a skilled fighter, having lived his life in comfy white-collar environs. And so he is more prone to committing these minor fuck-you infractions, like the traffic violation that has led us here.

Now, he will have to pay for it. Others have noticed Comrade Kim's penchant for rebellion. It is one of the qualities that attracted Min to her boss. "He's like my brother," she once told me. It's not hard to see why. They both spent a significant amount of their lives abroad and so have a good idea of how the outside world works; this tends to enlarge one's perspective on things; it also makes them a minority, among the world's sole cosmopolitan North Koreans.

Comrade Kim's boss has noticed it as well. That the comrade seems to suffer from a potentially life-threatening malady: loose tongue syndrome. An affliction that can have deadly consequences not just for the individual but for all those around him. Kim is bright and a big earner, and his boss happens to like him on a personal level. He is, after all, a formidable personality, always cracking jokes and dispensing his worldly wisdom while at the same time running a tight ship of discipline and order around the office. An asset to the organization, as it were.

So after a particularly raucous night out at a restaurant, when his tongue got perhaps a little too loose, his boss invited him into the office the next morning and bluntly asked him to refrain from the consumption of alcohol from now on. Comrade Kim nodded his assent. But he never apologized. He hadn't been reported. No point in expressing regret for things you may or may not have said when no one's forcing you. And anyway, his boss is no one to feel threatened by; Kim's protectors operate on a much higher level.

✪

After three quarters of an hour, Kim returns, followed by Min and Roe, Hwa's license in hand.

"Drive," he commands. Hwa accelerates.

I wonder how many fifties he had to peel off that roll of US dollars he keeps in his front pocket.

We make our way out of Wonsan in silence.

We're twenty-five miles outside the city when Min startles us with an announce-ment: "I forgot something."

That something is an SD card. Bringing out her MP3 player, Min stuck her headphones in her ear, but when she hit play, nothing happened. The card must have fallen out somehow, somewhere…And so she begins combing through the contents of her purse, sorting through the hand sanitizer bottles, lipstick contain-ers, eyeliner, phone charger, money clips grasping bills of different currencies, plus an array of gimmicky items she must have bought from sky shopping on her last flight: gold-plated credit card protectors, mini flashlight, a fitness tracker bracelet, container for anti-aging serum, pens with hidden USB sticks—but alas, no card.

A look of panic comes across her face as she mentally retraces her steps over the past two hours. "What's wrong?" Kim calls out from the front passenger seat, awoken from slumber by the disturbed energies behind him. She tells him. He shrugs but tells Hwa to keep driving. We've nearly reached our destination.

Winding around a steep and twisting mountainside road, we arrive at the entrance to Ullim Falls. Roe gets out at the entrance to give the staff stand-ing guard all the necessary details required at each stop of the journey—names, nationalities, passport numbers.

We pull into the parking lot, step out into the bloody orb of day. Day, cascad-ing like a waterfall down into the lot, where a brown-uniformed old soldier man emerges to stand guard, silver-toothed grin accenting his tanned visage.

We tread along the creek-parallel path leading up to the falls. Roe accompa-nies Alek and Alexandre and me. Kim stays behind with Hwa to help Min look for the card in her luggage.

"You know what this means, right?" Alexandre whispers tersely. "This could be a big fucking problem for her. An SD card. There's no way there's nothing foreign on it."

Roe's approaching from close behind, so I shush him. Yes, it's illegal, but now everyone does it, and every idiot knows. The big collective secret of the era: foreign media. This is why all the cinemas in the country are virtually barren now: people would rather watch what's on the USB sticks, SD cards, and, now less often, DVDs they acquire through black-market trade. Even the famous Taedongmun cinema in central Pyongyang, right on Sungni Street, has resorted to showing a Bolly-wood film this month. There was a time when fights would break out in the lines of people struggling to get into a cinema when the latest flick was showing—people were desperate for entertainment, and films, though filled with clunky propaganda, were at least a diversion. Clearly, there's no audience for the locally produced flicks any longer. The only time you watch one of those is when you're forced.

As Alek and Alexandre skip ahead, Roe catches up with me. "Travis," he says, "what about healthcare in Germany?"

"What about it?"

"Do you have to pay when you see a doctor?"

Well, yes and no, I tell him. There's an insurance system. It's complicated.

He pauses to consider this. "So you buy the insurance, and then the insurance company pays the doctor?"

"Yes. It's like that," I say.

"But is it expensive?"

"It can be, but it depends on a lot of factors. There's the state insurance system, and then there's private insurance, which can be cheaper, but only if you're young and healthy. And women usually have to pay more for it, since there's a good possibility that they might one day have maternity concerns, which gets expensive—or at least that's the position of the private insurance companies."

Roe considers all this carefully and then shrugs at the injustice of it all. "Here in Choson, healthcare is free for all citizens," he pronounces.

I nod, silently congratulate him for following the script so well. In fact, save for a few hospitals in the capital catering to the elite, healthcare is now subject to the same graft as every other facet of life. Outside hospitals and clinics, cigarette merchants have set up shop. Patients going in buy packs with which to gift the doctors in exchange for treatment; the doctors resell them to the merchants and pocket the cash on their way out at the end of their shifts. Medicine for most ailments is in such short supply that only hard currency will get you any. But, of course, none of this is mentioned to foreigners.

It's amusing at first, but as time wears on, the more you know about this place, the more annoyed you get when they lie to you. Because it reinforces the awareness that you, like they, are playing a role. And neither side has any choice in the matter—everything about the situation feels unnatural. As a tour guide, one of your primary duties is to lie to the foreigners in your charge, and as a foreigner, your role is to accept those lies unquestioningly. To give Roe and Min credit, they lie to us a lot less often than other tour guides I've had here. Roe barely speaks at all, but he generally follows Min's lead. This has less to do with Min's failure to abide by all she was taught during the long and rigorous training process that all tour guides have to undergo and more to do with her formative years spent abroad. From her own experience, she realizes that a lot of what she has been instructed to tell us we simply would not, could not believe.

Often they will lie about the most absurd things. On an architecture study trip I joined in 2014, we were given a tour of the Taedongmun Cinema House. Constructed in 1955, it was the first cinema erected in the country following the Korean War, and—with its columnar neoclassical facade, crowned with a triad statue of a gun-toting soldier, book-wielding peasant woman, and hoe-hoisting worker—is an architectural landmark of the capital. (The interior is a comparatively banal affair, owing to its refurbishment in 2008 with shiny marble flooring, following the "marblization" that similarly pervades official and commercial interiors throughout mainland China today: monkey see, monkey do.)

On this tour, we were accompanied by Simon from Koryo Tours, who asked our Korean guide, a middle-aged woman named Ms. O, whether we might be able to see the projection booth. Ms. O exchanged a few words with the manager of the cinema in Korean and then informed us that the booth was locked and no one on the premises had keys. Upon entering one of the two screening halls, Simon, his voice steeped in sarcasm, cried out, "Ms. O! Is that woman okay? Nobody has keys, so she must be trapped inside! Shouldn't we call someone to get her out?" We turned to the back of the hall, and sure enough, a cleaning woman could be seen busily dusting the inside of the brightly illuminated projection booth. We watched as Ms. O's face fell onto the shiny marble beneath us.

To be fair, the situation was outside Ms. O's control. The manager of the cinema told us it was not possible, she relayed the message; whether the fib was his or hers matters little. As Simon would tell me later, "In most countries, you are generally permitted to do anything you want, unless there is a law forbidding it. In the DPRK, it is the opposite: everything is forbidden, until you are told that it is allowed." Encountering these daily frustrations, the tendency is to ask your guides, "Why?" But in response, your guides will merely laugh at you. Because "Why?" is a question only a foreigner would ever ask.

★

The constant lying on those earlier visits only made me more curious. It was, after all, never an *unfriendly* lying; I always enjoyed cordial if somewhat stiff relations with my guides. And I'm certain that they never caught on that I knew I was being lied to. With the exception of Ms. O, who had worked in the 1980s at the DPRK Embassy in Vienna, none of my guides had ever been abroad. They had all heard of the internet and had a vague idea of what it was, owing to foreigners' descriptions and access to their own highly limited local version, the Intranet. Because of the continuing information blockade, most—but not all—North Koreans have no idea how much we actually know about their country.

"Are North Koreans free to travel abroad?" someone asked one of our guides on my first visit to the country.

"Oh yes, we can travel anywhere we want, anytime."

Of course, everyone knows that travel abroad is completely forbidden for all but the North Korean elite, who are only permitted to go on official business. Not only that, but North Koreans are not even permitted to leave their hometown unless they apply for and are granted a special travel pass that specifies their destination and the length of time they are permitted to remain there. Not only is there no freedom of speech, there is no freedom of movement.

Even when what your guide says blatantly contradicts the very scene before your eyes, they feel relatively unashamed about lying. "There are no special families here," a twenty-seven-year-old resident of Pyongyang, the capital of the elite, once told me—shortly after visiting the tony club of the Ryugyong Health Complex, with its ground-floor shops hawking Rolex watches and designer-label clothing. The triumph of socialism, indeed.

Such lies, I realized, point to a profoundly unsettling aspect of the zeitgeist: while capitalism has come to encroach upon virtually every facet of life, these activities are still technically illegal, as the regime has yet to officially change its ideological tune. No wonder, then, that the guides haven't changed theirs; they simply haven't been told to, and it would be dangerous for them to even bring it up. And were the authorities to do so, it would be a tacit admission of these contradictions, which are not supposed to be discussed.

Anyway, psychologically, lying does not have the same taboo here as it does in most cultures. North Koreans are reared with the implicit understanding that lying is a very natural thing to do. It is a survival mechanism. Because in this highly specific version of reality, the fabric of truth is woven with lies. Often, the lies are unknown to the citizens themselves, so tightly knit are they in the embroidery, everything they have been taught about the world and their country's place in it.

One of the most dreaded rituals of daily life—and arguably one of the more ingenious instruments of domestic psychological warfare installed by the regime—is self-criticism sessions, a practice commonly deployed in the Soviet Union and Maoist China. They begin in the classroom in elementary school and continue into the workplace in adulthood. In these exercises of self-diminution, you are expected to cite one of the teachings of the Great Leader, Dear Leader, or Respected Marshal and then illustrate how either you or, more usually, one of your comrades in the room has failed to live up to that high ideal. But like all aspects of daily life, self-criticism has come to be infused with a fair dose of the performative. As these sessions can result in permanently acrimonious relations between people—sowing the seeds of distrust is very much the underlying point—those who are a bit wiser tend to prepare for these sessions in advance by conferring with trusted friends and scripting slight offenses with which to accuse one another. Your turn this week, mine next week. In this way, you avoid igniting a feud that might inevitably develop into a more genuinely nasty series of back-and-forth accusations, which could potentially result in consequences far more serious and dangerous for both parties. By scripting the drama beforehand, the lie becomes a convenient truth for both accuser and accused.

So when my Korean guides would lie to my face, I didn't feel exactly offended, as I might anywhere else in the world. After all, I was essentially lying to them about a lot of things, in my own awkward, likely equally unconvincing way—who I am, the nature of the work I do, what I really believe. The question then becomes: How far can things really develop in any kind of relationship between two humans when virtually everything framing the situation is false, rooted in a lie?

For me, this is a question from which I can retreat, a question I can ponder from a safe, comparatively cozy distance each time I leave the country. While for my North Korean friends—if it is even possible for a foreigner to be friends with a North Korean—it is a question that they inevitably have to spend their entire lives ignoring.

The result, I have come to believe, is that at times, they do not even realize they are lying. They live in a perpetual ontological quandary, where truth becomes increasingly difficult to discern.

There are economic corollaries to all of this, of course. Tourism, after all, is a hard-currency business. And idealism is one of the official currencies. But its devaluation, over time, matches that of the North Korean won. It is yet a further reflection of the double consciousness of the North Korean psyche, where what you say and what you see with your own eyes markedly contradict each other, where that inner war between public duty and private necessity quietly rages.

Like the hills of Wonsan, the mountainous crags surrounding the Ullim Falls are said to resemble a folding screen, that most refined of East Asian household accoutrements. You can hear the echo of the falling water even before the falls come into view. As you cross a short bridge that takes you over the creek, the falls come into focus behind the summer foliage. From two hundred forty-six feet above, water cascades down from some hidden source midway up the boulder before hitting a shelf that spills down a second stream into a small pond below. Next to the falls, the date 2001—oddly not the Juche year—has been carved into the mountain in red ink. That is the year the surrounding construction was completed and it was deemed touristable, the road leading up the mountain paved, and the construction finished of the triangular teahouse on the other side of the pond that provides pristine viewing conditions—although Roe tells us it is no longer in operation.

I catch up with Alek and Alexandre. Roe goes off to speak to the old soldier guard who's been shadowing us the entire time.

"Maybe you should say something to Min," I whisper to Alek.

"Yes, man," says Alexandre, "this could be serious. What if the maid finds it in the room and turns it in to the security guys at the hotel?"

"We could say it's ours," I offer.

"So then what was it doing in her room?" Alexandre retorts. "Fuck that. I'm not getting involved. I don't want to go to prison here."

"It's more likely the maid would keep it for herself," says Alek. "You know, for personal consumption. Or to sell it on the Jangmadang or wherever."

"But if Min gets caught," Alexandre whispers, "you know what will happen. I feel sorry for her."

Actually, it's hard to know what *would* happen. Accounts vary as to the punishment doled out when caught with foreign media. It is still regarded as a crime, and a serious one at that. Though the punishment may no longer be as severe as the brutal incarceration Un Ju experienced in the early 2000s. Some defectors claim that nowadays, you can simply bribe your way out of the situation.

Back in the parking lot, Min has removed her suitcase from the back of the van, sprawled its contents across the pavement. Hwa and Kim stand by watching, smoking. Yes, even Kim—who quit years ago—is now smoking. The brown-suited guard stands at a distance, watching the scene suspiciously. This guy could cause us trouble if he wanted to. I remember I have a pack of Camels in my bag that I'd bought at duty-free in Beijing. I produce them and offer him one. He smiles and accepts, graciously. Alek follows my lead and, since he speaks the best Korean, proceeds to make small talk with the guy to distract him from Min's panic scene.

Min stands before her ravaged luggage, at a loss for what to do next. Kim mutters something, throws his cigarette down, climbs back into the van. Hwa follows after him. I give the soldier three cigarettes from my pack and a smile. He stashes them in his front pocket, gives me the universal gratitude symbol with hands clasped before him.

We're going back to Wonsan.

Could it be in the gallery? In the restaurant? No, there's no way. It could only be in the hotel, in her room. That's the only place it could have fallen out. Makes sense: a private space. There aren't any other women on the trip, so she gets her own room. A call to the reception desk while we were observing the falls produced no answers. Min requested that they halt cleaning the room until we could return to look for her lost belongings. She has lost something very very tiny, she explains.

Meanwhile, Min has opened up the plastic bag containing our snacks and is busy stuffing her face. "This is called panic eating," she deadpans.

Alexandre and I remain silent. The burden is on Alek. He's in the uncomfortable position of having to pretend he doesn't know the real reason why Min is panic eating while also wanting to offer his help out of genuine concern: the politics of friendship.

"So the card," he begins, "is there just... music on it? Or is there also data?"

Min masticates a cookie thoughtfully. "Data." She swallows.

"Hmm," he says. "Maybe... if it would help, you can tell them that it belongs to me? You know, this dumb Australian guy, losing stuff wherever we go, you're constantly having to pick up after him..."

His voice trails off.

Min looks at Alek, considering his offer. In that moment, she understands that he understands. That we understand. Through this secret nonverbal language of glances and gestural innuendo, mixed with all the events of the past hours, the past days, weeks—she recognizes the extent to which we are no longer innocent tourists.

"It's alright," she says. "I'll handle it."

Certainly no one is ecstatic about returning to Wonsan after Comrade Kim's face-losing run-in with the traffic cop this morning. *Get out of town* was the parting message. There aren't many backstreets to speak of in Wonsan, save for a few intended solely for pedestrians—but Hwa goes around the main square to lessen our chances of reencountering our white-uniformed friend and gets us back to the Tongmyong Hotel parking lot.

"Are you sure there's nothing I can do to help?" Alek asks a final time after Alexandre silently prods him.

"I'll take care of it," Min says. "You guys wait here."

Roe and Kim follow Min into the hotel. Hwa sticks a USB into the passenger-side monitor. An old black-and-white war movie plays. I ask Alek, the DPRK film buff, if he's seen this one. He shakes his head. Save for *The Flower Girl* and a couple others, the DPRK has canonized very few of its pre-1980 films with international DVD releases, though citizens can acquire domestic copies at DVD stalls that are off-limits to foreigners.

Suspense extends the length of the minutes through which we are forced to wait. Each time a car pulls into the lot, Hwa checks nervously to make sure it isn't one of the dreaded black BMWs with tinted windows, preferred vehicle of the *bowibu.* I can't stand the tension, so I step outside the van to smoke.

At the edge of the parking lot, behind a truck, is a large cage housing pigeons. Probably the source of the roast chicken we presumed we were eating at last night's dinner.

The hotel's ground floor is ringed by a wraparound terrace. I follow it past the lonely pile of stony rubble, the culmination of the morning's masonry endeavor. Behind the hotel, a middle-aged man in an undershirt smokes, guarding the drying sheets and towels from thieves. Down below, just off the jetty, two young boys crawl on rocks, dipping their hands into the sea. They're searching for shell-fish, crabs, anything they can eat or sell. Among other treasures, they've fished out a fallen pack containing three cigarettes, which they lay on a rock to dry beneath the rays of the noontime sun. Circling my way back to the parking lot, a group of hardhatted construction workers carry wooden planks toward the shoreline. They're in the early stages of building a new dock for the hotel. They stop to stare at the foreigner as I stroll past. I smile back at them, wave.

Finally, the Koreans reemerge from the hotel. They climb into the van. Without any exchange of words, Hwa turns the key in the ignition and pulls us out of the parking lot. Min stares sullenly out the window.

"Well," says Alek, "any luck?"

"No. It's not there."

We drive on in silence.

FORTY-TWO

DESPITE EVERYTHING SHE has been through, Un Ju fully intends to go home someday. Not to Wonsan but to Pyongyang, the capital. She knows she will never be able to change the system. But she dreams of helping others—other artists, like her. She will move to the US, to pursue a master's degree in drama therapy, before eventually returning to the North.

"Isn't that dangerous?" I asked her, incredulously.

She laughed. "To me," she said, "South Korea is a much darker place than North Korea ever was."

Sure, there were bad things in the North. But it is still the land of her childhood, the place that reared her—the place she understands best. In the South, she has worked so many menial jobs, been exploited by so many unscrupulous bosses who take advantage of North Koreans' ignorance of the legal system to overwork them and evade paying proper wages. When they find out where she is from, most South Koreans show no interest or curiosity whatsoever; some display outright hostility. At best, mentioning in a social gathering that you come from North Korea is sure to shut the conversation down. North Korean defectors quickly learn to *adapt*—get rid of their accents, try to blend in as well as possible. If someone asks where you are from, then lie—tell them Busan or some other distant city. South Korea has its own class system, after all, and the new North Korean arrivals are decidedly at the very bottom. Un Ju waited a year before telling her first boyfriend here. When she finally revealed her origin, he was shocked. He broke up with her a week later.

"Every message they've sent me since I've been here is the same: *You are nobody. You will never make it here.* If I try to protest, to even raise the issue, then the response is: 'Why are you saying that? Why are you causing trouble?'"

Many, if not most, North Korean defectors flounder in the South. Like Un Ju, they are scammed. They are abused. They are systematically discriminated against. Some commit suicide, including more than one of Un Ju's friends. In recent years, a number of defectors have opted to return to the North. And, in a recent survey, a quarter of those polled responded that they had seriously considered it.

★

What's more dangerous than anything, Un Ju maintains, is forgetting. She sees instances of it all the time. People often forget on purpose. But forgetting doesn't heal either the brutalizer or the victim. If anything, forgetting only worsens the damage.

Once, Un Ju gave a speech at a human rights fund-raiser. Afterward, a woman with a North Korean accent approached to offer her congratulations.

Un Ju looked at the woman closely. She knew who it was. It was one of the women who used to beat her up at the holding center in Thailand.

Un Ju began to cry.

"What's wrong?" the woman asked. "Why are you crying, my child?" She started to wrap her arms around Un Ju's shoulder.

Suddenly, Un Ju's fear and sadness turned to anger.

"You know damn well why I'm crying, who I am," Un Ju said.

She shook the woman's hands off her and walked away.

★

Listening to Un Ju speak, I realize that it is far more comforting to believe that reality is more black-and-white than it actually is. That *freedom* is a geographical location that can be marked on a map. That certain people who believe one thing are good while those who believe in something else are inherently evil. It is by far easier to understand the world we live in if we mold our consciousness according to the daily news cycle rather than trying to understand the historical circumstances that formed nations and regimes and systems of belief that seem so foreign and distant from our own—tragic circumstances that our own fore-bears played no small part in engineering. It is much easier to pat someone on the shoulder and tell them that they are now free rather than help them undergo the arduous process toward actual empowerment. It is much easier to demonize than to empathize, which is why the former is so preferable to politicians, who care more about protecting and promoting their own self-image than the risks of engagement with an Other whose needs, wants, and point of view are best left to fester in the realm of the unknowable.

In such circumstances, justice is more or less an attitude that can be adapted or feigned under the guise of righteousness, and the organs of public opinion are sure to support you, whether from fear or lack of any other idea of how to go about it. It is the tragedy of the world we live in that empathy is still too radical a tactic to take, that engagement is considered, by and large, a risk better left unexplored. The more we misunderstand something, the easier it is for us to destroy it. As though by destroying some force deemed evil and other, we were not also destroying ourselves along with it.

FORTY-THREE

HALFWAY TO MOUNT Kumgang, we pull over on some winding slope. Min needs a pee break.

We remain in the van, silently watch her through the rearview mirrors. At first, she turns down a narrow dirt path, gives out a startled laugh, and then turns back around, crossing to the other side of the highway before disappearing behind some choice foliage.

I slam the door behind me, stretch my legs. I follow in Min's footsteps, first to the little side road, curious as to the sight that gave her a jolt. I take a few steps behind a hilly bend, and suddenly a trio of filth-caked peasants appear, couched in the weeds. Their bicycles stand next to them, weighted down with bags of grain they're in the process of transporting to some market or other. One of them smokes a cigarette crudely rolled with a torn page of newspaper. The three just stare at me silently. I nod and turn around, walking slowly back to the highway.

Min emerges from the brush, bag of tissues still in hand. She walks back to the van, cleans herself up with some hand sanitizer, exchanges a few words with Roe and Kim. I climb back in, Hwa restarts the engine.

"...*Min?!*"

Now she's walking slowly down the highway, away from us. Wherever it is she's going, she doesn't seem too concerned about the time—the time of day or the duration we have left before the sun disappears completely, leaving Hwa to rely purely on the brights to get us to Mount Kumgang.

"What the hell is she doing?" asks Alexandre.

Comrade Kim curses. Nobody's moving, so I get out of the van, follow after her.

We're on a hill, so a long drainage ditch runs alongside the highway. Min is humming the melody of a Moranbong Band song, staring down into the ditch as she walks along beside it. Every now and then, she stops to pick a daffodil or one of the other tiny flowers growing wildly among the weeds. "Are you okay?" I ask her.

She continues to hum, mindlessly. Madly. Picking flowers. Making her own little bridal bouquet. Like she did when she was alone, a child, visiting her grandparents' house in the countryside.

She looks up at me with the eyes of someone who wants it all to be over. "Sometimes," she says, "I wish I were still a child."

"Min," I start to say. Until I realize there is nothing, absolutely nothing I can tell her.

The sun goes down not long after we start moving. Again, a sublime spectacle— the sky is so open here, the golden orb bleeds orange-purple hues all over the dry fields surrounding us, the village nestled in the field between the road and the mountains. You can hear the evening announcements blaring on the intercom as we swerve past. Everyone save Hwa and me falls into a slumber; instead, I slip into a bizarre daydream. It's sometime in the future, many years from now, when I am much older. Min is there with me. We are in some city; I'm not sure if it's Pyongyang—perhaps it's Seoul or somewhere else entirely, some European capital.

Anyway, we meet for coffee, old and gray. And it is clear that it has all crumbled, that North Korea as we both know it now, in these years, no longer exists. Or else maybe like Un Ju, she fled long ago, and has since come to know the bitterness and travails of exile more intimately and terrifyingly than she could have ever wished.

"Oh, but it was a beautiful dream we lived," she sighs, embittered by all the events that have occurred since then, the years.

"No," I reply. "It was always a nightmare. There were those rare few like me who were drawn to it out of some perverse fascination. But we all knew—even Alek—that it was awful. We could see it quite clearly each time we were there. And we yearned to tell you. But we couldn't. We were too scared. And for the exact same reasons you were, it turns out."

"But for us, it was home," she says, "and there were a lot of beautiful things we had that you couldn't even understand, that you wouldn't know. You're not Korean. Okay, maybe the regime was terrible. But at least we had a sense of *unity*. That doesn't exist anywhere else in this world, in any other country. I've been to practically all of them by now. I know what it's like. Sure, we encountered cruelty in Choson. But never the kinds of cruelty I've had to suffer since it all went away, when I was left afloat, a permanent exile on this planet—or what's left of it."

"You're right that we couldn't partake in those magic moments you describe," I reply. "We couldn't always learn the words to the songs, remember the steps to the dances. And no, we couldn't feel that sense of unity that bound you all together under the delusion of a common dream. But it is also true that we were able to see things that you weren't able to see. Things that we saw when we were looking at you there. We had that outside perspective, the one you lacked. We saw how you were suffering in silence. We saw it quite clearly. The pornography of that place is that you don't have to search to find those terrifying aspects, as I had thought early on. They're all right there in front of your eyes, staring you down the entire time, no matter what the regime tried to show us. That's the truth of that country you clung so hard to and still cling to in your golden years. And you have to admit that those terrors even informed those memories you say were beautiful, the ones you still cherish. That your conception of beauty is forever contaminated by, conflated with, terror."

The dream peters out as fast as it arrived. Now it's just the twilight, the sound of the whizzing motor and the bumpy road beneath us, the dim lights of Mount Kumgang on the horizon ahead.

PART NINE

RECONCILIATION

FORTY-FOUR

WE TAKE A wrong turn on our way to the resort. It's not exactly Hwa's fault. It's not like there's any such thing as GPS in North Korea. The road maps for this area are murky and filled with unmarked roads, as it's close to the ROK border and filled with secret military bases and installations. We find ourselves driving down a narrow lane surrounded by overgrowth, no different from any other of the run-down ungroomed roads we've been on in the countryside, when suddenly, out of nowhere, we hit a checkpoint—and not just one of the hundreds of mere permit-inspecting traffic checkpoints that dot the roads of this country, but a *military* checkpoint. Lots of soldiers, in and out of uniform, stand around the roadblock, looking at our van with a mixture of anger and suspicion.

Comrade Kim gets out of the van to ask whether this is the entrance to Mount Kumgang. The main officer in charge moves toward him with a pissed-off expression on his face: "What the *fuck* are you doing here, Comrade? This is the border, a restricted area, and you *do not* have permission to be here."

"I'm sorry, Officer, but our driver—"

"Tell your driver to turn that van around and get the hell out of here immediately."

It's a narrow, one-lane road, hard to turn around on. Hwa, in trying to maneuver a three-point turn, gets his front wheel stuck in a ditch. Alek and Alexandre and Roe and I all get out to push the van. We hop back inside and fuck off at high speed.

We pull over on the side of the road. Min rifles through her bag, looking for her list of contacts so she might call someone at the resort and figure out where we are, how to get us there. Hwa jumps out of the van, walks a few paces away, lights a cigarette. I watch him puff away in the rearview mirror. He's wearing dark sunglasses, lifts them for a split second to wipe away a tear.

When we finally arrive at the resort, we're greeted with a sort of ghost town. The official name is the Hyundai Kumgangsan Tourist Resort. At the entrance, we stop at a grouping of trailers. Min goes inside one of them to register our presence. The Koreans follow Min inside. The three of us climb out of the van, stretch our legs among the tumbleweeds. Fields of crops line the valley; a few scattered houses and apartment blocks up ahead denote some sort of village or settlement, though it hardly seems occupied. We walk along the road, studying our surroundings. The Koreans emerge about half an hour later and motion for us to get back in the van.

We drive through the roads of the resort, but it seems like they still don't have any clear idea of where we're going. I can only imagine what the conversation inside the trailer must have been like—it seems that no one was expecting us.

This is unlike any place I've ever seen in the DPRK. The resort was constructed as a sort of self-contained autonomous zone by the South Koreans in 2002. The Hyundai corporation spilled $350 million into renovating old structures while adding a whole plethora of luxury hotels, restaurants, bungalows, yurts, chalets, and caravan parks. It was the one place in the North where South Koreans could visit, an icon of the Sunshine Policy that was initiated by President Kim Dae Jung in 1998, meant to ease tensions between North and South. Kim was even awarded the Nobel Prize in 2000 for initiating the policy, and it was continued by his successor, Roh Moo Hyun.

President Kim borrowed the name from one of Aesop's fables—perhaps with a hint of sarcasm, as its title is *The North Wind and the Sun*. It concerns a competition between the two titular protagonists to determine which is the stronger natural entity. The lesson of the fable is meant to illustrate the conviction that persuasion always triumphs over force. This tactic resonates with the traditional Korean way of dealing with one's enemies: lavishing them with gifts so that they won't destroy you. Killing them with kindness, as it were.

Given its intended audience and the massive financial benefits it brought the DPRK, there is far less in the way of visual propaganda on display here—not a single image of either of the Kims can be seen, in fact. At its height in the mid-2000s, the resort attracted a quarter of a million tourists each year. These were optimistic times, and they continued under President Roh's administration.

Suddenly, reunification didn't seem like such a far-fetched fantasy after all. Under Roh, the Kaesong Industrial Park opened in the border city, one of the North's most historic, as Kaesong's shifting position on the thirty-eighth parallel throughout the war insured it against the US-led aerial bombing campaign. North and South Koreans didn't exactly get to work side by side in any of the hundred-some South Korean–owned companies operating within the zone— the workers were kept completely segregated, working in different buildings— but at least it was a step in the right direction.

But it was right here, in the Mount Kumgang resort, where the dream came to an end. In July 2008, a fifty-three-year-old South Korean woman, Park Wang Ja, ignored the warnings of her North Korean guides and wandered off a golf course. She was shot dead by a trigger-happy DPRK soldier. The South instantly suspended all tours to the resort. In 2010, as tensions escalated with military skirmishes between the two countries around the maritime border, the North seized control of the resort, effectively shredding the fifty-year exclusivity deal that had been signed with Hyundai. To put it mildly, this has made it difficult for the DPRK to attract other foreign investors to continue running the project, which would explain its desolate state.

The Sunshine Policy was declared a failure by the new right-wing government in Seoul in 2010, though in some senses, it took a bit longer to arrive at a complete impasse, fizzling out over the years as tensions escalated, culminating with the South's closure of the Kaesong Industrial Park in 2016. Moon Jae In, the new South Korean president, says he wants to reopen it, but as of this writing, no real progress has been made.

Still, there are a few other tourists present today, though all of them are domestic—most of them, it seems, well-heeled families from Pyongyang. We drive past a twelve-story hotel that looks abandoned, shrouded in darkness. "That's the family reunion center," Alek whispers. The resort here wasn't just built for tourists. During the Sunshine Policy years, several highly publicized family reunions took place, which allowed a select number of family members from the North and South, many of whom hadn't seen each other in sixty years owing to the peninsula's division, to finally meet. The vast majority were octogenarians. It was a bittersweet event—the reunions lasted three days, and it is unlikely that any of the briefly reunited family members will live long enough to see each other again. Driving past this sad site brings home the awareness that no matter what outsiders might say or think, this is ultimately a story about one country's division and the two very different systems, different solutions—now, different *countries*—that have emerged as the tragic result of that split.

We're probably the first Westerners to stay at the Kumgangsan Beach Hotel since it reopened a few months ago. Among the first guests, period. The quaint triangular wooden houses elicit fantasies of a luxury cabin nestled somewhere in the Rocky Mountains, though here the scenery includes not just the mountains but the sea, which can be reached from the road below us. The hotel is situated along an incline, at the top of which is a building with a sign marked "V.I.P." Our rooms are in the house next door. The rooms all boast seaview balconies, are large and airy, and come adorned with the quality of furnishings and amenities that clearly remind one of who built the hotel, replete with Samsung electronics—minus the Wi-Fi, naturally. Clearly by and for the comparatively well-heeled South Koreans, it is now left largely to vacationers from the upper echelons of the North, a demographic that is well aware of those disparities and, by staying here, can actually experience them in person. Those numbers, however, shouldn't be exaggerated—there are definitely more staff than there are guests kicking around the halls of the hotel at the moment. We don't have time to admire many of the other details. After dropping our bags off in our rooms and changing clothes, we meet back at the van. We're going hiking.

The guys run ahead, to scale the heights of the Diamond Mountain. Min and I give up halfway. I'm scared of heights; Min is too heavy to climb. We land in a pagoda where a couple of Korean hikers are resting, though soon they go away, uncomfortable and uncertain as to how to act in a foreigner's presence. A North Korean tour guide—that is, a guide for North Korean tourists—approaches us. She's wearing a name tag and a headset mic. As the economy has developed in recent years and a burgeoning middle class has begun to discover itself, domestic travel has become something of a trend. There is even a weekly television show on state TV that follows its attractive young hostess on her journeys to hotspots around the country. Today, with the exception of a family from the Indian Embassy in Pyongyang we bump into on our way up, we're the only foreign tourists on Mount Kumgang—the rest are all North Koreans. The guide asks Min who she is, who I am, what we're doing there. Min tells her, and the guide nods, satisfied, and continues down the trail to find her charges.

Leaving Min and me alone, seated on a bench, drinking in the majestic view. We have entered into a painting: it's the Kuryong Falls, the scene so lovingly described in the canvas by Lee Ryong Hee we saw yesterday at the gallery in Wonsan. The fall is steep but not completely vertical. The water rushes its way down in a white foamy crest, culminating in a tiny green pool at the bottom. The surrounding granite formations look as though they have been carved by a gigantic hand, a relief of carefully rendered linear forms jutting from the mountainous stone. It's supposed to look particularly impressive in winter, when the water freezes, the pure white of the snow glistening in contrast to the burnt umber of the surrounding cliffage.

We talk about fears rooted in our childhoods. Min confesses that she actually doesn't like travel, being away from home for a long time. If I'm most afraid of falling, Min's greatest fear is solitude.

"When I was a kid," she tells me, "my parents worked all the time. I was always left alone. After school, I'd come home, but my parents were never there—they'd always be working. I'd have to wait outside, alone, in the street until after dark."

Her experience of neglect is not unique. It is so pervasive, in fact, that a film was made on this subject. Released in 2007, *A Schoolgirl's Diary* is one of the few North Korean films in recent years that has found some small international success; it was picked up for distribution in France, where it inevitably bombed. The film tells the story of a teenage girl depressed by the perpetual absence of her scientist father. At the end of the film, when she receives news that her father has made an important scientific discovery and is being hailed for his contribution to the well-being of the fatherland, she realizes how selfish she has been.

Owing to the endless electricity shortages and all the tricks Min's family had to resort to around the house to get power generated, via batteries and kerosene and generators, her parents were afraid to give the children keys to the flat; the possibility of starting a fire was too great. Instead, she was left to play by herself in the streets of Pyongyang until they arrived home late at night. And in those years, the city really *was* dark.

"Weren't they worried something might happen to you?"

"No," says Min. "Pyongyang is a very safe city. Children can play freely, no one has to worry about getting kidnapped. But still...they left me. I mean, I don't blame them. They had to work. But at the time, it was very hard for me to understand. So I started to act out."

"Were you a rebel?" I ask, suddenly intrigued.

"Well, I never did anything in front of them. That's the thing. I'm a good daughter. Loyal, obedient. But when my parents weren't around...then I became the devil." She smiles. "I wasn't a bully or anything. But I was big for my age. And tough. A tomboy. I'd stick up for the girls in my class. If they were being picked on by a boy, then on the playground, I'd go with the girl, find the boy who was being mean to her. Beat him up in front of everyone. I was a monster!" She laughs.

"It must have been hard, coming back here after eight years in Cuba, all grown up. I mean...Was it hard to adjust? Was it hard to make friends?"

Min's laughter diminishes. "Yes," she says. "It was hard."

"You could have stayed. Finished your studies at the University of Havana."

"The thing is *I* chose to come back. My parents didn't send me. I actually came back a year before they did. I wanted...to prove something to them. That I could come here on my own. That I was independent."

"Were they worried?"

"Yes, a little. They tried to stop me, to persuade me to wait. The ambassador warned them that it was dangerous. You know, there are kidnappings, things like that."

One of the top recurring news stories in recent months has concerned a dozen DPRK employees of a North Korean restaurant in China. They had collectively left for the South one day this past spring. It was heralded as the largest group defection in history. The North insisted, however, that they were kidnapped by South Korean agents and demanded their repatriation to the North.

"Was there ever a chance that you would...get on another plane?" I ask.

She gets what I'm asking immediately, smiles. "No, there was never a chance. Like I said, I wanted to come back. To prove to them that I could do it. That I, in a way, didn't need them. In a weird way, it was my revenge for them leaving me alone all the time as a child."

Our conversation turns to work. I ask her whether she always intended to be a tour guide. I had always thought it was considered a relatively cushy, privileged job in the DPRK.

"It's not. Not really," Min says. "I actually wanted to go into the army. That's probably the best job you can get. But they wouldn't admit me."

Near the end of one's university studies, she tells me, you are asked to make a list of your top five choices for work. You are then invited for several interviews— among them, for Min, was one with Comrade Kim at the Korean State Travel Company. On graduation day, your new lifelong job is publicly announced. You have little to no say in the matter.

"*'Really? Tour guide?'* My friends were shocked. I was, too. Everyone thought I would get something better." Many graduates of the University of Foreign Studies, such as Comrade Kim, go on to potentially lucrative posts abroad at foreign diplomatic missions.

Still, she has grown resigned to her new life. It's a "fun country," she says. And Comrade Kim has become like a brother to her.

Suddenly, Min turns to me. "Remember the other night, after dinner? You said you might be able to help me?"

It was shortly after Min and Alexandre's Kimchi Baguette conversation. I was curious about how business actually worked here and also wanted to covertly push for her to introduce us to some artists I was eager to meet. So I mentioned that I had some friends in Berlin and London who own art galleries, who might possibly be interested in some joint venture. Min had also been dangling an IT business idea in front of Alek. She said she knew some guys who were computer geniuses here, guys who could do any kind of programming that was needed, and at a rate much lower than you'd find for such services in the West. Alek was at a loss, I know—he was torn between wanting to help Min but also having no clue how to go about it. Computers and programming aren't his field of interest—he comes from a family of academics; he's a college student majoring in East Asian studies.

Of course, none of us were really sincere in our interests. Alexandre isn't going to open up Kimchi Baguette with Min. And sadly, nobody in the West gives two shits about North Korean art. We are all just fishing for more clues about how everything works. Even if we were sincere, to pursue such activities would be to navigate the labyrinthine protocol of sanctions and could potentially land us in life-altering trouble.

I realize, now, however, that all that Kimchi Baguette talk might have been a joke for Alexandre, but it was something Min was very serious about.

"Because the thing is," Min continues, "Korea is strong. *Very* strong. Look at our army! We're one of the strongest countries in the world. So now, we just have to develop our economy so that it matches the strength of our army."

I nod my head. At times, there radiates a certain toughness from Min, when it's easy for me to see that little girl who beat up boys on the playground.

"The sanctions make that difficult," Min continues. A bold admission—since the official line is that sanctions have had no effect whatsoever on the economy.

"But it's a shame, really, because we can do virtually anything. It doesn't have to be computers, it can really be anything—we can sell hair for wigs, for instance. Artwork, sure, we can provide. Anything they need, we can do. But it takes a certain...adventurous spirit. What I mean is the person has to be either a little bit daring, to not care about the sanctions or else working in a sector that's not affected by them or else a person who comes from a country that's not participating in the sanctions. We need partners. So can you help me find one?"

I try to think of a diplomatic way to tell her that no one I know would be stupid or risky enough to do business with North Korea. I want to be as honest as possible without hurting her feelings.

"Your country has a little bit of a PR problem," I tell her, in what is probably the understatement of the decade. I explain that some countries will actually spend lots of money, millions of dollars, to hire a large public relations firm to help improve their country's image, to make it more attractive for investors. "I know you have no control over this, but I really wish someone, somewhere, at one of the higher levels, would think about doing something like that because it would make what you're trying to do a whole lot easier."

"It's never going to happen," Min states emotionlessly. She might not be willing or able to put it into words, but she understands implicitly a truth that citizens of a non-totalitarian state can never fathom. As Hannah Arendt wrote, what makes a totalitarian country so unpredictable to the rest of the world is its emancipation from the profit motive, that its wasteful incompetence in the economic sphere is very much intentional, calculated so as to exert total control over its populace. To what extent all these recent indices of wealth gleaned on the streets of Pyongyang represent sincere expressions of the new regime's intent, nobody can be certain.

"Anyway, why would we do that? Pay money for foreign propaganda?" Min asks. "To me, it's not a good business practice—to spend money on results you cannot see."

I sigh, studying the trail of the water down the gray-white sunbaked crags of the mountain.

"That's just how business *works* in the twenty-first century," I say. "You have to spend money in order to make money. It's all about image, marketing, PR... These PR firms hold some sway over the media, they have contacts, they can *place stories* to help improve the image of a place. I understand that *you're* business-minded, that you want to do business and be successful. But the people in power, in your government here, they're not thinking along those lines. They don't seem to care what the media says. But the media has great influence, Min. And it means that people—not just in America but everywhere—they're *afraid* of this place."

I make a broad, sweeping gesture with my arm and then I realize how ridiculous it looks and sounds; I'm standing, after all, in front of one of the most beautiful sites in Asia, probably one of the most scenic vistas in the entire world, one that so few people have seen—and calling it *scary.* Min nods her head, oblivious to the terrible irony of it all.

"This is why we need someone who is a little bit bold, a little bit risky. Because if they come here, if they see what Korea is *really* like, you *know* they won't be scared. They will see how it actually is here."

It seems like a fair enough pitch. But it's also naive. Because nobody believes that what they are shown here is real. But I don't say this to Min. Instead, I ask what kind of business she sees herself doing. What kind of partner should I look for when I go back out into the world?

Min doesn't have a clear answer. She keeps repeating: anything, anything. We can do anything.

"Then how does it work?" I ask. "Let's say I find a potential partner—"

"I can give you our office email. You can address it either to me or to Comrade Kim. We will get it, and we will respond immediately."

"Do you not have a personal email address where I can reach you?"

"No, there is just an office email. It all goes to one person, the secretary who deals with the emails. Otherwise, it would be chaos."

I have to bite my lip. It sounds like a comical excuse for the regime's restricting the vast majority of its citizens from communication with the outside world, though in actuality, there is probably not much more than one computer in their office, either. I have seen the inside of many offices by now, and almost none of them have computers.

"Okay, so I send an email to your office. How do I then introduce you to the foreign business partner? Are you and Comrade Kim able to travel? To come to, say, Berlin, and meet them to discuss details?"

"It's better they come here, to Pyongyang. That way we can show them everything we have to offer!"

Translation: It's very difficult to get permission to travel abroad. Especially to discuss a deal that might not result in anything.

I tell her that there are other issues. That the bad press isn't just about politics or nuclear weapons. That, in the business world, deals that have gone wrong here have also been reported in the media. That serious investors are loath to trust anything and anyone here because of that. So it would be a bit difficult to persuade investors to spend money to come and explore those opportunities.

She asks me what I'm talking about.

"Well, the biggest one is probably your Koryolink network. Your mobile phones. It was an investment by Orascom, an Egyptian company. It invested a 75 percent stake in the company, together with the government. Of course, Koryolink becomes wildly successful. You and everyone you know now has a mobile phone and uses it, right? Well, guess what happened to Orascom. Suddenly, it had a really tough time getting its profits out of the country. Its money, of course, was here, in a Korean bank. Eventually, your government seized control of the business altogether. Orascom leaves the picture empty-handed."

"What was the name of this company from Egypt?"

"Orascom," I tell her.

She makes a mental note. Clearly, she knows nothing of this. She doesn't try to make any apologies. What can she say? That that's the government, not private individuals like her and Kim? She can't say that. Because officially, the only business here is government business.

"What about discussion of the financial details?" I ask her, continuing to play along. "Is it safe to do that over email?"

"What do you mean?"

"I mean, say they are making a concrete offer. They want to negotiate a price. Can I include that information, those numbers, in the email?"

"It would be better for you if you didn't."

"I see."

And yet I don't. Or: I do and I don't. The duplicitous nature of how accounting is done in the new era: there are the official books, what it might look like were the company a state-run business, and the unofficial books, which reflect the reality of the situation, the profit-making stakes of all involved.

"Min," I say, "why don't you try to do business with the Chinese? There are Chinese businessmen *everywhere* in Pyongyang. They're so easy to meet."

"I don't *get* the Chinese," she says. "You know, I'm a lot more Western-minded in my thinking. Probably because I grew up in Cuba."

It's useless. The more I try to explain to her the potential objections of a Western investor, the more I realize that what I'm describing out loud is essentially a system of corruption. Of course it's not Min's fault; it is a system corrupted in equal measure by the incompetent totalitarian state, by the US-led sanctions that effectively criminalize economic activities regarded as mundane everywhere else in the world, and the neoliberal economics that is itself rife with inequalities, which North Koreans have no choice but to aspire to. A system whose corrupt qualities Min either tries to obfuscate or else naively admits to, apparently unaware of what is wrong with this business environment in which she is so keen to involve me. Then again, whether she's aware of it or not, I recognize it is all she really has, as the conversation reaches its inconclusive peak.

The Kuryong Falls, like much of the scenery in the Mount Kumgang area, is rife with legends. The name *Kuryong*, which means "Nine Dragons," is a reference to the creatures said to have resided here, in this well of water at the bottom of the falls, the ancient protectors of Mount Kumgang, with all its scenic—and perhaps other, more valuable—treasures.

In modern times, a different sort of dragon emerged to protect the riches of Mount Kumgang. While Min and I were having our conversation, the guys made it to the top of Kumgang, as Alexandre later relayed to me. Alexandre stood next to Comrade Kim, observing one of Korea's finest landscapes. "It's spectacular, isn't it?" said Alexandre.

"Yes," replied Comrade Kim. "A spectacle indeed. But do you know about Kumgang Mountain? What is *inside* the mountain?"

Alexandre hesitated. "Diamonds, right? They call it Diamond Mountain."

"No." Comrade Kim shook his head. "Not diamonds. *Gold.* The mountain we are now standing on. It is full of gold."

"Hmm, I see," said Alexandre. "So then...why hasn't it been mined?"

Comrade Kim shrugged his shoulders. "Before he died, Kim Il Sung said it's not meant for us. It should be kept for a future generation."

Alexandre nodded. He didn't say anything further, but he couldn't help but notice not just the desultory tone in Comrade Kim's voice, but that all North Koreans, when referring to any of the leaders in any language, are required to precede their names with one of their honorific sobriquets—the *Great Leader* Kim Il Sung, the *General* Kim Jong Il, the *Marshal* Kim Jong Un—a practice that Comrade Kim had just very pointedly neglected.

FORTY-FIVE

AFTER OUR HIKE, we cool off at the beach. Here there is no *foreigners-only* section, so we are able to freely mingle with the locals. Even the beach seems to have been specially designed to impress, with its combed white sand and placid waters. Everyone is in a happy mood, especially our Korean hosts, who frolic like children. Comrade Kim has rented or borrowed a raft from somewhere, and we take turns trying to knock each other off it into the water. Attracted by our screams and splashes and hysterical laughter, an older man comes over and joins us, clapping his hands and joining in the fun, unable to resist the opportunity to fraternize with the only foreigners in sight. Some soldiers engage us in a game of water soccer. It's a rather cruel version of the game that I will soon feel horrible for participating in, where a woman is chosen to serve as the human goal for each team—which leaves Min as ours. We play in waist-high water, and if the ball hits the woman-goal, then the other team scores a point. Of course we're all lousy at it and unable to protect Min from the opposing team's viciousness—she gets hit several times, culminating with the final score, when the soccer ball lands square on her nose and she bursts into tears. The soldiers cheer their victory, while Kim swims over to comfort his comrade.

Back on the shore, it seems we've crossed a demarcation line. Whereas in the water, everyone is eager to fraternize with us, as we rest in the sand, people are sure to keep their distance. Here comes the old man who was so eager to be our playmate a few minutes ago. I greet him in my elementary Korean and wave. He keeps his head down low and quickly walks past, as though he's never seen me before.

★

Public opinion in South Korea is mixed when it comes to assessing the merits and minuses of the Sunshine Policy. Some, including many defectors who have gravitated toward the right since arriving in the South, feel that it was a self-aggrandizing move by South Korean politicians who should have at least demanded from Kim Jong Il a demonstrable improvement in the human rights situation before handing over regime-sustaining aid of food and finances. Some say that the Kaesong Industrial Park was merely a cynical ploy for South Korean corporations to benefit from the North's cheap labor—a microcosmic foreshadowing of the exploitation that is bound to happen if and when reunification actually does occur.

But in many ways, the complicating factor in the Sunshine Policy of two liberal South Korean presidents was the United States, which at the time was in the hands of George W. Bush's conservative government. In the South Korean political divide, those on the right tend to be pro-American and pro-military, while those on the left favor a Yankee-go-home disarmament and a peaceful resolution to the inter-Korean crisis. As to what exactly that resolution might look like, there are a few ideas but not much consensus. For conservative South Koreans, the Sunshine Policy was an unforgivable act of defiance against the Washington status quo; above all, they fear that if the US were to pull its military presence out of the South tomorrow, the North would immediately invade and take over the entire peninsula. To make concessions to the North, then, is to weaken the South's alliance with the United States, an alliance without which right-wing South Koreans can't fathom their country's continual existence. Some conspiracy-minded right-wingers even went so far as to attribute sinister machinations to Kim and Roh's moves toward engagement; this is another old tactic of the right in South Korea, where anyone displaying the slightest liberal leaning is branded a commie, a Northern sympathizer, even a secret agent. (Current President Moon Jae In, from the center-left Democratic Party, had to endure such accusations from his right-wing opponents on the campaign trail.)

There is the by-now-routine complaint that, far from deterring the North from developing its *Songun*, or military-first policy, the financial benefits received from the South during the Sunshine years went directly into the nuclear weapons program. Then there is the matter of the North's continual military provocations throughout the Sunshine Policy, mainly skirmishes around disputed maritime boundaries that resulted in casualties on both ends. This is trotted out as proof that the South Koreans were being merely naive, that the North was never sincere in its desire for peaceful coexistence and eventual reunification.

However, such a conclusion relies on the assumption that the military in North Korea is always under the Supreme Leadership's command. There is a school of thought, among Pyongyangologists, that Kim Jong Il's instigation of the *Songun* policy was at least in part a concession to a contingent of the upper echelons of the military that was growing restless. A military coup is not something unheard-of in such unstable models of statehood, and fear of one would have been a good reason for Jong Il to add the Korean People's Army to his power base upon the death of his father in 1994. Doing so would grant the army a certain amount of authority, and with authority comes autonomy to act in certain cases. As the two Koreas remained technically at war throughout the Sunshine Policy, with no peace treaty ever signed, a wartime mentality was retained by the soldiers serving on the front line. Perhaps the Sunshine Policy was even an impetus for the fighting—just because you throw cash at us, it doesn't mean we'll give in.

Perhaps there's some truth, though, in the speculation that the North has not been sincere in its stated desire for reunification. At least not reunification of the overnight sort. Most reunification scenarios appear nightmarish to both the regime and its elites, save for the one Kim Il Sung envisioned and more or less fought for his entire life: a Korea united under his rule. If it is to be reunification by absorption, where the more economically and politically powerful country gets to do the absorbing à la Germany, then it would only mean, for the North Korean leadership, calamity: being put on trial for crimes against humanity at worst, exile at best; for the elites and *donju*, being forced to compete with South Korean business concerns; and for everyone else, second-class citizenship—or worse—next to one's rich Southern brethren.

But the truth is the South doesn't want an immediate reunification scenario, either. Economists' estimates vary, but many believe that if the North were to collapse tomorrow, the current economic disparity, perhaps ten times that of East and West Germany at the time of the former's collapse, is so great that it would be a burden impossible to shoulder by the affluent South; it would likely lead to a collapse of *their* economy or else a strain so great on its citizens that social unrest is all but guaranteed. It would, in other words, be a collapse of the existing social order in both countries, an event that neither North nor South is prepared for. This is why it was easy, after the first of two successive conservative governments came into power in the South, to slam the door shut on the Sunshine Policy.

To be fair, the left-leaning architects of the policy had no intention of overnight reunification. And they knew better than to rock the boat by dictating too many direct demands about food distribution, prison camps, and nuclear weapons to a regime they and the rest of the world regarded as belligerent, that has frequently weaponized belligerence. The underlying intent was for a far more subtle, slower means of transition, a gentle goading toward Chinese-style reform. The plan was more ambitious than its critics give it credit for. President Kim intended for a broad framework of cooperation that would include developing the North's crumbling infrastructure and, through a series of investments, gradually bringing the living standards of average North Koreans up to match the level of their Southern compatriots. By slowly but steadily increasing the North's economic dependence on the South, a relatively equitable reunification, it was hoped, would be the eventual outcome.

The failure of the Sunshine Policy was political. Meaning: it was a failure strictly on the level of politics and politicians. When the North executed its first nuclear test in 2006, it had nothing to do with the Sunshine Policy, despite what its critics might affirm. In fact, it was a reaction to the George W. Bush administration's hostile behavior and its refusal to engage diplomatically with the North, its tearing-up of agreements that had been made by the previous administration. It was Bush who, in the words of President Kim Dae Jung, reversed the age of warm sunshine back to the age of cold wind. The North's initial rapid and sudden moves toward nuclearization—leaving the nonproliferation treaty, kicking out inspectors from the International Atomic Energy Agency, testing long-range missiles—were all done with a clear goal in mind, that of gaining a bargaining chip with Washington. The subsequent administrations' failures fill in the rationale of the meantime. The Kim family has eyes. They have watched the downfall of Hussein and Gaddafi. That gives them a pretty good idea of what would happen if they gave in to the US's desire to denuclearize. Now, it is clear to everyone that they never will. If anything, the events of recent years make the North appear stronger than ever before. No wonder they display their missiles everywhere. This is where a refusal to engage has gotten us. In this version of the fable, the wind has won.

Dinner's at eight, and so around that time, we pull into a broad parking lot surrounded by brand-new buildings. Empty restaurants, empty convenience stores, empty supermarkets, empty duty-free—it could be any small mountainside town anywhere the day after the apocalypse.

"So where do we go?" Alek asks as we step out of the van. "Which one of these is our restaurant?"

"That one." Min points to the windowless rectangle before us. There's no sign denoting that it's a restaurant. Somehow she just knows.

All right then. Chow time.

The smiling young waitresses lead the sole diners to our table and immediately commence pouring drinks. The opening bars to "Pan-gap-sum-ni-da" swell out of some hidden speakers, and three waitresses with wireless mics fall into step and serenade us with the foreigners' welcome song. The mood quickly turns festive, and the waitresses encourage our debauchery, bringing us tambourines and funny little hats to put on each other and take photos.

Eventually, the room becomes a little less empty with the arrival of an extended family from Pyongyang, who occupy a large table on the side of the open floor that has become our makeshift stage. They stare at us shyly as we take our turns at karaoke but don't take up any of our invitations to mingle. I don't know the words to that many songs, especially compared to Alek and Alexandre. Instead, one waitress keeps bringing me the tambourine and pushing me toward the stage. By now, I've ingested enough liquid confidence to propel me through this, so with a crown of lilies on my head, I hop over next to Alek and begin banging the tambourine furiously in rhythm to the Moranbong number he's warbling through. My banging adds a pulse to the music I had always detected automatically but that most Koreans, it seems, hadn't. I sit back down, but each time I do, either Roe or Min or Kim or one of the waitresses places the tambourine back in my hands and pushes me up, and I start to rock out again, to their obvious amusement. In a country where spontaneity and looseness are unheard-of, the idea of dancing freely—of making it up as you go along, of losing yourself, of submitting to the rhythms of the music—is a novelty. Nobody goes so far as to join us and dance, but everyone watches, transfixed—except for Alexandre, who is busy laughing his ass off.

Finally, it's my turn to sing. In Wonsan, Min had written down the words to "Arirang," the beloved folk song of reunification. "It's your final assignment," she told me. "You have to do it at karaoke."

I'm helped along by one of the waitresses but surprisingly manage to make my way to the end. At least I am now able to read the words on the screen, thanks to Ms. Pak. Comrade Kim claps his hands. "Amazing," he says. "A month ago, he couldn't understand anything."

"And I still don't," I say, "but at least I can mouth the words."

He smiles. "That's enough to get by."

FORTY-SIX

OUR DRIVE BACK to Pyongyang the next morning takes us past rolling fields dotted with toiling farmers, decrepit villages, puttering wood-burning trucks spewing smoke and filled with tired, sunburnt day laborers. It's already near dark by the time we reach the checkpoint marking the entrance to the capital. Min hops out with all the permits and paperwork, hands them to the young soldier, who salutes our vehicle. They always give the guides a rough time when reentering the city, and this time isn't any different. The soldier spits and cooks up some bullshit excuse to chew Min out, something about how vehicles transporting foreigners are supposed to drive in a special lane—even though the highway is completely empty, as it has been all day, all week, all year...Roe hops out of the car to assist Min. Good, now the soldier has two people he can insult instead of just one. The main point, of course, is to remind these lowly citizens just how much of a privilege and honor it is to live in the capital. That they never forget it, never once take it for granted. A black Mercedes with tinted windows speeds toward the checkpoint. The soldier turns around, salutes the vehicle as it flies past. One of those cars with a 727 license plate; someone returning from official Workers' Party business, clearly in too much of a hurry to stop and say hello.

Finally, the soldiers wave us on.

Stopped at an intersection, we watch an argument between an old woman pushing a heavy cart and an older man. The old woman loses her temper, lunges forward, and begins pummeling the old man in the chest, nearly knocking him over, shouting obscenities all the while. The bored traffic girl stands on the street corner behind watching them. Finally she blows her whistle, steps forward into her position in traffic. The old woman and man separate, cross the street in opposite directions; our van moves past the scene. Up ahead, a golden sunset over the high-rises.

★

We have our final dinner where we had our first dinner: in a private room at the restaurant in the basement of the Kwangbok Street Shopping Center. Everybody's in a happy mood, though there's also a hint of melancholy. Nobody knows when or if we'll see each other again—especially we students and the North Koreans.

"May I ask you something, Travis?" Comrade Kim asks after we finish eating. "I don't know if you even want to answer this or not—if not, it's okay..."

My stomach tightens. "No, go ahead," I tell him.

"Are Americans even *allowed*, by your government, to travel to our country?"

I laugh wearily. I've never been so tired of being an American in all my life.

"Yes, of course we are. We can travel anywhere we want. Except for Cuba. Though—don't tell anyone—*I've been there, too.*"

"So there is no risk of you getting into trouble by coming here?"

"No," I said, "there's not. Not at this point in time, at least."

Comrade Kim chews on his toothpick thoughtfully.

"Of course," I say, "I don't know what will happen, what with the, uh, Warmbier case and everything..."

"Warmbier." Kim laughs. "Yes, you were very brave for coming here!"

I laugh too. I never felt at risk, I tell him, somewhat truthfully. "I mean, Warmbier brought this on himself, clearly. If you try to steal something like that, of course you are going to get arrested."

"Well," says Kim with a sharp edge to his voice, "I don't know what happened with Warmbier. But you, Travis. I can assure you." He shakes his finger at me warm-naturedly. "You will always be safe when you travel here with us. That I can personally guarantee you." He smiles.

"But what about the letter?" Alexandre interrupts.

"Letter?"

"The letter of recommendation. I asked you to get me that from the school. Is it still possible?"

Alexandre has some fantasy that securing a *letter of recommendation* from the university will aid him in his quest to apply for a longer, more official course of study at Kim Il Sung University next year. He has asked several times, but the Koreans clearly have no idea what he's talking about. It's not like this is a normal country, where one fills out an application form and submits letters of recommendation when applying for admission to a university. For everything he knows, Alexandre still doesn't get that that's not how things work here. That there is, in fact, no standard procedure for a foreigner in applying to study at any university. There is no precedent. And he should know, since we're among the first to have ever done it.

"The certificate you got today." Comrade Kim calmly picks his teeth. "That should be sufficient."

"Okay. What about the phone number?"

"What phone number?"

"For the university."

"There is no phone number."

"The university doesn't have a phone?"

"It is internal. It is impossible to call from a foreign number."

"But what if I want to come here again to study?"

Comrade Kim shoots him a calculatedly pensive look. "It is best if you come again with Tongil Tours," he replies coolly.

Alexandre can't let it go. We're leaving tomorrow, and he can't handle it.

"Yes, but this is only for one month. And it's on a tourist visa—not a student visa. What if I want to come back and study for a longer period? How do I get the visa? Who do I talk to? Can you give me the number of someone in the Ministry of Education? Maybe your guy in the Ministry of Foreign Affairs?"

"It is not so easy, I'm afraid."

"Well, then what can I do?"

Kim eyes Alek with a sly smile. "Twenty-nineteen," he says. "I think 2019 will be a very good year."

"But what if I want to come back before?"

Witnessing this conversation is almost unbearably awkward. Kim doing things the noncommittal Norko way, all understatement and whispered inference, Alexandre with this disturbing eruption of pushiness that defies all subtlety.

"Twenty-nineteen," Kim repeats. "Twenty-nineteen."

What everyone knows but can't say aloud is that Alek has been awarded a scholarship to study at a university in Seoul for the next three years. But as it is subsidized by the Australian and South Korean governments, one of the stipulations is that he is not allowed to enter the North for the duration of his study. Twenty-nineteen is the year it finishes, the year he'll be able to return.

"I understand what you mean," says Alexandre tensely. "But what if I want to come back before then?"

Kim removes the toothpick from his mouth. "I don't know that I understand what *you* mean. Tell me something: *Why* do you want so badly to study here in Korea?"

"Because I want to learn the language."

"Then why don't you go to study in the South? It would be much easier for you to arrange."

"I'm not interested in the South. I am interested in this country."

"That's what I can't understand. Why are you so interested in my country? What is it, exactly, that you want to do here? I don't understand what your business is. I can understand Alek, for instance. He is running a company specializing in tours. Okay, I get it! But you. I still don't understand what it is you are doing, what it is you want. Why do you even want to learn Korean?"

"I don't know for sure. I'm still figuring out what I want to do. I am just a student for now."

Kim stares at him suspiciously. *What kind of answer is that?* his eyes seem to say. "And your father is okay with this? Just studying for no reason, until you find what it is you want to do?"

"Yes. My parents are fine with it. I mean, wasn't it the same for you at my age?"

"No."

"So you knew exactly what it was you wanted to do with your life?"

"Yes."

"What?"

"To serve the motherland." Kim nods, satisfied at having given the correct answer.

That answer should have put an end to everything. Certificates, medals, rank—all insignia of a world we don't belong to, that we never will. It is a conversation we've had before and not one that needs to be had again—and certainly not with those forced to endure its consequences. This should be readily comprehensible and easy, by now, to accept. Instead, it only rankles Alexandre further. He is, I realize, experiencing something we all do upon leaving this place—that knife-sharp cognizance of not-belonging. Not just of not-belonging, but of our tremendous failure to ever understand.

Alexandre is free falling into the same trap that every would-be Pyongyangologist who comes here and becomes obsessed with the place falls into: the question of *access*. Of which doors we are allowed to open, which are locked for us, and why. Behind those locked doors, so the assumption goes, is where the truth must hide.

"*I will never come back here as a tourist,*" Alexandre sneers. As though it is one's tourist status that prevents one from unlocking that door. As though having a different visa status, which gives one a *minder* instead of a *guide,* will somehow alter your perception of everything that lies before you. Coming here under some other visa category, whether as a diplomat or NGO worker, does not give you more access. You are still not allowed to enter any North Korean's home. You are still forced to have two North Koreans accompany you in most contexts. So what, exactly, is he trying to achieve?

The *truth,* however, is in actuality so banal that it usually eludes us. The truth is that neither Alexandre nor Alek nor I will ever be regarded as one of them. The system is what it is, it predates us, and it will likely endure in some form or other until well after we are gone. The *truth* is being disclosed unwittingly to Alexandre in the very conversation he is now having with Comrade Kim, in this drama between the irreconcilable worlds of the liberal arts model of "finding yourself" via education versus the self predefined as a vessel of the state. The truth is, in short, right in front of us, everywhere we look, lucent as the light that burrows its holes into the morning fog until it dissipates in the clarity of day. The only thing missing is the stories of the faces we see around us—stories, indeed, that yearn to be told but cannot be for now. And we have to leave it at that because in the end, they are not our stories to tell.

FORTY-SEVEN

AFTER DINNER, WE head to the Taedong River Beer Festival. It's the first year they're holding it, on the banks off the square right across from the lit-up Juche Tower, the same banks where we ditched our guides and took our risky walk that afternoon. Arriving past the barricades, Min presents us each with three tickets redeemable for our choice of light or dark drafts of the local Taedong-gang brew. Foreign tour groups intermingle with a crowd of Pyongyangites, and nobody tries to separate them. The mood convivial, uncontrived, relaxed—it's certainly the most *normal* social gathering I've ever attended here, and it fills me with hope for the future. Walking among the laughing, beer-swilling groups, I spot one table with three twenty-something guys I'm absolutely certain are gay. Neatly dressed, with fashionable South Korean–style haircuts, they giggle as they show each other photos on their smartphones. I'm tempted to pull up a chair, join them, but then I think better of the idea.

Roe claps me on the back. "How are you, Comrade Travis?"

"Comrade Roe! I'm fine, thanks. Are you having fun?"

"No!" He smiles.

"Really? Why not?"

"I will have fun tomorrow," he says. "When I can come here with my wife and daughter!"

Well, then. At least we know *someone* isn't going to be missing us!

Later, we drop Comrade Kim off in front of a newish apartment block in east Pyongyang. Definitely not the poor area by our school—electricity abounds, everything is lit up. A low-rise—only five floors, a huge benefit given the power outages that often leave the elevator-dependent stranded. At least I think it's his building. As we pull away, I look behind and notice Kim standing there, watching our car disappear into traffic. I want to believe he is sad to see us go, but perhaps he just wants to be sure we don't see which house he is about to disappear into.

★

To be truthful, I don't really know who Comrade Kim is or what goes on in his head when he closes the door to his apartment behind him and retires for the night. All I can do is employ that sharpened tool relied upon by every aspiring Pyongyangologist: speculation.

To me, Comrade Kim is a Pyongyang man of the moment, an idyll of the Kim Jong Un era. A cynic, an optimist, and a gambler, all rolled into one. He hates the system because he's spent enough time outside to see it for what it is, but he also knows how to work it and, anyway, believes it will all probably crumble in a few years. And if it takes too long to do so, then, perhaps in the back of his mind, he has a plan to get out once his father passes away. In the meantime, the goal is to get as rich as possible.

He turns the bedside lamp off as he crawls into bed next to his wife. He has to wake up early tomorrow to see us off at the airport, and after that, another business trip, this time to Nampo on the west coast. He's building a factory there. But as to what will be made in that factory—well, as with most things these days, it's complicated . . .

No, I don't know much about Comrade Kim. But I somehow feel I will see him again someday—in Pyongyang or elsewhere.

FORTY-EIGHT

AND SO WE depart the land of morning calm. Min is waiting for us in the lobby, to assist with the checkout procedure. She hands us each our passports, sniffling. Hwa has already pulled the van up to the entrance. Roe is inside, waiting. We make our final bows to the bellhop and then climb into the van for one last ride through the city.

Today is not so misty. In fact, the sun has risen quite early, casting a startling clarity upon all the familiar scenes we drive past. We hit a red light right in front of the Ryugyong Hotel, that majestic, never-to-be-finished relic. It is Pyongyang's Eiffel Tower, it now occurs to me. Just as that epochal structure, which can be seen everywhere one looks throughout the city, stood for something more than itself in the Paris of the nineteenth century when it was erected, so the Ryugyong, in its perpetual state of incompletion, is an icon of the larger incompletion of Korea as a nation. It stands tall and proud in its brute bluntness, but its shimmering facade is all there is; its glass windows reflect the city back onto itself, concealing whatever lies within, a temple that can only be pondered from without.

Hwa turns on the radio. The opening bars to a Moranbong Band song, "Voice of My Heart." Another paean of patriotism, sure, but this one gently moving in its sweet simplicity, its melody a lullaby. Min softly sings along:

> *The deepest thoughts of my heart*
> *I tell my Mother*
> *All truthful, hiding nothing*
> *And my mind gets relieved*

Because you are a caring Mother
With warm and deep compassion
My wounded sore heart was healed
By your warm affection

If there had been no love
I would have gotten sores as from a whip
But although I was a foolish child
Mother raised me lovingly

Without fear or hesitation
I was embraced in her bosom
I was not afraid to tell my faults and mistakes
All truthfully and openly

As we coast through the streets, I study the faces of all the people we pass by. People on their way to work, to school. I wonder about their lives, all those stories yet to be told. All the ones I see, but also the ones who are absent. The ones who were born into this city, this society, and have been able to thrive. But also the ones who have failed to adapt. The poor ones who grew up to become rich. The rich ones who grew richer and then, one day, lost it all and fled. The ones who still struggle to understand the world around them, their place in it. The ones who said the wrong thing, got into trouble. The ones who said the right thing, got into trouble anyway. The ones who got sent away and were called for again, only to be sent back. The ones who were sent away and never seen or heard from thereafter. The ones who devoted their entire lives to the cause, only to watch it implode before them, their efforts wasted, taking them and everyone they truly loved down with it. The ones who never really believed in any of it to begin with but were still richly rewarded. The ones who stood by while others suffered, using the grand cause as their excuse for inaction. The selfish ones; the selfless ones. The ones who were shattered by the generosity they received and didn't expect, having never believed that their lives were worth all that much. The ones who were raised to believe in something else entirely and died still believing in that thing. The ones who were won over by it all, who thought if they only believed hard enough, dedicated themselves a little more, great things would eventually come their way. The ones I have met and spoken to, the ones I will never know. The ones who still dream and the ones who can no longer.

> *In this bosom, millions of children*
> *Have been raised as one single heart*
> *In order to live a shining life*
> *I will follow only my Mother*
>
> *Selflessly and forever*
> *I will love only you*
> *Mother, Mother, oh great Mother*
> *I will forever remain in your arms*

EPILOGUE

HISTORY CONTINUES TO write itself at a frenetic pace. Although less than two years have passed since that summer of 2016, much has happened in the intervening period. Otto Warmbier was released by the DPRK authorities, flown back to the United States in a comatose state, and died shortly thereafter. A newly elected US president, who appears to have only the vaguest understanding of the tense political malaise that has afflicted East Asia for more than half a century, issues flippant threats of nuclear war. Punishing sanctions continue to cripple the North's moribund economy, which will only force the people of North Korea to find new, undoubtedly illegal, means of generating hard currency. The US has elected to slam shut the final door on engagement by banning its citizens from visiting as tourists, threatening those who choose to violate the statute with the draconian confiscation of their passport—which means effectively taking away one's right, as a US citizen, to freedom of movement, a right that ironically is denied to the people of the DPRK by their government—a form of punishment that has no precedent and is probably illegal.

Much has happened, and even more will happen before this book goes to print—so much, in fact, that I find it somewhat pointless to comment on any one of these issues, since, given the volatile nature of the conflict, any of them could be sidelined or eradicated by tomorrow's events.

Suffice to say that the threat of war is very real, and its implications must be fully understood. Because ultimately, it would have a dire effect on virtually all of us. Were a new Korean War to erupt, hundreds of thousands, if not millions, would die. The battle would not be confined to the Korean peninsula. China, which does not wish to have American soldiers at its border, would inevitably be forced to side with North Korea, and the result would effectively be a proxy war between China and the United States; given Russia's recent warming of ties with North Korea and its own shared border with the country, there is a chance that it would also become involved. All conflicts that have long been festering in this troubled region would erupt; China would be impelled to make a grab for Taiwan, sparking yet another bloody confrontation. With South Korea, the world's eleventh-largest economy, under nuclear siege, the global economy would likely collapse. In short, this would not be a regional war; it would be World War III. In such a conflict, there would be no winners—only losers. We have to ask ourselves—as citizens of the world, regardless of nationality—whether such a battle is truly worthwhile.

In the summer of 2017, Tongil Tours held its second Pyongyang Summer Language Program. This time, ten students signed up. None of us originators were able to attend—Alek wanted to go but was still on his scholarship in Seoul—but I've heard it was a roaring success. It was not without its challenges, however. The biggest one was posed by one of Tongil Tours' competitors, Juche Travel Services, which began to offer the exact same study program at the same university. Even worse, JTS's publicity for the tour was filled with erroneous claims: that the students would take classes at Kim Il Sung University, the country's most prestigious, rather than Kim Hyong Jik; that students would be able to stay on campus in the dormitories alongside North Korean students; that this program was the first of its kind. All claims that turned out to be false. It seems that the cowboy capitalism that predominates in Pyongyang, which is but a pale reflection of our own neoliberal economic system, has also infected the bear market economy of DPRK tourism. Nonetheless, Tongil Tours soldiers on. Because of all the new Westerners in her charge, I've heard that Ms. Pak has now been required to take English classes and is well on her way toward fluency.

Alek got back together with his girlfriend—actually, she had been receiving his text messages all along, but for whatever reason, her responses to those messages were not being transmitted. As I was finishing this book, I received an invitation to their wedding this spring. Sadly, I will not be able to attend, as the ceremony is to take place—where else?—in Pyongyang.

Alexandre continues to plot his return to North Korea. His latest scheme is to pursue a doctorate in DPRK law at Kim Il Sung University. Problem is, his Korean is still not good enough. When he heard that a representative from Kim Il Sung University was going to be in Beijing, where he has spent the past year studying, he asked Alek, with his superior Korean, to imitate him over the phone in the hopes that he would win admittance. I'm not sure how it will pan out, but it wouldn't surprise me if Alexandre wound up working for the French Cooperation Bureau in Pyongyang someday and eventually writing a book on his own experiences.

Writing this book has effectively prolonged my stay in Pyongyang. Each day, I relive the events, the people, the places I experienced on my trips to the country over the past five years. At night, I frequently dream that I'm back there, walking the streets, the violins and synths of a Moranbong Band pop tune faintly discernible in the background.

There's one memory in particular that I prefer to revisit. It's from 2012, my first trip to the country. We're at the Demilitarized Zone on the border with the South, about to be given a tour of the historical stalemate that has solidified the division of this peninsula for the past fifty-nine years.

The soldier giving us the tour is a young guy, around the same age as me. We look at each other and smile; something clicks. His job is to stand across the dividing line and stare down the enemy each day. But I'm the first American he's ever actually spoken to. We are led from the gift shop into a small lecture room. With a wooden pointer, the soldier briefly explains the engraved wall map of the surrounding area. He leads us outside, where we are made to walk single file through an entrance gate. On the other side, our bus is waiting for us. We climb in along with the officer. We drive along a dirt road surrounded by weeds, in which no doubt a number of mines have been embedded, past all the moats, the block obstacles, the drop-down barriers that imply that *Demilitarized Zone* is something of a misnomer. We arrive at the Armistice Talks Hall, a modest hut fronted with a small stele. Next door is a large, single-story building with a dove on the roof. This is where the Armistice Agreement was ultimately signed on July 27, 1953. In the center of the room, the chairs, tables, and flags that were there that day have been faithfully preserved. Surrounding this display, a museum has been erected on the walls, with blown-up photographs of Kim Il Sung and all the expected evidential images of war and torment and US aggression and the ultimate triumph of the Korean People's Army.

We are guided to the Joint Security Area. Here, I lay eyes on South Korea for the first time. Across the dividing line, a row of blue-and-white huts. This is where the armistice talks are held, have been held ever since the war ground to its standstill. We stand on the platform of the Stalinist-style building overlooking the scene. Across from us, the South's equivalent is a high-tech mammoth that fuses edgy postmodern aesthetics with traditional Korean style. But the South Korean side is completely vacant, devoid of soldiers and tourists, while on our side, there is just our small group and a couple of soldiers who have been placed before the main dividing line, as though to prevent any of us from crossing over.

We go inside the central hut. This is the Military Armistice Commission Conference Hall. We are invited to sit at the large round table in the center of the room, which is lined with live microphones. Here, whenever North and South must hold official talks, is where it's done. Two more North Korean soldiers stand inside the hut, blocking the exit on the South Korean side. On the walls, a display of flags of each of the countries that participated in the Korean War against the DPRK.

We take our photos, and after finishing his narration in somber voice and answering all our questions, the soldier leads us back to our van. We climb in and begin our drive back to Panmunjom, the name of the truce village, which no longer actually exists—now, it is little more than a name for this place where a divided land attempts to acknowledge its past and move toward an ever uncertain future. The melancholic mood lifts instantly as the soldier climbs into the back of the van and plants himself next to me. He's handsome, with unblemished, untanned complexion, and looks well fed. No doubt from a well-to-do and well-connected family, as it takes both money and connections for a soldier this young to get a prestige post like this. A poor soldier from nowheresville would more likely be assigned to a grueling construction post as his first assignment. Perhaps he has also been chosen for his height—at six feet tall, he is a towering antidote to the common perception that the majority of soldiers' growth has been stunted as a consequence of the Arduous March. As he speaks to me enthusiastically, he gestures with his hands, rough and swollen from his daily tae kwon do training, breaking wooden slabs and concrete bricks with his fists.

He's full of questions—who I am, what I do—and our guide laughs delightedly as she translates our exchange. Mostly, he wants to know what I think of his country. Have I been to the South before? I say no—because at the time, I hadn't. I ask him where he's from. Pyongyang, he says proudly. He misses it. It is, after all, the place he calls home, the place he knows best, and the place he's been away from now for countless months, maybe years. I can relate—I haven't been home for a while, either. Though for different reasons.

But right now, at least, we find ourselves on common ground, and we both know it, without having to say it. I'm from where I'm from, he's from this place, and there's nothing we can do about it. We are both the products of countries determined to do their own thing, to pursue their agendas and interests with cunning and aggression. Maybe there's a part of both of us that tends to look at the worlds we come from and wonder what's real and what's not.

He looks at me, and I look at him. He smiles and shrugs, says something in Korean. My guide laughs.

"What did he say?" I ask her.

"'Countries are countries,'" she translates. "'But people are people.'"

BIBLIOGRAPHY

BOOKS

Abt, Felix. *A Capitalist in North Korea.* Tokyo: Tuttle Publishing, 2014.

Arendt, Hannah. *The Origins of Totalitarianism.* New York: Harcourt, Brace, Jovanovich, 1973.

Armstrong, Charles K. *Tyranny of the Weak: North Korea and the World, 1950–1992.* Ithaca, NY: Cornell University Press, 2013.

Bird, Isabella. *Korea and Her Neighbours.* Seoul: Yonsei University Press, 1970.

Breen, Michael. *Kim Jong Il: North Korea's Dear Leader.* John Wiley & Sons, 2004.

Corfield, Justin. *Historical Dictionary of Pyongyang.* London: Anthem Press, 2013.

Cumings, Bruce. *North Korea: Another Country.* New York: The New Press, 2004.

Cumings, Bruce. *The Korean War: A History.* New York: Modern Library, 2010.

Fischer, Paul. *A Kim Jong-Il Production.* New York: Flatiron Books, 2015.

Frank, Rüdiger, ed. *Exploring North Korean Arts.* Nuremberg: Verlag für moderne Kunst, 2012.

Gessen, Masha. *The Future is History: How Totalitarianism Reclaimed Russia.* New York: Riverhead Books, 2017.

Golomstock, Igor. *Totalitarian Art in the Soviet Union, the Third Reich, Fascist Italy, and the People's Republic of China,* trans. Robert Chandler. New York: Overlook Press, 2012 (first published October 1990).

Groys, Boris. *The Total Art of Stalinism.* Princeton, NJ: Princeton University Press, 1992.

Guyotat, Pierre. *Eden Eden Eden.* Creation Books, 1995.

Hwang, Sok Yong. *The Guest.* New York: Seven Stories Press, 2008.

Jang, Jin-Sung. *Dear Leader.* New York: Atria, 2014.

Kang, Chol Hwan. *The Aquariums of Pyongyang.* New York: Basic Books, 2001.

Khrushchev, Nikita. *Khrushchev Remembers.* London: Sphere Books, 1971.

Kim, Jong Il. *For the Development of Juche-Orientated Literature and Art.* Pyongyang: Foreign Languages Publishing House, 1990.

Kim, Jong Il. *On the Art of the Cinema.* Pyongyang: Foreign Languages Publishing House, 1989.

Kim, Jong Il. *On the Juche Philosophy.* Pyongyang: Foreign Languages Publishing House, 2002.

Kim, Suki. *Without You, There Is No Us.* New York: Crown, 2014.

Kim, Suk Young. *Illusive Utopia: Theater, Film, and Everyday Performance in North Korea.*

Lankov, Andrei. *From Stalin to Kim Il Sung: The Formation of North Korea, 1945–1960.* New Brunswick, NJ: Rutgers University Press, 2002.

Lankov, Andrei. *The Real North Korea.* Oxford: Oxford University Press, 2015.

Lim, Jae-Cheon. *Kim Jong Il's Leadership of North Korea.* New York: Routledge, 2009.

Martin, Bradley K. *Under the Loving Care of the Fatherly Leader: North Korea and the Kim Dynasty.* New York: St. Martin's Griffin, 2006.

Morris-Suzuki, Tessa. *Exodus to North Korea: Shadows from Japan's Cold War.* Lanham, MD: Rowman and Littlefield, 2007.

Myers, B. R. *The Cleanest Race: How North Koreans See Themselves—and Why It Matters.* New York: Melville House, 2010.

Myers, B. R. *The Juche Myth.* Busan: Sthele Press, 2015.

National Tourism Association. *Pyongyang.* Pyongyang: Foreign Languages Publishing House, 1999.

Oberdorfer, Don. *The Two Koreas: A Contemporary History.* New York: Basic Books, 2014.

Orwell, George. *1984.* New York: Signet Classics, 1961.

Orwell, George. *Animal Farm.* New York: Signet Classics, 1956.

Portal, Jane. *Art under Control in North Korea.* London: Reaktion Books, 2005.

Schönherr, Johannes. *North Korean Cinema: A History.* Jefferson, NC: McFarland & Co., 2012.

Springer, Chris. *Pyongyang: The Hidden History of the North Korean Capital.* Budapest: Entente Bt., 2003.

Suh, Dae-Sook. *Kim Il Sung: The North Korean Leader.* New York: Columbia University Press, 1988.

Tudor, Daniel, and Pearson, James. *North Korea Confidential.* Tokyo: Tuttle Publishing, 2015.

Willoughby, Robert. *North Korea.* Guilford, CT: The Globe Pequot Press, 2014.

ARTICLES

Andrew, Roy C. "Exploring Unknown Corners of the 'Hermit Kingdom.'" *National Geographic,* July 1919.

French, Paul. "A Day in the Life of Pyongyang: How North Korea's Capital Goes to Work." *The Guardian,* May 2, 2014. https://www.theguardian.com/world/2014/may/02/north-korea-a-day-in-the-life-pyongyang

Gabroussenko, Tatiana. "Benoit Symposium: Writers in the DPRK: The Invisible Stars." *SinoNK,* September 27, 2013. http://sinonk.com/2013/09/27/writers-in-the-dprk-the-invisible-stars/

Han, Sunghoon. "The Ongoing Korean War at the Sinchon Museum in North Korea." *Cross-Currents: East Asian History and Culture Review,* E-Journal No. 14, March 2015.

Jeppesen, Travis. "Critical Mass." Artforum.com, May 22, 2014. https://www.artforum.com/slant/travis-jeppesen-on-architecture-for-the-masses-in-north-korea-46727

Jeppesen, Travis. "In the Studio: Tania Brugeura." *Art in America,* September 2015.

Jeppesen, Travis. "Mass Media." Artforum.com, September 7, 2012. https://www.artforum.com/diary/travis-jeppesen-at-the-arirang-mass-games-33414

Jeppesen, Travis. "Norko Realism." *Art in America,* June 2014.

Lankov, Andrei. "The Evolution of North Korea's *Inminban*." *NKNews,* April 28, 2015. https://www.nknews.org/2015/04/the-evolution-of-north-koreas-inminban/

Lankov, Andrei. "North Korean Heroes." *The Korea Times,* March 1, 2009. http://www.koreatimes.co.kr/www/news/opinon/2011/04/166_40496.html

O'Carroll, Chad. "Dredging Disadvantage? Pyongyang's Never-Ending Sand Problem." *NKNews,* January 10, 2017. https://www.nknews.org/2017/01/dredging-disadvantage-pyongyangs-never-ending-sand-problem/

O'Neill, Mark. "Kim Il Sung's Secret History." *South China Morning Post,* October 17, 2010. http://www.scmp.com/article/727755/kim-il-sungs-secret-history

Shih, Gerry. "Gung-ho Culture at Tour Agency Warmbier Used on North Korea Trip." Associated Press, June 22, 2017. https://apnews.com/bb7f026e872c49409ca2d4443d83e31b.

Sigley, Alek. "Crisps and Coffeeshops: North Korea's New Consumerism." *The Diplomat,* March 1, 2017. http://thediplomat.com/2017/03/crisps-and-coffee-shops-north-koreas-new-consumerism/?__s=xbhqrunkotxqppthh16u

Sigley, Alek. "A Few Things You May Not Have Known about the Pochonbo Electronic Ensemble: Part 2." *Tongil Tours Blog,* November 26, 2017. https://tongiltours.com/blog/the-north-korea-blog/things-may-not-known-pochonbo-electronic-ensemble-part-2/

Skåtun, Ole Jakub. "Capitalist Credentials: N. Korea Sympathizer Group's Huge Profit on Access to Country." *NKNews,* January 15, 2015. https://www.nknews.org/2015/01/capitalist-credentials-n-korea-sympathizer-groups-huge-profit-on-access-to-country/

Unsigned. "N. Korea's Per Capita Income Slightly Up in 2016: Data." *Yonhap News Agency,* December 15, 2017. http://english.yonhapnews.co.kr/search1/2603000000.html?cid=AEN20171215003000320&__s=xbhqrunkotxqppthh16u

Žižek, Slavoj. "Capitalism Has Broken Free of the Shackles of Democracy." *Financial Times,* February 1, 2015. https://www.ft.com/content/088ee78e-7597-11e4-a1a9 -00144feabdc0

WEB

Pyongyang Metro. http://pyongyang-metro.com/

FILMOGRAPHY

Wilking, Raphael, dir. *Friends of Kim.* Netherlands, 2006.